Physiological Techniques in Behavioral Research

Devendra Singh
UNIVERSITY OF TEXAS AT AUSTIN

David D. Avery
COLORADO STATE UNIVERSITY

Brooks/Cole Publishing Company
Monterey, California
A Division of Wadsworth Publishing Company, Inc.

ISBN: 0-8185-0110-3
L.C. Catalog Card No.: 74-82037
Printed in the United States of America
10 9 8 7 6 5 4 3 2 1

Interior Design: *Bernard Dix*
Cover Design: *Linda Marcetti*
Composition, Printing, & Binding: *Kingsport Press, Inc., Kingsport, Tennessee*

Preface

In recent years it has become increasingly obvious that the study of relationships between brain and behavior necessitates the acquisition of laboratory skills not readily available in most behavior laboratories. Although a student may have been exposed formally to one specialized physiological technique during the course of training, rarely has he had the opportunity to gain competence in several skills. Thus, it was our intention to compile a practical guide to the techniques most commonly used in neuropsychological research.

Our approach has been to explain and describe the techniques with which each of us has become familiar in the course of our own research—lesioning, electrical stimulation, and chemical stimulation. In chapters contributed by specialists in their fields, other methods have been described, including electrophysiological recording by Donald A. Irwin, histology by Barbara L. Case, and miscellaneous surgical techniques in the rat by Charles T. Snowdon and by John D. Davis and Constance S. Campbell. In each of these chapters, the emphasis is on basic procedures as well as practical hints that are usually learned through costly mistakes. Elaborate, theoretical, and involved explanations are not included; however, additional sources of information appear in the references and suggested readings at the end of the chapters. In the first two chapters, materials of a more nonspecific nature, such as basic animal care and basic surgical skills, are presented. These chapters provide necessary knowledge for successful acquisition and use of the more sophisticated techniques in the remaining chapters. In addition, the appendix of manufacturers and suppliers not only should help the reader who must acquire necessary materials for the implementation of the techniques described in this book but should be of general benefit for any neuropsychological laboratory.

We would like to thank Jackson Beatty of the University of California, Los Angeles, Thomas E. Breen of Fresno State College, Ben M. Clopton of the University of California, Santa Barbara, Robert Dyer of Towson State College, Glenn I. Hatton of Michigan State University, Dale W. McAdam of The University of Rochester, Charles Rebert of Stanford Research Institute, John M. Rhodes of The University of New Mexico, and Robert Stutz of the University of Cincinnati for their helpful reviews of the manuscript.

Devendra Singh

David D. Avery

Contents

Introduction

In the increasingly specialized world of the biological sciences, a behavioral scientist who wishes, in his quest for understanding, to manipulate physiological variables finds himself in a strange situation. Often, the achievement of his ultimate goal—that is, to understand behavior—depends on how skillful he becomes in using skills and techniques of many diverse and highly specialized fields such as anatomy, physiology, surgery, and biochemistry. Thus, the behavioral scientist, an apparent jack-of-all-trades, is really expected to be the master of many diverse techniques, including, of course, his own behavioral tools.

Paradoxically, most behavioral scientists get very little opportunity to learn intricate techniques within a structured academic setting. Exposure to techniques occurs often through observing or assisting professors, helping senior colleagues, or engaging in a "learn-while-you-work" project—which is laden more often with errors than with trials. We do not wish to imply that the student can learn without working or that there is a substitute for diligent practice. However, in most academic institutions, limited facilities and the specialized interests of professors result in technique training that is often quite narrow. Since few source manuals are available, a student who wishes to employ a technique to which he has not been exposed has little recourse to it. He can, of course, give up his desired research and work with such projects that fit into the scheme of his environment. Or, if he is persistent, he can write to other scientists who are using the desired techniques and, with the help of a few sketchy notes, begin by trial and error to pursue his goals. Clearly, he will waste much valuable time.

Another problem frequently encountered concerns the transference of techniques among species. For example, a person who has learned a technique, say surgical ablation, on a given species may find himself quite incapable of performing electrical or chemical stimulation, or even surgical ablation, on another species. Such difficulties often result in a very restricted approach to research problems, especially if the investigator's institution is small and the opportunities for interdisciplinary cooperation are few.

This book compiles and discusses common physiological techniques and related subject matter. Although not exhaustive by any definition, it presents a number of different techniques that psychologists often employ. It is specifically directed to (a) those who would like to perfect new techniques but (b) do not have much opportunity for interdisciplinary help and (c) desire a compilation of different procedures and practical hints that are often learned only through costly mistakes. However, we make no pretense whatsoever of inventing new techniques.

Briefly, the book takes a practical point of view, and, we hope, will be useful as a guide and practice manual. In planning it we have tried to answer questions that are basic to the maintenance of a laboratory: What is the space requirement for a given animal? How much and what should animals be fed? How can one detect and prevent common disease? What kinds of drugs are to be used and where are they to be obtained? Rather than giving elaborate, theoretical answers, we try to be very precise, simple, and nontechnical. We are assuming that most research workers would like to have this information to help them but do not plan to become experts on animal breeding or diseases. However, for those who would like more details—for example, of the etiology of certain diseases or of a special technique—we provide lists of suggested additional readings. We employ a similar rationale in the chapters on anesthesia, experimental lesions, and so forth, where we present only those aspects that are practical and leave theoretical involvement to more elaborate books in the respective fields. For a handy reference, we list the brand names of drugs and the manufacturers' names and addresses for different supplies in the Appendix.

Obviously, it is impossible to include in the book all the techniques that could be of use to the behavioral scientist. Therefore, we discuss only those techniques that (1) are necessary for overall comprehension (from animal care to perfusion, histology, and reconstruction of the brain for reporting) and (2) have been most frequently used in the past. The selection of the animals and techniques is the result of a thorough review of the *Journal of Comparative and Physiological Psychology* (JCPP), 1948–1972 (the change of name from *Journal of Comparative Psychology* to *Journal of Comparative and Physiological Psychology* reflected a tremendous increase in the use of physiological technique).

The most popular subject for physiological research has been the rat, followed by the monkey *(rhesus),* the cat, and the dog (see Table 1). That the dog has lost popularity in psychological

TABLE 1. Physiological Techniques Used on Different Species, as Reported in JCPP, 1948–1972

	NUMBER OF STUDIES REPORTED						
	MOUSE	RAT	CAT	DOG	MONKEY	OTHERS	TOTAL
ELECTRICAL LESION	6	195	12	0	18	15	246
ASPIRATION	2	67	37	7	91	14	218
ELECTRICAL STIMULATION	4	92	31	2	9	4	142
CHEMICAL STIMULATION	0	52	3	0	0	4	59
ELECTRICAL RECORDING	1	47	16	11	5	24	104
X-IRRADIATION	0	29	0	1	9	0	39
ECS	4	97	0	0	4	1	106
FISTULA	0	12	0	0	1	0	13
OTHERS	3	51	3	0	3	6	66
TOTAL	20	642	102	21	140	68	993

research is, in a way, very fortunate, since the dog is one animal that is sure to arouse antivivisectionist feelings in the general public. The most popular technique has been electrical lesion, followed by aspiration. Recently, there has been an extreme increase in the use of electrical and chemical stimulation and electrical recording. This book, therefore, emphasizes rat, cat, and monkey care and general surgery; the techniques of lesioning, chemical and electrical brain stimulation, electrical recording, and histology; and special surgical techniques for gastric and venous cannulation.

CHAPTER 1

Preoperative Care of Animals

Devendra Singh
UNIVERSITY OF TEXAS AT AUSTIN

This chapter provides information essential for proper animal care and maintenance. The first section deals briefly with animal quarters, safety measures for personnel, routine checkups, sanitary measures, and disposal of animals. The second section deals with general care and management of rats, cats, and monkeys, and, for each of these animals, discusses handling, feeding, breeding, and common physiological data. Finally, the chapter briefly describes the symptoms and treatment of common diseases.

PRINCIPLES OF LABORATORY ANIMAL CARE

Most people engaged in animal research would agree that very few legitimate experiments that required inhumane treatment have been conducted. Aside from the obvious moral and ethical reasons, animals should be treated humanely to avoid the risk of inaccurate experimental conclusions that result from abnormalities created through reckless treatment. It is very difficult, however, from the viewpoint of research, to define precisely "humane treatment." Perhaps the most adequate definition would imply that, without a legitimate scientific reason, animals should not be subjected to conditions considered harmful to their growth and welfare. Moreover, all research grants awarded by federal funds require that animal facilities and care meet certain criteria developed in accordance with Public Law 89–544 (amended December 1970). The booklet "Guide for Laboratory Animal Facilities and Care" (Public Health Service, Publication No. 1024) provides information about animal facilities and care as required by PL89–544.

The Board of Scientific Affairs' Committee on Precautions and Standards in Animal Experimentation of the American Psychological Association has published guidelines that should be followed at all times. The guidelines, which satisfy the legal requirements for proper care and humane treatment of laboratory animals, are as follows:

1. All animals used for experimental purposes must be lawfully acquired and their retention shall be in strict compliance with federal and local laws and regulations.
2. Care and feeding of all experimental animals shall be in accordance with accepted laboratory practices, with due consideration for bodily comfort, kind treatment, and sanitary environment.
3. Every effort must be made to avoid unnecessary discomfort to experimental animals. Research subjecting animals to discomfort should be conducted only when an experienced scientist is convinced that such discomfort is required and is justified by the significance of the research.
4. Surgical procedures should be done under suitable anesthesia; major ones under general anesthesia, and only minor ones under local anesthesia. If the nature of a study is such as to require the animal to survive, acceptable techniques to avoid infection must be followed throughout. If the study does not require survival, the animal must be disposed of in a humane manner at the conclusion of the operation.
5. The postoperative care of animals must minimize discomfort during convalescence in accordance with accepted practices.

6. When animals are used by students for their education or the advancement of science, such work should be under the direct supervision of an experienced teacher or investigator. The rules for conduct of such work shall be the same as those for the conduct of research.

A copy of these rules shall be posted in all rooms where animals are housed and where animal experimentation is conducted. Violators of the above rules shall be promptly reported to the director of the laboratory and by him to other administrative authorities if he deems it necessary.*

Since many laboratories are unable to afford certified animal technicians, it is beneficial for all personnel, including students, involved in animal experimentation to be trained in the handling and maintenance of the animals. Laboratory personnel should also be familiar with the symptomatology of common diseases and be thoroughly indoctrinated in the principles of hygiene necessary for preventing diseases. Strict adherence to the rules of cleanliness not only reduces the incidence of disease but has a useful psychological effect on the students in that it tends to reinforce an impression of the serious nature of their research. Furthermore, compulsory procedures, as preliminaries to entering the animal quarters, are an effective means of discouraging visitors, who may introduce diseases into the colony.

Animal Quarters and Equipment

The animal quarters should be equipped with proper lighting and ventilation, and be free of drafts. Though uniform lighting is necessary, animals should be protected against direct exposure to the light source, whether artificial or natural. Air-conditioned animal quarters are advantageous; however, if air conditioning is not feasible, thermostatic temperature regulation and humidity control should be maintained. The animal room should be arranged so that it can be disinfected and cleaned from roof to floor. If funds and space are available, the National Academy of Sciences-National Research Council specifications must be followed; however, where existing space has to suffice, it should be modified to meet the specifications as closely as possible. The proper size of the animal room obviously depends on the type and number of animals housed in it. Under no circumstances should two different species be housed in the same room; inclusion of different species in the same room not only increases the probability of cross-species infection but introduces many variables (for example, amount or type of noise that may frighten the animals, effect of smell) that may seriously affect the behavior of the animal and confound experimental findings. If maintenance of two species is essential but space is limited to one room, partition the room. The animal quarters should contain a cabinet for storing records, a first aid kit, and a sink with a generous supply of hot and cold water.

Among the most important items in the animal quarters are the cages. The proper size of the cages depends on the type and number of animals housed in them. Most commercially manufactured cages meet research specifications, and constructing the cages oneself is seldom more economical than buying them.

In behavioral research many experiments are conducted concurrently; thus affixing to each cage an identification card or tag displaying the name of the experimenter and the conditions of the experiment is imperative. Tags should display such relevant instructions as "destroy," "no water," and "no food or water." Since most behavioral experiments require the animals to be maintained on a rigidly scheduled intake of food and water, the experimental conditions should be posted on each cage to enable the caretaker to determine whether an apparent abnormality is natural or experimentally produced. Records of the body weight of the animal should be maintained, and any severe deviation from normal food and water intake or physical growth should also be recorded.

* From *Guiding Principles for the Humane Care and Use of Animals,* Committee on Precautions and Standards in Animal Experimentation, Board of Scientific Affairs. Copyright 1962 by the American Psychological Association. Reprinted by permission.

Safety Measures for Personnel

All persons responsible for handling animals should be immunized against tetanus and other infectious diseases. The importance of immunization is considerably increased if monkeys are to be used. Every 2 to 6 months, all personnel should have a skin tuberculin test, followed by a chest X ray. Anyone who has a break or cut in the skin should not handle monkeys or clean the cages. A good habit is to wash one's hands with detergent before entering and leaving the animal quarters. When in the animal room, all personnel should wear shoes and clothing reserved exclusively for use in the animal room. All personnel should wear face masks when cleaning the room or cages. If any injury or cut occurs in the course of work in the animal quarters, the wound must be thoroughly cleaned with soap and water, and some topical antiseptic must be applied. The slightest monkey bite is potentially very dangerous; if one occurs, the area of the bite should be cleaned with hydrogen peroxide, and the patient must undergo an immediate medical examination.

Sanitary Measures

The best way to reduce the incidence of disease is to formulate clearly defined sanitary and hygienic procedures in accordance with PL89–544, which must be observed at all times.

Whenever feasible, animals should be housed in individual cages. Group housing, though economical in terms of space, is a likely source of communicable diseases and other problems resulting from crowding. For example, rats, especially pups, have a tendency to crowd and heap together; if too many pups are housed in the same cage, they are likely to suffocate. Two monkeys may be housed in the same cage only if they have similar dispositions; physical injury, bites, and the dominant animal's consumption of most of the food and water are frequent outcomes of community living. Therefore, group housing requires constant care and attention. Another reason to avoid group housing, at least in psychological experiments, is that most animals are kept on some type of food- or water-deprivation schedule that is difficult to maintain in the group situation. However, one possible way to alleviate the dilemma of different schedules for different animals is to feed the animals separately outside the cages.

As a sanitary precaution, food should never be placed or scattered on the cage floor; always attach food hoppers to the cages. Water should be provided for each animal in a bottle used exclusively for that animal. If the water supply is in another room so that the bottles have to be carried in and out, mark the bottles with identification numbers so that they can be returned to the proper animals. Soak bottles in soapy hot water and thoroughly clean them before using for a new batch of animals.

Clean animal quarters and cages as often as possible, and change the animal bedding at least once a week. If numerous cages and sufficient funds are available, use a commercial sterilizer or mechanical cage-washer. However, in the absence of mechanical cleaning equipment, commercially produced chemical disinfectants (for example, Lysol) can be used successfully. Other disinfectants are hot water and soap, and steam jet pressure. When a sterilizer is not available for seriously contaminated cages, a butane torch can produce sufficient heat to disinfect the cages, or the cages can be immersed for half an hour in a solution of carbolic acid in a ratio of 1 part to 20 parts water. Boiling cages in water for 20 minutes is also an effective means of sterilization. Control airborne infection by using infrared light in the animal room.

The problem of odor in the animal quarters is difficult to solve, since the odor always can be detected by people not accustomed to it. Commercially available deodorants can be used, though the introduction of a strong chemical odor may affect the behavior of the animals. Most odors can be greatly reduced if quarters are kept clean and properly ventilated and if the animal bedding is changed as frequently as possible. Keeping animal quarters clean not only minimizes unpleasant odor but is also one of the most effective ways to prevent disease.

Euthanasia and Disposal

Animals can be killed by physical means (for example, stunning) or chemical means (for example, an overdose of anesthesia). The physical method produces violent convulsions and appears to be inhumane; it especially is not recommended for killing cats and monkeys (Animal Welfare Institute, 1968). The chemical method is easy and is preferred over physical methods (for details on physical and chemical methods, see Smith, 1965). Animals can be killed by administering an overdose of barbiturates (for injection procedures see Chapter 2) or by letting the animal inhale ether or chloroform vapor. If large numbers of rats are to be killed, killing by ether or chloroform is more convenient and less expensive. Ether is both highly flammable and explosive and therefore should be handled with great care. Chloroform is not explosive and is much safer to use than ether. Both chemicals, however, are irritating agents and on bodily contact can produce serious burns and discomfort.

A simple method for ether or chloroform killing is to place the animals in a large wooden or metal box containing the chemical. A trash can with a tight-fitting lid can be used. Place cotton or some other absorbent material in the bottom of the can and place a chicken-wire screen a few inches above the bottom to prevent the animals' direct contact with the chemical. Place the animals into the can and close the lid; pour chloroform or ether through an attached tube. Death ensues in about 4 to 5 minutes, but, to be sure, leave the animals in the chamber for at least 10 minutes. The lid should be opened in a room with a proper exhaust system by a person wearing a face mask.

Cats and monkeys should be killed by injecting them with an overdose of barbiturates such as pentobarbital, which is not very expensive and can be purchased in 5-pound lots. The Animal Welfare Institute (1968) suggests the following formula to prepare a highly potent solution: Mix 75 g pentobarbital sodium in 50 cc 95 percent alcohol; to this mixture add physiological saline to make a total solution of 500 cc. The suggested dose is 0.4 cc/1 kg body weight. The solution can be stored for a long time in a dry place without affecting its potency. If injected intraperitoneally, the solution will cause unconsciousness and death in about 10 minutes. However, to be sure that the animal is dead, do not dispose of the body until about 30 minutes have elapsed. Absence of the heartbeat and breathing and coldness and stiffness of the body indicate death.

The best method for the disposal of dead animals is to burn them in an incinerator. If an incinerator is not available, the animals can be buried. Use a fenced area for burial to prevent stray dogs and other animals from removing carcasses. Place the dead bodies deep in the ground and pack them with salt (to accelerate decay) before covering the grave. Dead animals should not be left in garbage cans inside or outside the animal quarters; preferably, they should be disposed of immediately after death. However, if the incinerator is located at an inconvenient distance from the animal quarters, collect the bodies and store them temporarily in a refrigerator or freezer. Later, cart the animals in airtight garbage cans to the incinerator.

GENERAL CARE AND MANAGEMENT OF ANIMALS

This section discusses the handling, feeding, breeding, and general care of rats, cats, and monkeys. Also included here are brief descriptions of the symptoms of various common diseases and, in some cases, treatment.* This information is intended strictly to help the caretaker in making decisions about discarding and isolating animals or asking for professional help.

As a general rule, a sick animal should be destroyed. If a sick animal is indispensable for research purposes, quarantine procedures should be followed and proper records of medication should be kept, since treatment can confound sensitive behavioral tests. Laboratories that use cats or monkeys must seek the help of a veterinarian and should keep proper records of the animals' body weights and physical growth.

* The author gratefully acknowledges the assistance of T. G. Bradfield, DVM, in describing diseases and treatment.

Rat *(Rattus norvegicus)*

HOUSING

According to the Animal Welfare Institute (1968), a room temperature of 18° to 21°C and a relative humidity of about 50 to 60 percent should be maintained to ensure the proper growth and health of the animals. Rats should be protected against extreme fluctuation in temperature. Sudden loud noises should be minimized. Rats are nocturnal creatures and should be maintained on a light-dark cycle unless the experiment specifically requires otherwise. Since variation in light-dark cycles produces a variety of endocrinological changes in rats (see Wurtman, 1966), a stable light-dark cycle is crucial. Install an electronic timer that automatically turns the lights on and off in the animal quarters at preset time intervals.

Most of the commercially manufactured individual and group (dormer) cages are satisfactory for housing rats. Usually, for ease of moving and cleaning, placing 30 to 60 hanging cages on a cage stand or truck mounted on casters is preferable to placing cages on an immobile rack. If possible, use stainless steel cages and cage pans, since, unlike those made of galvanized steel, they do not rust. Fill the cage pans with wood shavings, shredded paper, or commercially manufactured bedding material (San-i-cel). Change the bedding material as frequently as possible, once a week at the very least, to minimize odor.

Food should be placed in food hoppers attached to the cages. If powdered food is used, food tunnels (Wahmann Company) can be attached to the cage. Food tunnels reduce food spillage to a much greater extent than the so-called nonscattering food cups. Although automatic watering devices are available, they are expensive and, furthermore, of no great utility, since in behavioral research animals are frequently on a water-deprivation schedule. Water can be supplied in quart-size bottles fitted with a rubber stopper and steel nipple.

HANDLING

Most commercial breeders can supply rats of any age or sex on short notice. Rats reach maturity in about 50 to 60 days; however, most behavioral laboratories work with 90- to 100-day-old animals. Therefore, 90- to 100-day-old rats should be used to provide comparable data, unless the experiment specifically requires otherwise.

On arrival from the supplier, rats should be handled for a few days until they cease vocalizing, urinating, and defecating when touched or lifted. The procedure for handling is as follows: Lift the animal and place it on a table. Let the animal explore the table top and repeatedly pass the animal from one hand to the other. This method of handling, which approximates the way in which animals will be handled during subsequent experimental procedures, is very helpful in reducing the animal's aversion to being picked up.

Unlike mice, rats should never be picked up by their tails, which have a tendency to break. The standard method for lifting a rat is as follows: "Place the hand, palm downwards over the animal's back, with thumb and forefinger around the neck and remaining fingers around the body to take the weight; then firmly but gently lift the animal" (Animal Welfare Institute, 1968, p. 31). If one further precaution is taken—that is, crossing the forelegs of the animal with the thumb and forefinger—the animal cannot bite and gloves are unnecessary. If a rat must be lifted by the tail, pick it up as close to the base of the tail as possible. It is further recommended that, even with "handled" rats, the animal be allowed first to feel the presence of the hand; touch it on the back before lifting it out of the cage to reduce the animal's tendency to display startle reactions and fright.

IDENTIFICATION

If animals are individually caged, identification is not a problem as long as each rat's number is clearly displayed on its cage. For group living, the most common identification procedures are color-marking the fur, tattooing a number in the ear (Farris, 1950), and punching the ears. Color-marks (made with picric acid, carbolfuchsin, or gentian violet) are good for only a short period of time and must be reapplied every two weeks. Tattooing numbers in the rat's ears is, at best, very tedious. Ear punching is the most satisfactory identification since it is permanent and can be accomplished easily by the use of a chicken toe-punch, which produces a notch in the ear of the animal; however, ear punching should not be tried on adult animals, for they tend to bleed profusely.

Ear punching requires a definite coding system. The following numerical coding system works very well. The left ear of the rat is used for notches indicating multiples of 10 (10, 20, 30, and so on), whereas the right ear is used for notches indicating single digits (1, 2, 3, and so on). Numbers are read in ascending order from the lowest notch (closest to the cheek) to the highest notch (closest to the skull). A notch in the center of the right ear signifies 100, whereas a notch in the center of the left ear signifies 1000. Thus, by using one ear or the other, or both, a great many permutations are possible. For example, a rat with left-ear notches in the lowest peripheral and the central positions, plus a right-ear notch in the lowest peripheral position, would be identified as 1011 (see Figure 1.1).

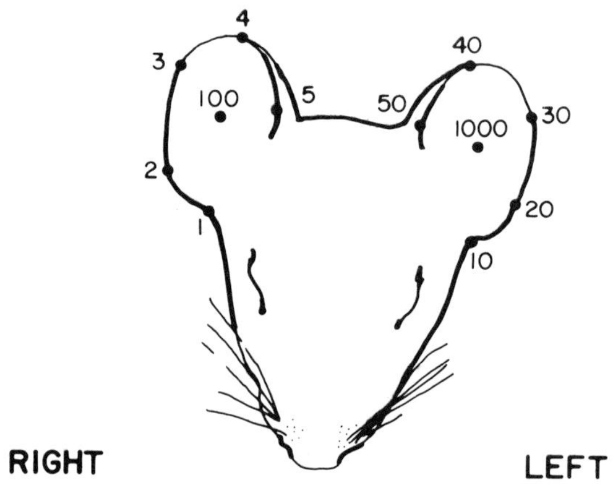

FIGURE 1.1. A Numerical Coding System in Rats Using Ear Punching.

FORCE-FEEDING

In many instances, either because of illness or experimental treatment, the animal cannot voluntarily eat or drink and must be force-fed. The easiest method is to use a rubber catheter (French No. 8, 2 and two-thirds mm diam) attached to a 10 to 20 cc syringe. Mark the catheter to indicate the average length required to reach the stomach. Place the rat on its side on a hard, flat surface and, with the index finger and thumb, pull the skin up over the cheek; the pressure opens the rat's mouth. Slowly thread the catheter over the tongue through the interdental space (see Figure 1.2). As the catheter passes over the tongue, the rat will invariably start chewing and swallowing. If the catheter passes into the esophagus, mild choking but no visible discomfort occurs. If the catheter enters the trachea, voluntary choking and coughing occur; in such a case, pull the catheter back immediately. Once the catheter reaches the stomach, quickly inject all the desired material and pull out the catheter.

Moreland (1965) suggests using a 7- to 10-cm-long 15- to 16-gauge hypodermic needle instead of a catheter. Slightly bend (20° to 30°) and blunt the needle. Apply a small ball of solder to the distal end of the needle to facilitate passing the needle. Attach the needle to an appropriate syringe. The feeding procedure is the same as described for the catheter technique, but the needle technique requires more care, since a metal needle can cause injury if the animal struggles. However, a needle can be used when a small amount of material is to be administered and when the experimental condition does not require placing the material directly into the stomach.

BREEDING

Rats can be bred throughout the year. Since their gestation period is short (21 days), breeding some in the laboratory may be economical. For breeding purposes, place two females and two males of an identical age-group (130 to 200 days) together in a large cage. Though puberty occurs

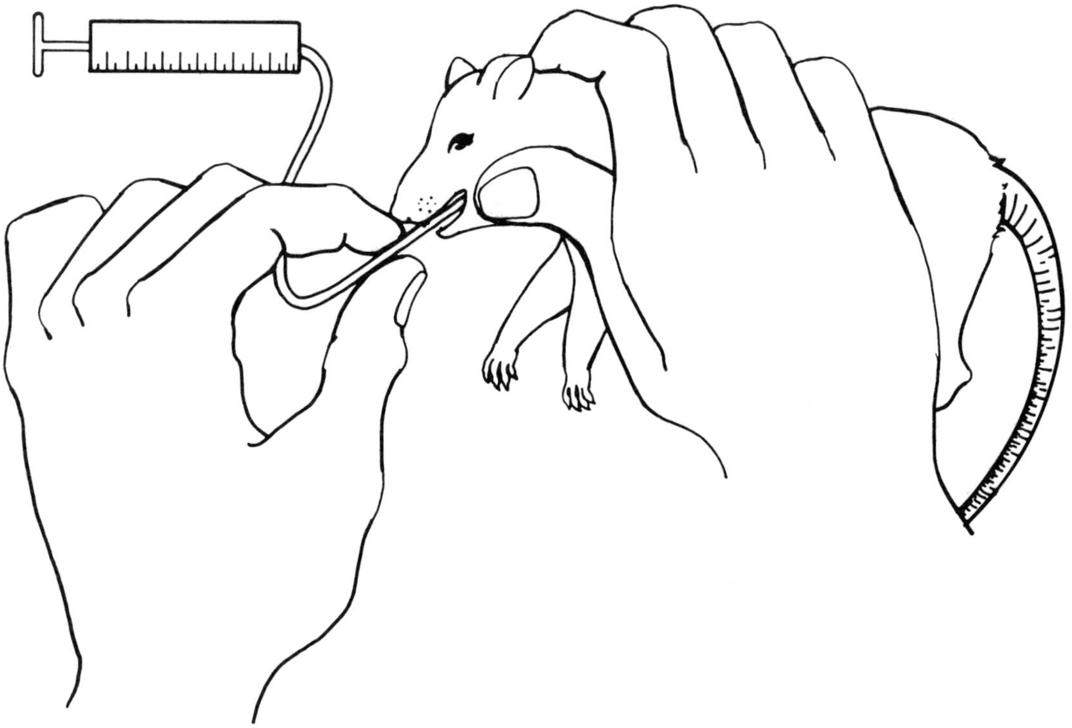

FIGURE 1.2. Force-Feeding in Unanesthetized Rats. The body of the rat is held on the tabletop with the pressure of the palm, and the skin over the cheek is pulled up by the thumb. The catheter is slowly threaded over the tongue through the interdental space.

at 50 to 60 days, better breeding results if somewhat older animals are used. The estrus cycle (every 4 or 5 days) can be detected either by vaginal smears or by the ear-quivering test suggested by Farris and Griffith (1949). When a female is in heat, gentle stroking of the head or back elicits ear quivering; however, this reaction occurs only in the late afternoon or early evening. Light should be dim or off in the animal quarters where breeding is planned. Separate the females from the males after about 20 days. An enlarged abdomen indicates pregnancy; if the abdomen is not enlarged, leave the female with the males.

If the experiment requires a large number of infant rats but the proper space is not available for breeding a large number of animals, timed sperm-positive females can be commercially obtained. These females later can be mated with males to continue a small breeding colony.

Usually about 8 to 12 young comprise a litter, each infant weighing about 4 to 5 grams. The ears open at 2.5 to 3.5 days after birth, whereas the eyes open at 14 to 17 days after birth (Farris & Griffith, 1949). When the males are about 40 days old, the testes descend. Before 40 days, the only method of definitely ascertaining the sex of the animals is checking ano-genital distances (distance between the papilla and the anus); the ano-genital distance is greater in the male (see Figure 1.3). Furthermore, the male genital papillae are generally larger.

An animal weighing less than 30 grams at the age of weaning should be discarded (Farris & Griffith, 1949). Rats are usually weaned at about 23 to 28 days, but they can be given solid food at 19 to 20 days. If experimental conditions require that pups be raised with a foster mother, the pups (which replace the foster mother's own offspring) should be permitted to acquire the nest odor before the foster mother has access to them, to increase the probability that she will accept the pups (Farris, 1950). Commercially available diets (for example, Purina Rat Chow) are nutritionally balanced and require no further supplement other than a few drops of multivitamin (liquid baby multivitamin for humans can be used) in their water supply.

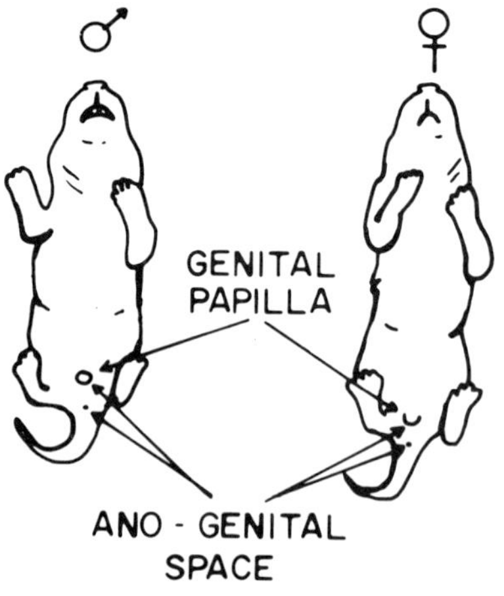

FIGURE 1.3. External Sex Differences in Young Rats. Adapted from *The Rat in Laboratory Investigation,* by J. Farris & J. Q. Griffith. Copyright © 1949 by J. B. Lippincott Company. Used with permission.

COMMON USEFUL DATA

*Physiological**

ITEM	AVERAGE	RANGE
Rectal temperature (C)	37.1°	34.3°–37.7°
Heart rate (beats/min)	328	261–600
Respiration (min)	85	66–115
Daily food consumption (g)	14	10–20
Daily water consumption (cc)	14	13–31
Estrus cycle (days)	4	4–5
Gestation period (days)	21	21–30
Weaning age (days)	21	18–28
Puberty (days)	65	56–70
Menopause (days)	450	427–512
Life-span (years)	2	2–3

Sensory

Rats are behaviorally color-blind, and their retinal elements are predominantly rods. However, rats can probably learn wavelength discrimination on the basis of differential brightness associated with each color. The upper limit of the hearing range is about 40 kHz. The lower limit, on the basis of single-unit recording from the inferior colliculus, lies within the range of 3.2 to 3.5 kHz (Clopton & Winfield, 1973). The laboratory rat can emit pure tones between 20 and 30 kHz (Anderson, 1954). Both behavioral and electrophysiological evidence indicate that the rat has fully developed gustatory (see Hagstrom & Pfaffmann, 1959; Pfaffmann, 1959) and olfactory mechanisms (see Pfaffmann, Goff, & Bare, 1958).

COMMON DISEASES: SYMPTOMS AND PREVENTION

Rats are remarkably resistant to disease and infection but, nonetheless, are susceptible to chronic respiratory disease (CRD). The common symptoms of CRD are nasal discharge, watering eyes, weight loss, and dyspnea (a distinct harsh wheezing above the breathing, which is irregular and shallow). CRD is a slowly progressive disease and often can be prevented by giving tetracycline

* All reported physiological data for rat, cat, and monkey pertain to adult animals. The main sources used in compiling these data were W. S. Spector (Ed.), *Handbook on Biological Data* (Philadelphia: Saunders, 1956); P. L. Altman and D. S. Dittmer, *Biology Data Book* (Washington, D.C.: Federation of American Societies for Experimental Biology, 1964); and the information supplied by the National Research Council, Institute of Laboratory Animal Resources (personal communication, Jan. 1971).

antibiotics (American Cyanamid). The prescribed dose is 300 mg/l water, or one level teaspoon per gallon of water. As a precautionary measure, give all animals this drug for at least three days before starting an experiment, especially during the winter months. Since the diluted drug loses its potency after two days, a fresh supply should be obtained frequently.

Another disease, very common in winter months, is ringtail, the principal symptom of which is annular constriction in the tail. Ringtail is associated with low relative humidity and can be prevented and controlled by keeping the relative humidity at about 50 to 60 percent.

Middle-ear disease also occasionally occurs in the rat. An animal that suffers from this disease cannot run in a straight line and will tilt its head to one side. As there is no cure for middle-ear disease, an inflicted animal must be destroyed.

Rats should also be protected from parasites (lice); otherwise, they spend most of the time scratching or licking themselves—behavior that is not very desirable in behavioral testing. Control lice by dusting the animals with a mixture of .1 percent gamma benzene hexachloride, 2 percent methoxcychor, and 97.9 percent talc. A commercially available product, Ectocide Powder (Norden Laboratory), is very effective. Dust the animals on at least two occasions—on arrival from the supplier and again before the start of the experiment.

Cat *(Felis domesticus)*

HOUSING

Cats are most commonly obtained from a city pound, though some behavioral laboratories prefer to purchase cats directly from a supplier. In either case, a holding room, in which newly acquired cats can be caged individually and observed, is essential. After at least three weeks of initial holding, the animals can be permitted to live with each other or with older residents. Cats found to be sick during the holding period should be destroyed.

The most suitable living quarters for cats are outdoor-indoor combinations—that is, a backyard enclosed by chicken wire and a connected room. Here the animals always have ready access to sunshine, fresh air, and plenty of room for exercise. If an entirely indoor existence is planned, install an exhaust fan or a system capable of 5 to 8 changes of air per hour; stagnant air in a room can contribute to respiratory problems. Public Law 89–544 requires that each adult cat be provided a minimum of $2\frac{1}{2}$ square feet (.23 m^2) of floor space and that not more than 12 adult nonconditioned cats be housed in the same room. Whenever possible, one of the walls or partitions between pens (which should reach from floor to ceiling to prevent the cat moving from one pen to another) in the room should be wire mesh; cats seem to enjoy climbing, and a wire-mesh wall is a safe means of exercise. The room should contain an elevated rack for sleeping and boxes containing sawdust, sand, or oil absorber (from an auto-parts dealer) to serve as toilets. Toilet facilities are important, since most cats obtained from pounds are housebroken and have a tendency to withhold stool if toilet facilities are not available. The temperature in the room should be maintained at about 21° to 22°C and the relative humidity at 50 percent. Cats, unlike rats, can regulate body temperature by shivering as well as by panting. Living quarters should be cleaned and toilet ballast changed at least once a day.

Cats are easily identified by their own natural markings, but, to be safe, each cat should have a collar showing an identification number and name. A more tedious identification method is to tattoo the number on the ear of the cat.

Cats respond to affection and gentleness and rarely present problems in handling. Rough treatment such as lifting a cat by the scruff of the neck makes the cat fearful and creates later handling problems. If a cat is to be carried for a short distance, place it on the arm, support the legs, and hold it against the body. For carrying a long distance, a carrying cage may be better than the arms, especially if the cat is new to its surroundings or fearful. Commercially available coated cardboard carrying cages are satisfactory, inexpensive, and readily obtained from any veterinary hospital supplier.

When restraining is required, lay the cat on its side on the table or floor. "Place a forearm over his neck and with both hands take a firm grasp of his legs, placing one finger between each pair of legs, then apply light pressure with the forearm" (Animal Welfare Institute, 1968, p. 59).

DIET

Cats require a diet with a high caloric density and protein content. Liver, muscles, and other bodily organs are the most suitable food items for cats, though these items should not be used as a complete diet for long periods of time, as such a diet can cause nutritional secondary hyperparathyroidism (Kirk, 1968). Cats can also consume fat in exceptionally high concentration, though their tolerance for food containing lactose or sucrose is not high. Carbohydrates are not essential for cats (Scott, 1960). A cat's caloric requirement depends on the growth period; a growing animal requires many more calories than a fully mature cat does. For example, a fully grown and not very active cat can be maintained on 60 calories/kg body weight a day (Waterhouse & Carver, 1962). Generally, the daily intake of most cats is about 4 percent of their body weight, though kittens and pregnant or lactating mothers may eat approximately double this amount (Paterson, 1963).

Water requirements are low if cats are fed a diet of moist food, but they will increase their water consumption by seven to ten times if they are fed dry food.

Those who have worked with cats are familiar with their reluctance to accept some foods. The severity of the problem is much greater if cats are to be trained to perform certain specific tasks to obtain food reinforcement. Crawford and Kenshalo (1965) report that homogenized calf's liver mixed with equal amounts of water is quite appealing to cats.

Another highly favored liquid reinforcer is a mixture of "C & D" cat food (Hill Packing), condensed milk, and multivitamin tablets (Pep, Upjohn). Cats can be maintained exclusively on this mixture. To prevent tooth decay, cats should always be fed some solids such as liver, fish, or chicken (J. I. Lacey, personal communication, Jan. 1968). For sick cats, Mull-Soy (Borden) provides an excellent high-energy liquid diet (Knapp, 1962). Debilitated cats or cats placed under stress require higher levels of vitamin B, which can be provided by mixing Vi-sorbin (Norden) in the regular feed.

FORCE-FEEDING

Force-feed cats by passing a tube through the mouth. The following intubation procedure is based on a method developed by Knapp (1962). The stomach tube consists of a 40-cm, soft-rubber catheter (French No. 12, 4 mm diam) attached to a 30 cc hypodermic syringe. Lubricate the tube with oil or some other water-soluble lubricant (for example, methyl cellulose) before passing the tube into the stomach. An assistant holds the cat upright against the chest, supports the hindlegs with one hand, and holds the forelegs with another. The operator keeps the head steady (parallel with the floor) and with the index finger presses one cheek between the upper and lower teeth. With the other hand, the operator passes the tube over the lower incisors, between the canine teeth. To prevent the cat's chewing the catheter, insert a hard plastic tube (readily made from a syringe case by cutting off the smaller end). Insert the catheter in the outer tube and gently push backward to the throat and down the esophagus. Once the catheter is inside the stomach (distance from the mouth is 15 to 30 cm, depending on the size of the cat), deposit the desired amount of material and gently remove the catheter. This method can be repeated for many days without producing any detectable damage to oral or pharyngeal surfaces.

BREEDING

Most behavioral laboratories do not engage in systematic breeding, mainly because adult animals are used in practically all experiments. Most laboratories are more interested in preventing pregnancy so that it does not interfere with the relatively extensive testing periods. However, if breeding is intended, the following points should be noted.

First, the breeding season in cats varies according to geographical location. In North America the breeding season falls roughly between December and July. Second, for good breeding results, at least 15 square feet (1.2 m^2) of space should be provided (Paterson, 1963), though successful breeding in small quarters has been reported. Third, ascertain that the female is in estrus, or heat; the estrus cycle in laboratory conditions may not occur at regular intervals. In most females estrus occurs about every 2 weeks and is maintained for 3 to 6 days, although in the presence of a restricted male estrus may continue 9 to 10 days (Dawson, 1950). The simplest way to ascertain whether or not a female is in heat is to gently rub the genital region. If the female is in heat, she will assume lordosis. Furthermore, before the onset of estrus, the female becomes excessively playful and rolls and rubs herself. Finally, take the female to the room where the male normally lives; males have a strong sense of territory and may not mate in strange places. If the female is mated successfully, she will roll violently on the ground (Paterson, 1963).

A pregnant female should be placed in an individual cage with a generous supply of cloth and paper scraps for building a nest. The gestation period is usually about 52 to 69 days, and the normal litter size is 3 to 6 kittens. The birth of only 1 or 2 offspring indicates dietary deficiency or endemic disease.

Newly born kittens are apparently deaf, and their eyes do not open until about 10 days after birth. Kittens wean at about 7 weeks, but they should be given solid food starting about the 4th week. Both male and female kittens grow at about the same rate until the 8th week, after which males grow more rapidly, and by the 13th week the male kitten usually reaches about 40 percent of the weight of the adult male (Dawson, 1950). The addition of procaine penicillin or penicillin G ((30 mg/kg wet food weight) to their feed increases the growth rate in kittens (Dickinson & Scott, 1953). While lactating, the female does not go through estrus. She can be used again for breeding 2 months after delivery.

COMMON USEFUL DATA

Physiological

ITEM	AVERAGE	RANGE
Rectal temperature (C)	37.7°	37.0–38.7°
Heart rate (beats/min)	116	110–140
Respiration (min)	25	20–30
Daily food consumption (g)	140	130–160
Daily water consumption (ml)	200	100–300
Estrus cycle (Polyestrous; induced 4 days) (Ovulation seasonally)	4	3–6
Gestation period (days)	63	52–69
Weaning age (weeks)	7	7–9
Puberty (months)	6	6–15
Life-span (years)	13	8–21

Sensory

A great deal of behavioral and electrophysiological research has been conducted to ascertain whether cats have color vision. Whereas the electrophysiological data indicate wavelength discrimination, behavioral evidence suggests that cats are color-blind but can learn wavelength discrimination on the basis of brightness differences between colors (R. Anderson, personal communication, Oct. 1966). The electrophysiological work suggests a lower limit for hearing at 30 Hz and an upper limit at about 45 kHz. The detection threshold for 100 Hz is about 38 dB SPL, whereas 500 Hz can be detected at about 6 dB (Spector, 1956). Gustatory mechanisms have been investigated, primarily by electrophysiological methods, and differential responses can be recorded for salt, hydrochloric acid, and quinine.

COMMON DISEASES: SYMPTOMS AND PREVENTION

The most common and dangerous disease in cats is distemper (feline panleukopenia). Distemper in early stages is marked by vomiting, followed by a high fever (39.6° to 40.2°C) that is either diphasic or polyphasic. A cat suffering from distemper is likely to assume a crouching position with the head hanging low. Distemper is contagious; immediately remove and destroy afflicted animals. To protect a cat from distemper, give one of the modified virus vaccines immediately after acquiring the cat for the laboratory. Each cat should be given one ml of the vaccine (Felocine®, Norden; Deltab®, Dellens) either subcutaneously or intraperitoneally. Cats over 10 to 14 weeks are given one injection of vaccine, then a yearly booster. Kittens under 12 weeks should be given a series of two injections. Such treatment will produce immunity in 48 to 72 hours.

In the case of known exposure to disease, injection of 2 to 5 cc Anti Feline Distemper Serum (Fort Dodge) subcutaneously or intraperitoneally gives immediate protection that will last 5 to 10 days. However, do not give a live virus vaccine during the 5- to 10-day period because serum antibodies will neutralize it.

Another common disease, also contagious but less prevalent than distemper, is feline rhinotracheitis (FVR). The symptoms of FVR are a high fever, accompanied by excessive salivation and ocular and nasal discharge, and excessive sneezing. FVR can be controlled by giving Aureomycin® (Lederle) orally at an initial dosage of 55 mg/kg body weight and continuing every 12 hours in reduced doses of 22.5 mg (Kirk, 1968).

Anorexia is very common in kittens, mainly because of breathing obstructions. Decongestive drugs or antihistamine, or both, usually help to relieve this condition. Kittens suffering from this condition should be given one (8 mg) capsule of Teladron® (Norden) every 12 hours. Subcutaneous injection of Antiphrine (Haver Lockhart) at a dosage of .055 cc/kg body weight brings fast relief. Orphan kittens can be maintained on human baby formula if the protein content is doubled.

Another disease common to young kittens (2 to 4 weeks old) is purulent conjunctivitis, an eye infection that usually lasts 4 to 5 days. Paterson (1963) reports complete recovery if the eyes are cleaned twice a day with lukewarm water and an eye ointment (such as Neo Cortif® or Mycitracin®, Upjohn) is applied under the lid.

A word of caution about using a rectal thermometer in cats: The anal sphincter of the cat is quite strong, and most cats resist insertion of the thermometer. Therefore, dip the thermometer in oil or apply a little petroleum jelly to it before using.

Monkey *(Macaca mulatta)*

Maintaining a monkey colony is an expensive, long-term project. Monkeys should be used as experimental animals only if financial and technical resources are assured for an indefinite period of time. The problems related to monkey maintenance, care, and training are unique, and the best way to prepare oneself for them is to gain first-hand knowledge by working in laboratories that use monkeys in behavioral research. Though monkeys have been used in behavioral research for quite some time, little has been written to adequately prepare the behavioral scientist for working with them. However, Sidowski and Lockard (1966) provide a brief summary, written with the psychologist in mind, of monkey care and maintenance.

HOUSING

Generally, monkeys should be purchased when they are about 1 to 2 years old, since the infant mortality rate in monkeys is rather high. The age of the monkey can be determined by the eruption of teeth, which follows a definite developmental sequence. Eckstein and Zuckerman (1957) have shown that the first molar erupts at about 20 months, followed by the central incisor (32 months), lateral incisor (35 months), second molar (42 months), first and second premolar and canine (43 to 44 months), and finally the third molar (70 to 90 months).

Purchase monkeys only from an authorized dealer. Practically all authorized dealers can supply monkeys that have been stabilized (that is, isolated and observed) in the United States. Each state has its own requirements, but invariably all require at least 30 days quarantine in the United States and two negative tuberculin tests. An added precaution is to keep the newly acquired monkeys in isolation for a few weeks; only after inspection and certification of good health by a veterinarian should they be introduced into the monkey colony.

Monkey quarters should be situated in an enclosed area that has a concrete floor with proper drainage. Although monkeys normally inhabit tropical regions, they can be housed exclusively indoors if their quarters are kept warm. Monkeys can tolerate a wide temperature range (10° to 26°C) as long as sudden fluctuations are avoided (Eckstein & Zuckerman, 1957). Ideally, the room temperature should be maintained at 15° to 26°C, with a relative humidity of 40 percent. As a rule of thumb, temperature and humidity should approximate conditions that are optimal for man.

The quarters themselves should consist of a large wire-mesh enclosure, either in the open air or, if the monkeys are to be kept indoors, inside the room that has been prepared for housing. Arrange the individual living cages within the enclosure. Public Law 89–544 stipulates that the individual cage provide a minimum floor space equal to an area of at least three times the area occupied by the monkey when standing on four feet. Placement of the cages in a larger enclosure presents considerable advantages. When the attendant enters to clean or feed the monkeys, the animal can be allowed to run around outside its living cage as a good way to help prevent cage paralysis. The outer enclosure also minimizes the possibility of escape, especially when the cage is housed in an indoor room, for it would rarely happen that the doors of both the cage and the room would be left open at the same time. Fitting all doors with strong closure springs to protect against carelessness in closing doors is advisable. Also, if some unauthorized person were to enter the main enclosure, as some people are apt to do in spite of warnings and signs to the contrary, little harm could be done.

Arrange the cages in a single or double-decked row, but, in either case, firmly secure them to the floor or walls of the room, since monkeys have a tendency to jolt and shake their cages vigorously. The cages preferably should be made of stainless steel and should have wide wire-mesh floors so that excrement and waste can drop into a catch pan placed below. The pan should be filled with sawdust, San-i-cel, or water. Cleaning pans daily not only is a sanitary precaution but also is economical, since, with daily attention, the pans need be filled only with water. The cage doors should be secured with padlocks, though some manufactured cages have bolts in places where the animals cannot reach them. Give food through a hopper attached to the cage or place food in small stainless-steel pans that slide into the cage. Water should always be available to the animal unless the experiment specifies otherwise.

Clean cages with soap and hot (70°C) water at least once a month and hose the floor of the enclosure room daily. A garden hose attached to the hot water faucet facilitates cleaning immobile cages.

HANDLING

Monkeys are very active and aggressive animals, but they respond well to handling. Frequently, monkeys must be captured to be removed to another place for physical examination, drug administration, or experimental work. Catch nets are usually used to remove animals for physical examination, whereas monkeys are trained to enter voluntarily into a transport cage for experimental work.

In order to catch an animal for physical examination, open the cage door very slightly—that is, enough for a net to be inserted through the crack but not enough to allow the monkey to escape. Place the net over the monkey, and, once the monkey is inside, twist and lower the net to the floor. Van Wagenen (personal communication, January 1971) suggests that, if the catching net is made of cloth or some other material through which the monkey cannot see, the monkey will readily enter the net. Grasp the head of the monkey from the back and open the net; grasp the monkey's arms and hold them together behind its back. Because monkeys can bite hard and inflict severe wounds, wearing heavy duty gloves that come up to the upper arms when catching monkeys is advisable.

Another effective procedure for capturing a monkey, in appropriate circumstances, is to let him loose into the outer room. Since monkeys are apt to get winded rather quickly, they can usually be captured by hand or in a net after a short chase (Van Wagenen, 1950).

The transport cage is one of the most important pieces of equipment in behavioral research of the monkey. The transport cage is essentially a metal box (usually 46 cm × 46 cm × 76 cm; adequate dimensions depend on the size of the animals) that has two guillotine-type doors with spring locks. The sides of the cage are usually heavy wire mesh, whereas the top and doors are solid metal sheets. A handle on the top of the cage facilitates carrying the cage.

To train an animal to enter a transport cage, open both the doors and spread a few peanuts on the floor at the front of the cage. It takes some time before a monkey will enter the cage to pick up the peanuts from the floor; usually, the animal reaches into the cage in an attempt to obtain the peanuts without entering. However, progressively increasing the distance from the door to the point where the peanuts are placed lures the monkey farther into the cage. After the animal has entered the cage a few times, lower the far door. Feeding the monkey from the side of the cage through the wire mesh tends to increase the length of the animal's stay in the open cage. After a day of such training, also lower the near door. Feed the monkey for a few minutes and then release him. On the following day, after the monkey has entered the cage of his own volition, lift the cage and carry it around the room before releasing the animal. If some monkeys do not respond to such training procedures and must be chased into the cage, use a brush to frighten the animal into a transport cage that has been placed next to the door of the living cage.

IDENTIFICATION

Because of the long-term nature of most behavioral research, dye-marking is not very useful as a means of identification, as it fades too quickly. The most frequently used identification is a tattooed number on the chest of the animal, the chest being preferred over other parts of the body because the hair on the upper chest is sparse. For tattooing, use heavy-duty clippers to remove hair; apply the number in either black or red ink. Commercially available plastic bands with numbers can also be used for identification, though monkeys have a tendency to play constantly with such bands.

DIET

Proper nutrition is the best means of preventing most diseases. Ruch (1959) states that the origin of a great many cases of monkey disease is acute malnutrition.

Monkeys can be maintained in good health on commercially available diets (Purina Monkey Chow) if the diet is properly supplemented with fresh fruit, green vegetables, and vitamins. The use of a particular kind of fruit or vegetable usually depends on which seasonal fruits are available and thus inexpensive. Ideally, fruits and vegetables should be varied from day to day. Table 1.1 compares the diets used to maintain monkeys in three different types of research laboratories.

Monkeys can be fed sweet potatoes, cooked rice, and raw or cooked eggs—in fact, practically any food except meat. Highly preferred foods are bananas, grapes, peanuts, raisins, and currants, which are usually employed as food reinforcement. Most laboratories provide one meal a day, to which monkeys adapt very readily.

TABLE 1.1 Diets Used for Laboratory Monkeys

NAME OF LABORATORY	TYPE OF LABORATORY	BASIC DIET (ADULT)	FRUITS AND VEGETABLES	VITAMINS AND SUPPLEMENTS
Wisconsin Primate Center	Behavioral	Commercial Monkey Chow	Lettuce Orange Apple	Irradol-A Isoniazid
Texas Radiobiological Laboratory	Biological	Home-Cooked Meal	Orange Apple	Vi-Daylin Ascorbic Acid Isoniazid
New York Lederle Laboratories	Pharmaceutical	Commercial Monkey Chow	Apple Banana Orange Carrot Green Bean	Vi-tyke

FORCE-FEEDING

The simplest method for force-feeding monkeys is nasal intubation as described by Moreland (1965). The basic equipment for feeding is a rubber catheter (French No. 8, $2^2/_3$ mm diam; or No. 10, $3^1/_3$ mm diam), or a pediatric human nasogastric feeding tube, and an appropriate-size syringe. An assistant restrains the monkey by holding its arms together behind its back with one hand and immobilizing its head with the other. A second assistant restrains the feet. The operator gently passes the lubricated tube into a nostril. When the tube reaches the throat the animal swallows the tube. If the tube should enter the trachea, the monkey will struggle violently and choke. In such a case, pull the tube out a little and gently push down again until it reaches the stomach.

CHAIRING

Many experiments require restricting the monkey to a small area that contains stimulus display and response panels. A restraining chair, basically a regular chair with a large neck plate, can be used to hold the monkey in place by the neck and support his hands and feet. Monkeys can be left in the restraining chair for long periods of time without any distinctly harmful effects. However, long-term, continuous chairing can cause ulcers at the point of contact with the seat, edema of the legs from lack of use, and intestinal blockage from lack of exercise. If long-term chairing is essential, Riopelle and Thomsen (1968) suggest the following precautions to reduce health problems: First, whenever feasible, release the animal from the chair (24 hours of release for every 96 hours of confinement). Second, clean the chair and the animal daily. Finally, to take the pressure off the limbs, tilt the chair to a semireclining position at periodic intervals.

A recent restraint device developed by Henry and Bowman (1971) eliminates almost all the problems normally encountered in long-term chairing. The device permits the monkey to stand or sit at will and leaves the hands free to reach the mouth for self-feeding; yet the monkey cannot touch an implanted electrode or cannula. Furthermore, adjustable parts permit using the same setup for monkeys of different sizes. (See Figure 1.4.)

The main components of the Henry and Bowman device are as follows: (1) an adjustable collar and bib; (2) an adjustable waist restraining device; and (3) the chair that can "float" above the base of the device (to permit freedom of movement). A nylon strap looped around the neck and brought to the back of the chair through a slot eliminates the problem of the neck's making contact with surrounding metal (see Figure 1.4, bottom). A wingnut tightened friction clamp in back of the chair (see Figure 1.4, center) keeps the strap in place. A nylon band restrains the waist of the animal. Raising or lowering the waist device adjusts the distance between the waist and neck bands. The chair is welded onto a .94 cm × 76 cm × 127 cm steel base (see Figure 1.4, top). The perpendicular frame of the chair is made of 2.5-cm angle irons welded to the base, through which are drilled .94-cm holes every 3.8 cm. Bolts are passed through the .94-cm hole (at a height appropriate for the size of the animal) in the two perpendicular angle irons. To these bolts movable parallel bars are attached on each side. The parallel bars, which are attached by means of joints to the back of the chair, have on each side coil-expansion springs. Finally, the springs are adjusted by hooking their ends into holes in the parallel bars, so that the chair floats (thus permitting freedom of movement to the animal) above the base.

When preparing the monkey for chairing, allow the animal to adapt to the chair for a few days for periods of short duration. During initial adaptation, tranquilizing drugs are frequently given to facilitate handling and training, although Young (1957, 1958) has devised a simple training technique that requires no drugs or physical contact with the monkey. Some investigators have even succeeded in training nonaggressive monkeys to chair themselves by using a procedure very much like that used in training a monkey to enter a transport cage. During training the monkey was allowed to enter "an enclosed space between upper and lower plates of the restraining chair which is placed against the home cage. When trapped in this space, the animal was enticed, with small pieces of fruit, to place its head through the head hole of the upper plate. This allowed the neck plate of the restraining chair to be positioned" (Barrow et al., 1966, p. 680). The authors report that after 2 to 3 days of such training, monkeys readily chair themselves.

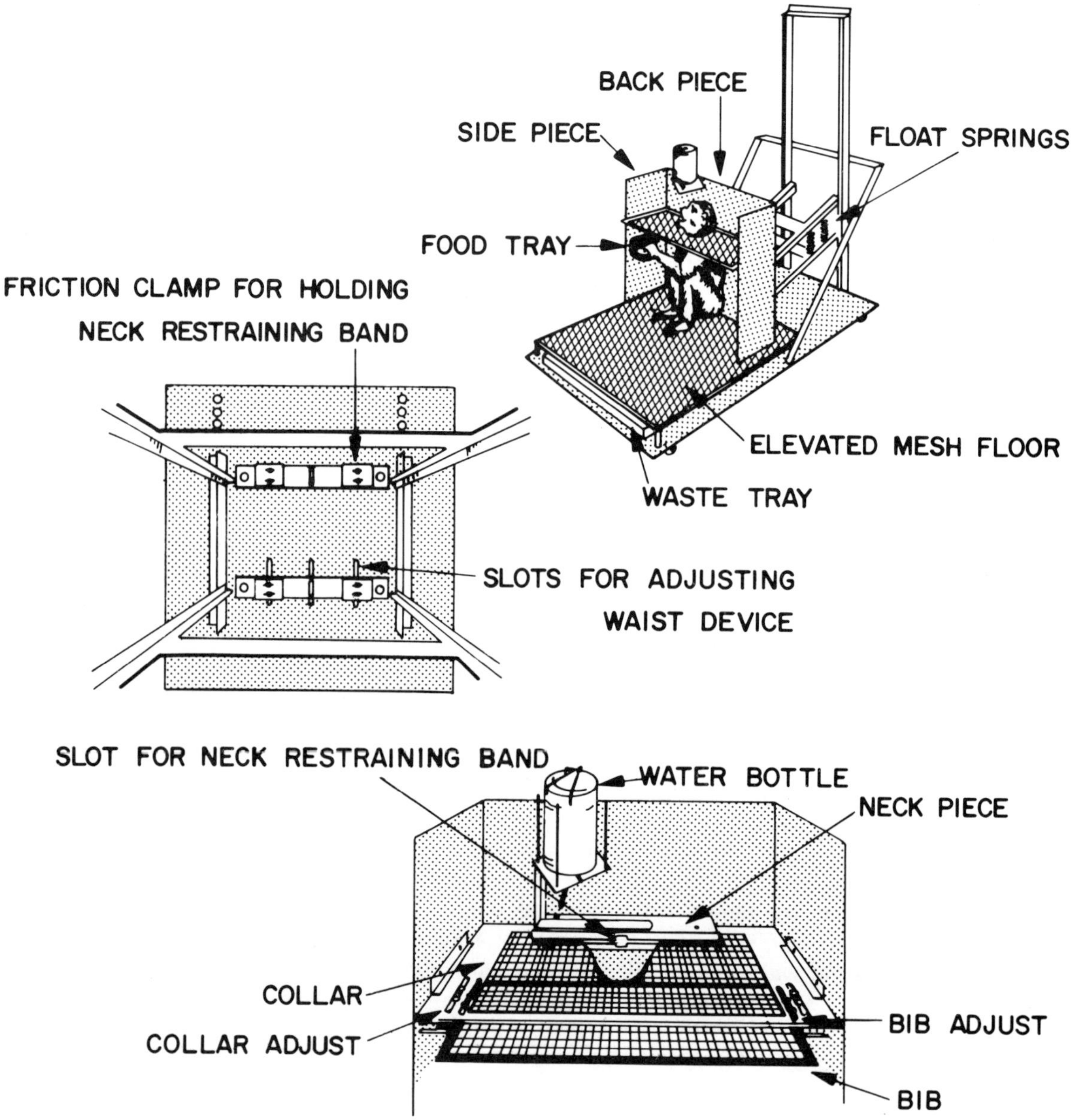

FIGURE 1.4. A Long-Term Restraint Device for Monkeys. The collar and bib (lower) allow the monkey's hands to reach its mouth. The neck and waist bands are made of nylon and can be adjusted (center). The float springs, adjusted by hooking the ends into holes in the parallel bars (upper), make it possible for the chair to float above the base. From K. R. Henry & R. E. Bowman. A long-term restraint device for primates. *Physiology and Behavior,* 1971, **7,** 271–272.

BREEDING

The soundest practice is not to breed, since laboratory breeding is an expensive, extremely frustrating, and completely unpredictable venture. If there is a specific need for infant monkeys, it is far better to buy pregnant females. However, the following brief discussion is included for those who wish to breed monkeys.

Ideally, the breeding pair should be about 4 years old. Females reach puberty at about 3 years. Sex-skin development characterizes the onset of puberty; the skin at the side of the midline pubic region thickens, acquires a deep-pink color, and takes on a turgid appearance. Females complete the menstrual cycle, indicated by the occurrence of drops of blood on the cage floor or in the catch pan, every 28 days. Female monkeys will accept a male at any time of the year and do not exhibit any distinct behavior when in heat.

It is important that the male and female become acquainted before mating, as familiarity increases the probability of a successful mating. The pair should be housed in the same room within sight of one another. The female should be introduced into the male cage on the 11th or 12th day of the menstrual cycle.

There is no sure method to diagnose pregnancy until about 3 months after mating, when the pregnant female shows enlargement of the abdomen and an increase in body weight. The gestation period is between 146 and 180 days. At birth, which is invariably at night (Van Wagenen, 1950), the infant monkey weighs approximately 300 to 600 grams. Normal infants show well-coordinated movements by 1 week of age.

Infants can be raised away from their mothers on a human baby formula. Accounts of infant care are available in Mason and Harlow (1958, 1959), Blomquist and Harlow (1961), and Van Wagenen (1950). Place the infant on a heating pad and wrap it in a towel. Administer the liquid diet in the Brecht feeder, designed for use by premature human infants. Hold the nipple to the infant's lips, since the infant does not have directive head movement. For the first two weeks, the infant's hands and feet must be permitted to grab a towel or some other soft material; otherwise, the sucking and swallowing reflexes are not properly elicited (Van Wagenen, 1950).

Sidowski and Lockard (1966) describe the procedure of infant care and liquid diet used at the Wisconsin Regional Primate Center. According to these authors, 8- to 12-hour-old infants are given 5 percent dextrose and water every 2 hours for 11 to 12 feedings. The infants are then fed Similac with Iron (Ross) mixed with equal parts of water. Solid formula (human baby formula) can be offered at about 1 to 1½ months. The young monkey can be raised in a group of age-mates beginning at about age 3 months.

COMMON USEFUL DATA

Physiological

ITEM	AVERAGE	RANGE
Rectal temperature (C)	38.5°	38.5°–39.1°
Heart rate (beats/min)	200	185–260
Respiration (min)	50	31–60
Daily food consumption (g)	120	90–150
Daily water consumption (cc)	410	171–710
Menstrual cycle (days)	28	23–33
Gestation period (days)	164	146–180
Weaning age (months)	From birth	4–6
Puberty, male (years)	4.5	3–5
Puberty, female (years)	3.5	2–4
Life-span (years)	15	10–30

Sensory

The visual system in monkeys is highly developed and functionally comparable to that of man. Monkeys are diurnal animals and have excellent color vision. They can readily learn wavelength discrimination except for yellow (589 mu) and longer wavelengths. The hearing range is between 60 Hz and 40 kHz (Stebbins, 1973). Stebbins (1973) reports that monkeys can detect changes of about 5 Hz in frequency and 2 dB in intensity at 1000 Hz at 60 dB above the threshold of audibility. The gustatory system is fully developed; monkeys have some clear taste preferences (Weiskrantz, 1960). Monkeys can also readily learn olfactory discriminations (see Schuckman, Kling, & Orbach, 1969).

COMMON DISEASES: SYMPTOMS AND PREVENTION

Monkeys are very susceptible to respiratory diseases, especially tuberculosis. Administer the tuberculin test immediately to the newly arrived monkeys. The procedure is as follows: Inject one ml (25 mg) undiluted Mammalian Intradermic Tuberculin (U. S. Dept. of Agriculture, Bureau of Animal Husbandry) in the eyelid with a 27-gauge, one-half-in. needle. To inject, pull down the upper portion of the eyelid with the thumb and keep the syringe parallel to the eye. The results of the test can be determined within 48 hours; swelling and redness of the tested eyelid characterize a positive reaction. Though investigators have noted false positive reactions, it is wise to destroy those monkeys that show a positive reaction. (It is also good policy not to house two monkeys in the same cage before administering this test, since a nontubercular monkey that has been housed with a tubercular monkey must also be destroyed.) Repeat tuberculin tests as often as possible, but at least every three months. Also give newly arrived monkeys tetracycline soluble powder (200 mg/animal) in their drinking water for a week after arrival and routinely during the winter months thereafter. As a preventive measure for tuberculosis, add Isoniazid (20 mg/kg body weight) to the diet.

Dysentery is also very common in monkeys, especially in newly shipped animals and in infants. An animal suffering from dysentery is very inactive and shows little interest in food and drink. Chronic dysentery is invariably caused by bacteria, and afflicted animals should be isolated from the others. The disease responds to chloramphenicol palmitate (Chloromycetin®, Parke Davis), which should be administered intramuscularly at a dosage of 55 mg/kg body weight. Chloromycetin is also available for oral administration (55 mg/kg) and, if preferred, should be added to the feed twice daily for four days. Entromycin® (Pitman-Moore) mixed in drinking water (4.5 gm powder/1 liter water) is reported to be extremely effective (Snodgrass, 1955). Alternatively, 4 ml of 125 mg paregoric elixir (Abbott) can be given in the feed (Kirk, 1968). In severely ill animals, replace bodily-fluid losses with daily intraperitoneal injections of saline-dextrose solutions.

Another disease, though not very common, is Virus B (*Herpes simiae*). Animals suffering from Virus B usually have lesions or ulcers about the buccal cavity and lips. Virus B is transmitted to humans by bites or contamination of wounds by infected material. It can be fatal. An animal suffering from this disease must be destroyed immediately. Avoid physical contact with the diseased animal's body, saliva, or excreta. Sterilize the cage and other objects with which the animal had contact. All personnel working in the animal room must report for physical examinations.

REFERENCES

Altman, P. L., & Dittmer, D. S. *Biology data book.* Washington, D. C.: Federation of American Societies for Experimental Biology, 1964.

Anderson, J. W. The production of ultrasonic sounds by laboratory rats and other animals. *Science,* 1954, **119,** 808–809.

Animal Welfare Institute. *Basic care of experimental animals.* New York: Author, 1968.

Barrow, S., Luschei, E., Nathan, M., & Saslow, C. A training technique for the daily chairing of monkeys. *Journal of the Experimental Analysis of Behavior,* 1966, **9,** 680.

Blomquist, A. J., & Harlow, H. F. The infant rhesus monkey program at the University of Wisconsin Primate Laboratory. *Proceedings of the Animal Care Panel,* 1961, **11,** 57–64.

Clopton, B. M., & Winfield, J. A. Tonotopic organization in the inferior colliculus of the rat. *Brain Research,* 1973, **56,** 355–358.

Crawford, F. T., & Kenshalo, D. R. A liquid reinforcer for the cat. *Journal of the Experimental Analysis of Behavior,* 1965, **8,** 29.

Dawson, A. B. The domestic cat. In E. J. Farris (Ed.), *The care and breeding of laboratory animals.* New York: Wiley, 1950.

Dickinson, C. D., & Scott, P. P. The effect of penicillin on the weight gained by kittens. *Proceedings of the Royal Society,* B, 1953, **61,** 24–25.

Eckstein, P., & Zukerman, S. Monkeys. In A. N. Worden & W. Lane-Petter (Eds.), *UFAW handbook on the care and management of laboratory animals.* (2nd ed.) London: University Federation for Animal Welfare, 1957.

Farris, E. J. The rat as an experimental animal. In E. J. Farris (Ed.), *The care and breeding of laboratory animals.* New York: Wiley, 1950.

Farris, E. J., & Griffith, J. Q. *The rat in laboratory investigation.* Philadelphia: Lippincott, 1949.

Hagstrom, E. O., & Pfaffmann, C. The relative taste effectiveness of different sugars for the rat. *Journal of Comparative and Physiological Psychology,* 1959, **52,** 259–262.

Henry, K. R., & Bowman, R. E. A long-term restraint device for primates. *Physiology and Behavior,* 1971, **7,** 271–272.

Kirk, R. W. (Ed.) *Current veterinary therapy.* (3rd ed.) Philadelphia: Saunders, 1968.

Knapp, W. A., Jr. Feeding hospitalized cats. *Veterinary Medicine,* 1962, **57,** 46–51.

Mason, W. A., & Harlow, H. F. Learned approach by infant rhesus monkeys to the sucking situation. *Psychological Reports,* 1958, **4,** 78–82.

Mason, W. A., & Harlow, H. F. Initial responses of rhesus monkeys to solid foods. *Psychological Reports,* 1959, **5,** 193–199.

Moreland, A. F. Collection and withdrawal of body fluids and infusion techniques. In W. I. Gay (Ed.), *Methods of animal experimentation.* Vol. 1. New York: Academic Press, 1965.

Paterson, J. S. Cats. In W. Lane-Petter (Ed.), *Animals for research: Principles of breeding and management.* New York: Academic Press, 1963.

Pfaffmann, C. The sense of taste. In J. Bield (Ed.), *Handbook of physiology.* Vol. 1. Section 1. Washington, D. C.: American Physiological Society, 1959.

Pfaffmann, C., Goff, W. R., & Bare, J. K. An olfactometer for the rat. *Science,* 1958, **128,** 1007–1008.

Riopelle, A. J., & Thomsen, C. E. Use of primates as behavioral subjects. In W. I. Gay (Ed.), *Methods of animal experimentation.* Vol. 3. New York: Academic Press, 1968.

Ruch, T. C. *Diseases of laboratory primates.* Philadelphia: Saunders, 1959.

Schuckman, H., Kling, A., & Orbach, J. Olfactory discrimination with lesions in the amygdala. *Journal of Comparative and Physiological Psychology,* 1969, **67,** 212–215.

Scott, P. P. The cat. *Veterinary Record,* 1960, **72,** 6–9.

Sidowski, J. B., & Lockard, R. B. Some preliminary considerations in research. In J. B. Sidowski (Ed.), *Experimental methods and instrumentation in psychology.* New York: McGraw-Hill, 1966.

Smith, D. C. Methods of euthanasia and disposal of laboratory animals. In W. I. Gay (Ed.), *Methods of animal experimentation.* Vol. 1. New York: Academic Press, 1965.

Snodgrass, T. B. The management of diarrhea problems in a monkey colony. *Veterinary Medicine,* 1955, **50,** 185–186.

Spector, W. S. (Ed.) *Handbook of biological data.* Philadelphia: Saunders, 1956.

Stebbins, W. C. Hearing of old world monkeys (Cercopithecinae). *American Journal of Physical Anthropology,* 1973, **38,** 357–364.

Van Wagenen, G. The monkey. In E. J. Farris (Ed.), *The care and breeding of laboratory animals.* New York: Wiley, 1950.

Waterhouse, H. N., & Carver, D. S. Growth rate, food and caloric consumption of laboratory cats. *Proceedings of the Animal Care Panel,* 1962, **12,** 271–274.

Weiskrantz, L. Effects of medial temporal lesions on taste preference in the monkey. *Nature,* 1960, **187,** 879–880.

Wurtman, R. J. Effects of light and visual stimuli on endocrine function. In L. Martini & W. F. Ganong (Eds.), *Neuroendocrinology.* Vol. 2. New York: Academic Press, 1966.

Young, F. A. A primate control system. *Proceedings of the Animal Care Panel,* 1957, **7,** 127–137.

Young, F. A. A simplified loading technique for a monkey chair. *Proceedings of the Animal Care Panel,* 1958, **8,** 161–163.

SUGGESTED READINGS

Farris, E. J. (Ed.) *The care and breeding of laboratory animals.* New York: Wiley, 1950.

Gay, W. I. (Ed.) *Methods of animal experimentation.* Vol. 1. New York: Academic Press, 1965.

Lane-Petter, W. *Animals for research: Principles of breeding and management.* New York: Academic Press, 1963.

Lane-Petter, W., Worden, A. N., Hill, B. F., Paterson, J. S., & Vevers, H. G. (Eds.) *UFAW handbook on the care and management of laboratory animals.* (3rd ed.) London: Livingstone, 1967.

CHAPTER 2

Equipment, Anesthesia, and Basic Surgical Skills

Devendra Singh
UNIVERSITY OF TEXAS AT AUSTIN

This chapter presents practical, elementary aspects of the surgical setup, anesthesiological techniques, and some common surgical skills. The first section deals with the management of frequently used surgical equipment and instruments. Whenever possible, inexpensive substitutes for costly equipment are suggested. The second section discusses dosage, administration, maintenance, and management of anesthesia in rats, cats, and monkeys. The final section deals with the preparation for aseptic surgery, some common suture patterns, and postoperative care of the animal.

SURGERY

Room and Equipment

Practically any room can be converted into a surgical room. The physical dimensions are dictated by the nature of the surgery and the kinds of animals used. If work is restricted to rats alone, elaborate arrangement of space is not necessary; any solid, sturdy table and a good light source are sufficient for most surgery involved in behavior research on the rat. On the other hand, if space is available, the operating room should be planned for aseptic surgery. A room designed for minor surgery can be adapted readily to major surgery with little additional equipment and practically no instrument duplication. Thus, assuming that future plans will call for surgery on the cat or the monkey, the surgery room should be big enough to install a good-size surgical table, an instrument cabinet, a surgical lamp, a container for waste disposal, and oxygen equipment. It should be large enough to provide working space for a surgeon and at least one assistant. The room should be designed in such a manner that it can be thoroughly cleaned. Since natural light will not be used, windows are not essential and might best be avoided since they tend to attract dust. If additional space is available, an adjoining room should be used as a preparation room, which should contain a hot and cold water supply, a perfusion setup (see Chapter 7), and a table for preparing the animal before surgery. The preparation room should also have several cabinets or closets for the storage of surgical and anesthetic accessories (for example, hair clippers, disinfectant, hypodermic syringes and needles, scissors, cotton roll and gauze, and adhesive tape) and cleaning supplies (for example, nail brushes, hand soap, and soap for cleaning instruments). Ideally, the autoclave should be installed in the preparation room.

The most important pieces of equipment in a surgery room are the surgical table and lamp. A human surgical table, adapted to animal surgery, is an unnecessary expense. Furthermore, commercially manufactured animal surgical tables lack flexibility and are also rather expensive. With very simple tools and inexpensive materials, however, an old barber's chair can successfully be converted into an operating table that meets all the requirements for flexibility (see Figure 2.1).

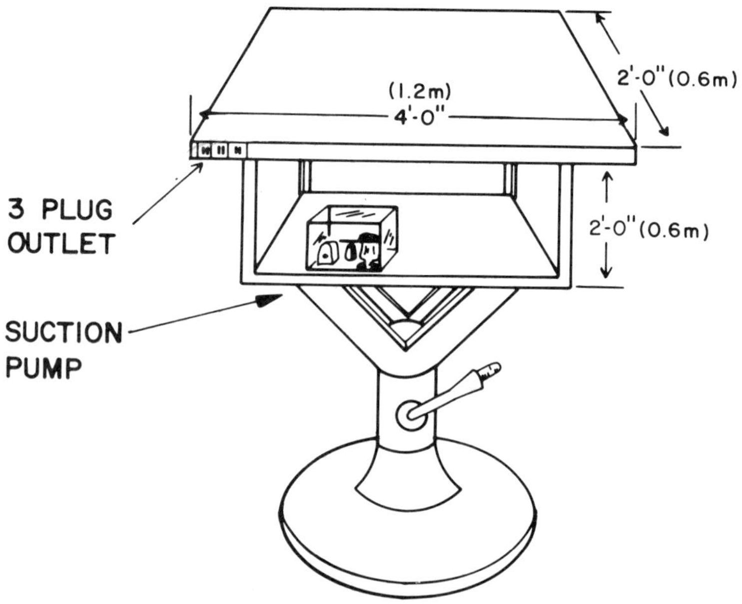

FIGURE 2.1. A Surgical Operating Table Made from a Discarded Barber's Chair.

The light source should produce a minimum amount of heat and should be easily manipulated to illuminate any desired area. An overhead source that minimizes both glare and shadow provides the most satisfactory illumination. The operating room should never be flooded with bright light. The gowns worn by the surgeon and his assistants should be soft green or gray, since a white gown, which reflects more light than a green or gray one, frequently causes eyestrain.

Other pieces of required equipment are a good portable suction pump (Harvard pump) and an incubator. A suction pump, with catheter, is not only essential for aspiration (see Chapter 3) but also is useful for removing blood from a wound or for removing saliva obstructing the oral cavity of an anesthetized animal. Furthermore, many suction pumps (for example, Starline) can also expel air and therefore can be used for positive-pressure ventilation of the lungs of anesthetized animals. An incubator, which is essential for convalescent animals (to prevent drug-induced hypothermia), can be converted from a discarded human-infant incubator. Or, an incubator can be constructed easily from 1.3 cm-thick, clear Plexiglas, through which a hole is drilled for filtering oxygen through a basket of ice (see Figure 2.2). (The chamber can be converted into an ether chamber for anesthetic purposes by replacing the oxygen with ether vapors or by attaching a spray bottle of ether onto the side of the chamber.) Place a heating pad on the floor of the recuperating chamber. Though not ideal, the box can provide acceptable temperature and humidity control during postsurgical recovery.

Instruments

If one must choose, a wise policy is to buy a few of the best surgical tools rather than large quantities of mediocre ones. Through practice one can develop a great deal of skill and flexibility in the use of a small number of instruments. Furthermore, although high-quality surgical instruments are very expensive, they will last almost indefinitely if given proper care. Surgical instruments from the following functional categories will usually meet the requirements of a laboratory planned for conventional surgery.

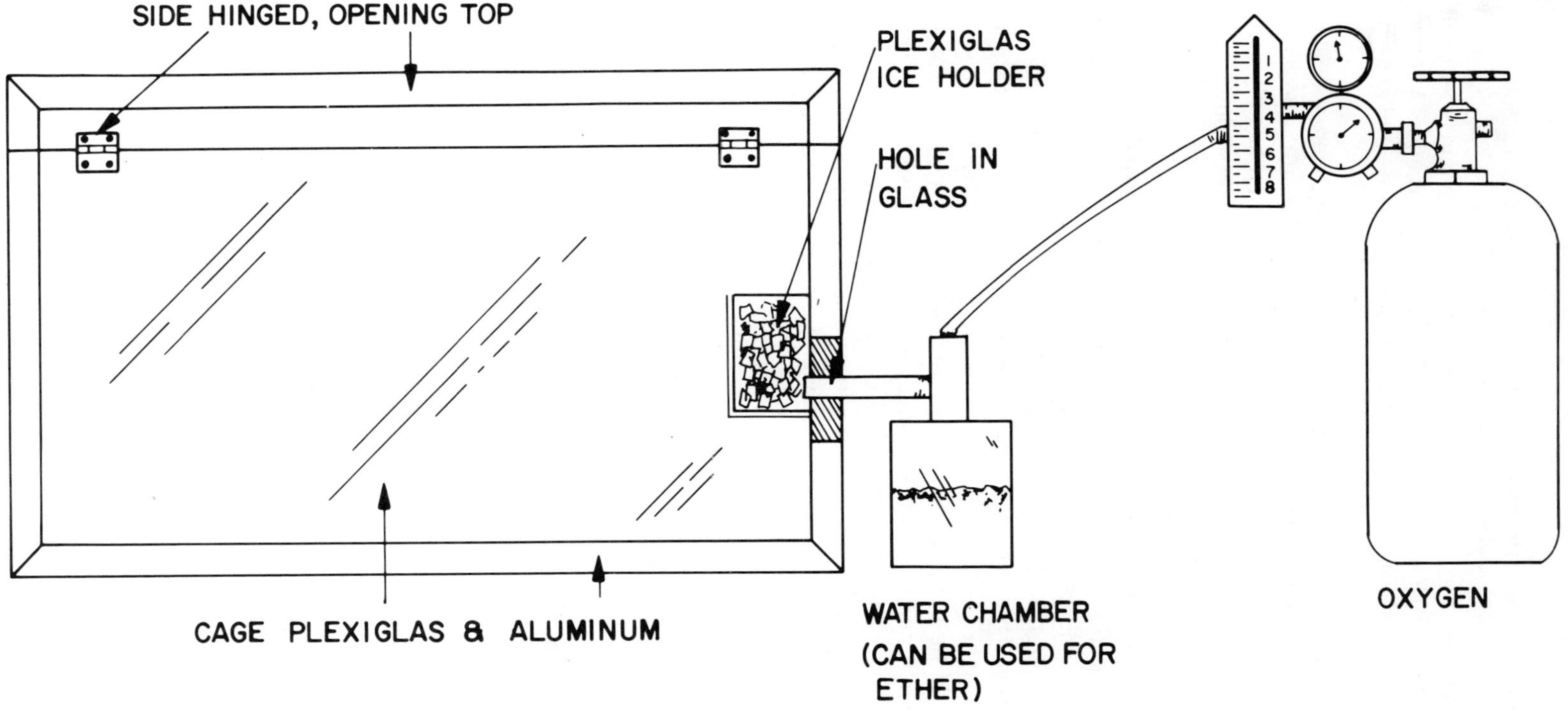

FIGURE 2.2. An Inexpensive Custom-Made Incubator or Ether Chamber. When used as incubator, humidity is maintained by filling the Plexiglas holder with ice and passing oxygen through it; a heating pad on the floor of the chamber maintains temperature. When used as an ether chamber, the tube carrying oxygen is disconnected and a spray bottle containing ether is attached.

CUTTING

The most common cutting instruments are knives, or scalpels, scissors, rongeurs, saws, and drills. Knives are most frequently used for making skin incisions. Knife handles and blades have numbers representing various types, and only certain types of blades fit certain types of knife handles. For example, blades 10, 11, 12, and 15 fit handles 3 and 7; blades 20, 21, and 22 fit handle 4. Many researchers prefer knife handle 4 with blade 20 for cat and monkey surgery, and knife handle 3 with blade 10 for rat surgery.

Scissors, which are used to cut tissues and sutures, come in different lengths and styles. Dissecting (Mayo) scissors are used for cutting overlying and exposed tissue, whereas Metzenbaum scissors, which are long, are used for dissecting in wounds and cavities. Frequently used scissors are straight dissecting (sharp-sharp point; blunt-blunt point), Mayo curved dissecting, Iris (straight and curved), and Metzenbaum.

Rongeurs, saws, and drills are used for cutting bones. Rongeurs are used for chipping bone away (for example, to enlarge a hole in the skull or to remove the brain from the skull). Saws are used for cutting larger pieces of bone (for example, to make a bone flap) (see Chapter 3). The most frequently used bone-cutting instruments in behavioral research are surgical drills for drilling holes in the skull to insert electrodes. Surgical drills can be electrical (for example, a dental drill) or hand-operated (Hudson cranial drill). The size of the hole depends on the size of trephines and burrs. Most of the required drilling can be performed with a conventional dental drill or an electrical hobby drill (Dremel). The drill should be wired through a rheostat so that its speed can be controlled. A foot-pedal rheostat can be purchased from any dental-supply store. For use on cats and monkeys, a hand drill is better since it not only allows better control of direction and pressure but also reduces the amount of heat generated. Since the skulls of cats and monkeys are relatively thick, a dental or electrical drill, if used continuously, could produce enough heat to affect cortical tissues.

GRASPING

Grasping instruments (hemostats and forceps) are designed to grasp tissue to hold, clamp, or pull it out of the way. Grasping instruments may have serrations, or teeth, to provide a firm grip. Forceps with serrations (dressing forceps) are used to grasp delicate tissue with minimal damage. Heavy teeth forceps (tissue forceps such as Kocher forceps) are used for grasping muscles. Towel clips, which have sharp points, are used to clip towels together or to the skin. A variety of hemostats (for clamping) such as the curved, straight, and mosquito types should also be purchased.

RETRACTING

Retractors are used to hold back the edge of a wound or cavity, to expose the operative area, or to hold back superficial tissues to expose deep tissues. Self-retaining retractors with blunt and sharp prongs (various spreads from 6.3 cm to 18.8 cm) meet most surgical requirements.

SUTURING

Michel wound clips and surgical needles can perform most skin and tissue suturing (closure). Michel wound clips are applied with a clip applier, which has a specially designed bite. Wound clips can be used to close large skin incisions (such as that of an ovariectomy or adrenalectomy); however, their use is not highly recommended, since they can be irritating and animals can pull the clips out.

Suturing should be done with surgical needles, which come in a variety of sizes, thicknesses, and shapes. Needles are numbered on a fine-to-coarse scale (the smaller the number, the larger the needle; for example, 1 is coarse and 20 is very fine) and can be straight or curved. Finally, needles can have a tapered (round) point or a cutting (triangular) point. Straight needles are used primarily for skin closure, whereas curved needles can be used for both deep and surface closures. Most researchers prefer curved needles, which are always used with a needle holder. Tapered, or round-point, needles are used on delicate tissue such as dura mater since the tapered needle tends to push tissue aside rather than cut it. Cutting, or triangular, needles are used for skin and other tough tissues.

ANESTHESIA

Because local anesthesia is rarely used in behavioral research, this section deals only with general anesthesia. General anesthesia, which makes the animal manageable and insensitive to pain during surgery, can be induced by inhalation or injection of anesthetic drugs. Regardless of the method employed, the effectiveness of the anesthetic agent depends on a variety of factors, the most important of which is the metabolic rate of the animal. Therefore, conditions that affect the metabolic rate also alter the effects of anesthesia. According to Lumb (1963), size (the smaller the animal, the larger the dose per unit of body weight), age (infants and older animals are very sensitive), amount of fat deposit (animals with large quantities of fat are more sensitive than muscular animals), and general physical condition (fatigue and strain increase sensitivity) are important factors. Furthermore, a variety of other factors such as concentration of the anesthetic agent (dilution reduces effectiveness), rate of injection (a slower rate is less effective), anesthetic treatment history (repeated administration of certain anesthetic agents produces tolerance in the animal and reduces effectiveness), concurrent administration of other drugs (certain drugs such as sulfonamides increase sensitivity to ether as well as to barbiturates), and recent feeding (feeding alters the metabolic rate and reduces the duration of the anesthesia) have also been shown to modify the effect of anesthesia (Lumb, 1963).

Routes of Administration

INHALATION

The inhalation method is often used to administer volatile anesthetic agents such as ether by dropping the agent on a cotton gauze mask placed loosely over the muzzle of the animal. Because this procedure causes the animal to struggle, it is not advised for cats and monkeys, for which, instead, an ether chamber should be used. Ether should be administered in a room having proper exhaust facilities, since ether can cause irritation and dryness of the eye. As a precaution, apply eye ointment (veterinary ophthalmic ointment, Sussex) to the animal's eyes. Ether should not touch the animal or irritation will result. Ether can also cause excessive salivation and bronchial secretion, which can be reduced by pretreating the animal with atropine sulfate, but it is wise to drain or aspirate saliva from the animal after surgery.

Ether is an excellent, short-acting anesthesia and should be used when surgery can be completed in a short time. Because ether is highly flammable and explosive, extreme care should be taken. A distinct and boldly printed sign indicating that ether is being used should be displayed at the entrance to the surgery room to keep smokers from entering. Ether should not be used for long-term anesthesia, since it is rather cumbersome and long-term use requires arrangements such as endotracheal tubes with a breathing apparatus and continuous monitoring. Barbiturates are better for long-term anesthesia since they can be injected in measured dosages and require no elaborate arrangements during surgery.

INJECTION

Barbiturates and other drugs can be given by subcutaneous (sc), intramuscular (im), intraperitoneal (ip), or intravenous (iv) injection. The selection of a given injection route is determined primarily by whether the experimental condition requires a fast or slow absorption rate of the drug; sc is used for slow absorption, whereas iv is used for fast absorption. A few precautions should be taken whenever any drug or chemical is to be injected. First, thoroughly clean the injection site with a disinfectant (for example, iodine); use a sterilized hypodermic syringe and needle to prevent infection. Second, if the drug is stored in a refrigerator, warm it to room temperature before injecting; introduction of a cold solution will cause vasoconstriction and a resultant retardation of absorption. Finally, if the drug is in a bottle with a rubber stopper, eliminate the danger of blunting the needle by first puncturing the stopper with a large-gauge needle; then insert the needle to be used for injection through the previously punctured hole to withdraw the drug. Once the syringe is filled, expel any air bubbles by holding the syringe vertically and slowly pushing the plunger while tapping the syringe until bubbles disappear. Apart from causing physiological complications, the presence of air bubbles makes an accurate estimate of dosage impossible.

Subcutaneous

The subcutaneous route is used when the chemical is not irritating to tissue and a slow rate of absorption is desired. The rate of absorption can be further reduced by combining the drug with oil, a vasoconstriction agent (for example, epinephrine [adrenaline chloride, Parke Davis]), or some vehicle in which it is insoluble. In some instances, for effectiveness over periods of weeks or months, a chemical in solid pellet form can be implanted under the skin (Goodman & Gilman, 1970).

An injection can be given at practically any part of the body where loose skin is found. One commonly used site is the skin behind the neck. Lift the skin with the thumb and index finger; then insert the needle behind the raised skin. Rub the site to distribute the drug and remove the lump.

Intramuscular

Drugs injected in deep muscle tissues are rapidly absorbed. A slow, even rate of absorption can be achieved by injecting oil-suspended drugs. The commonly used site for injection is the heavy musculature of the hind limb. Insert the needle parallel to the animal's muscles in order to avoid striking bones or puncturing the sciatic nerve. Before injecting the drug, slightly pull out the plunger of the syringe in order to see if the needle is in a blood vessel; if blood draws into the syringe, slightly pull out the needle or insert it again. Then rub the injection site to distribute the drug.

Intraperitoneal

Intraperitoneal injection is the most commonly used route for introducing drugs into animals. Drugs injected in the peritoneal cavity are rapidly absorbed and rapidly enter circulation. Restrain and hold the animal in a vertical position for injection. Almost any site between the diaphragm and the pelvic area can be used, except the abdominal midline, where the tissues do not readily heal and where injection can cause ulcers (Croft, 1960). Take care not to inject the liver, bladder, or gastrointestinal tract, since injection in any of these sites will alter the rate of absorption (Lumb, 1963). The best site is lateral to the midline in the center of the abdomen. Before injecting the drug, slightly pull out the plunger to make sure that the needle is not in a blood vessel or the bladder. Inject the drug rapidly to minimize the stress to the animal.

Intravenous

The intravenous route is used when an almost immediate effect of any drug is desired. Because of its rapid effect, it is the most frequently used route for introducing anesthesia. Furthermore, the rapid effect makes it possible to take into account the idiosyncrasies of the animal's response to the drug and to adjust the dosage accordingly. Therefore, unlike other routes, intravenous injection does not require calculation of the anesthetic dose on the basis of the body weight of the animal; injection is continued until the desired depth of anesthesia, as determined by certain reflex tests (see the following section), is obtained.

For intravenous injection it is wise to mix equal amounts of physiological saline with the anesthetic, since the mixture provides a greater range of safety. Initially, inject the anesthetic agent rapidly in order to minimize the struggle and excitement; after the initial dose has taken effect, slowly administer further amounts. If the surgery is to last several hours, leave the needle in the blood vessel and securely tape the needle and syringe to the limb. To prevent the plunger from being pushed out of the barrel by the blood pressure, secure the plunger to the barrel of the syringe with a piece of tape. Flush the syringe and needle with some anticoagulant solution (for example, heparin sulphate 1:1000 solution) to prevent the blood from coagulating in the needle and syringe so that additional intermittent dosages can be given easily.

Stages and Signs of Anesthesia

The classical stages of general anesthesia, based on neuromuscular signs, are presented in Table 2.1. The main objective of presenting these stages is to provide the experimenter with some broad guidelines with which to determine whether or not the animal is underanesthetized or overanesthetized. Note that the stages overlap and that animals show considerable variation in response to anesthesia.

In stage I the animal remains conscious, and all the sensory and motor reflexes remain functioning. The animal starts losing consciousness in stage II, but sensory and motor reflexes remain functional. Muscular relaxation and depression or abolition of reflexes characterize stage III. Following human anesthesiological convention, stage III divides into four planes. For animal experimental work, planes 1 and 2 represent light surgical anesthesia, whereas planes 3 and 4 represent deep surgical anesthesia. Finally, stage IV represents extremely deep anesthesia, under which the animal will die quickly unless immediate countermeasures are taken.

All surgical procedures should be carried out under deep surgical anesthesia, which can be assessed by reflex tests. Markowitz et al. (1964) list the following indications of depth of anesthesia: a rigid abdomen, spontaneous blinking, swallowing movements, and rapid breathing in a forceful manner indicate light anesthesia; shallow, feeble breathing indicates overanesthesia. Croft (1960) suggests that, in cats, reduction of the pupil of the eye to a small slit is a sign of overanesthesia.

All the signs are useful to determine depth of anesthesia, but their proper interpretation requires a great amount of practice and experience. The animal's reactions to certain stimuli are better indicators of depth of anesthesia, as they are more objective and reliable than the clinical signs.

Administration and Management of Anesthesia in Individual Animals

This section describes effective anesthetic agents and dosages, injection sites, injection procedures, reflex tests to determine depth of anesthesia, techniques of artificial respiration, and other related procedures for rats, cats, and monkeys.

RAT

Ether can be used to anesthetize rats for short durations. Dip a cotton gauze pad in ether and place it loosely on the face of the rat, or, because rats often struggle and must be firmly grasped, place the rat in a bell jar or a box containing the ether-soaked cotton. Short-term anesthesia (lasting 3 to 10 minutes) can be induced in one-day-old infants by hypothermia (Farris & Griffith, 1949). Wrap the infant in a filter paper and place in a dry test tube; immerse the test tube in a bucket filled with ice until the infant becomes immobile.

Long-acting anesthesia is most frequently induced by intraperitoneal injection of pentobarbital sodium (Nembutal, Abbott). Though the anesthesia can be given intravenously (in the tail or saphenous veins), intravenous injection, considering the difficulty of administration, should be avoided. Subcutaneous injection of pentobarbital maintains anesthesia for a longer duration than intraperitoneal injection, but the induction is much slower (Schaffer, 1965). Deep surgical anesthesia

STAGES OF ANESTHESIA		DEPRESSION OF CENTRAL NERVOUS SYSTEM	NERVES DEPRESSED	MUCOUS MEMBRANE COLOR (1)	PUPIL SIZE	EYEBALL ACTIVITY	MUSCLE TONE	RESPIRATION	PULSE AND BLOOD PRESSURE (B.P.)	REFLEXES: LID	CORNEAL	SKIN	SWAL-LOWING	COUGH	PEDAL	MISCELLANEOUS
I analgesia (stage of voluntary movement)		sensory cortex		normal / flushed	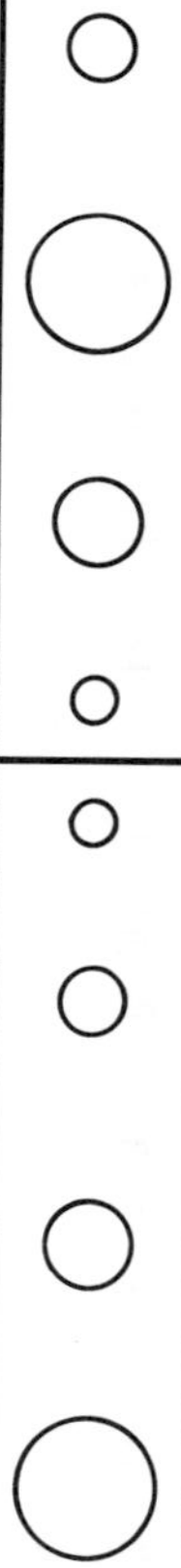	voluntary	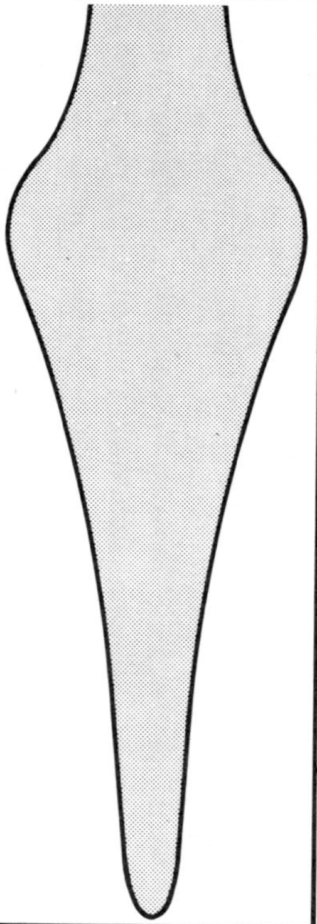	rapid and irregular	rapid pulse and elevated B.P.	+	+	+	+	+	+	pain abol-ished
II delirium (stage of involuntary movement)		motor cortex / decerebrate rigidity		flushed		++++		very irregular (erratic)	rapid pulse and elevated B.P.	+	+	+	+	+	+	unconscious / swallowing, emesis, may occur
III surgical	plane 1	midbrain	III	flushed / normal		+		slow and regular	normal pulse and normal B.P.	+ / — / —	+	—	—	+	—	
	plane 2	spinal cord (increased depression)	V / X	normal		fixed		slow and regular	normal pulse and normal B.P.	—	+ to — / —	—	—	—	—	
	plane 3	spinal cord (increased depression)	VI	normal / pale		eyelid relaxed		delayed thoracic / chiefly abdominal	rapid pulse and fall in B.P.(2)	—	—	—	—	—	—	smooth mus-cle depressed / pedal reflex absent (3)
	plane 4	spinal cord (severe de-pression)		pale				abdominal (shallow)	rapid, weak pulse and fall in B.P.	—	—	—	—	—	—	anal reflex present
IV paralysis (death follows)		medullary paralysis		pale and cyanotic			none	none (diaphragm paralyzed)	shock level	—	—	—	—	—	—	anal and bladder sphincters relaxing

TABLE 2.1. Characteristics of the Stages of Anesthesia without Premedication. (1) Cyanosis occurs in any stage of oxygen want. (2) It has been estimated that 15 minutes in plane 3 is as shock producing as 2 hours in plane 2. (3) Pedal reflex activity is abolished with ether in plane 1 but may persist as long as plane 3 when barbiturate anesthesia is employed. Reprinted by permission from *Veterinary Pharmacology and Therapeutics*, 3rd Edition, L. Meyer Jones, editor, © 1965 by the Iowa State University Press, Ames, Iowa.

can be induced in mature rats by injecting 5 mg/100 g body weight intraperitoneally. (Most of the commercially manufactured pentobarbital sodium solutions contain 65 mg/ml, which can be diluted to any desired strength by mixing 10 percent ethyl alcohol, sterile distilled water, or physiological saline.) As female rats apparently are more sensitive to pentobarbital, administering only three-fourths of the male dose to females greatly reduces mortality. For infant rats under 50 g body weight, Schaffer (1965) recommends a dose of 1.0 to 3.0 mg/100 g body weight. The safety margin of pentobarbital can be greatly increased by mixing it with chloral hydrate (Valenstein, 1961), which is commercially available (Equi-Thesin, Jansen; Chloropent, Fort Dodge) and safely used on one-day-old rats (Valenstein, Case, & Valenstein, 1969). The Equi-Thesin dose for mature male rats is 4 ml/kg; for females, use three-fourths of the male dose. Valenstein et al. (1969) suggest a dosage of 2.0 ml/kg for infant rats.

For intraperitoneal injection in mature rats, use 20- to 24-gauge hypodermic needles. For infant rats, use a 30-gauge needle with a tuberculine syringe (1 cc) to increase the accuracy of injecting small quantities. In order to inject the rat, hold the rat vertically and introduce the needle lateral to the midline in the center of the abdomen (see Figure 2.3). Though not essential, atropine sulfate (.25 cc of 1/120 grain/cc) can also be injected intraperitoneally at this time to control excessive saliva. Deep anesthesia, indicated by the absence of foot retraction (pedal reflex) when the foot is pinched, is evident in 5 to 10 minutes. Anesthesia lasts about 45 to 60 minutes but can be extended further with the help of ether or additional doses (one-fourth of the initial dose) of pentobarbital or chloral hydrate. If the anesthetic period is extended, atropine sulfate should also be repeated to minimize respiratory problems.

If the animal shows signs of overanesthesia, Farris & Griffith (1949) suggest .33 mg/100 g body weight subcutaneous injection of strychnine sulfate.

If breathing stops, check the oral cavity for obstructing saliva and, if present, aspirate it. If aspiration does not restore breathing, one of the following methods should be employed. Pass air

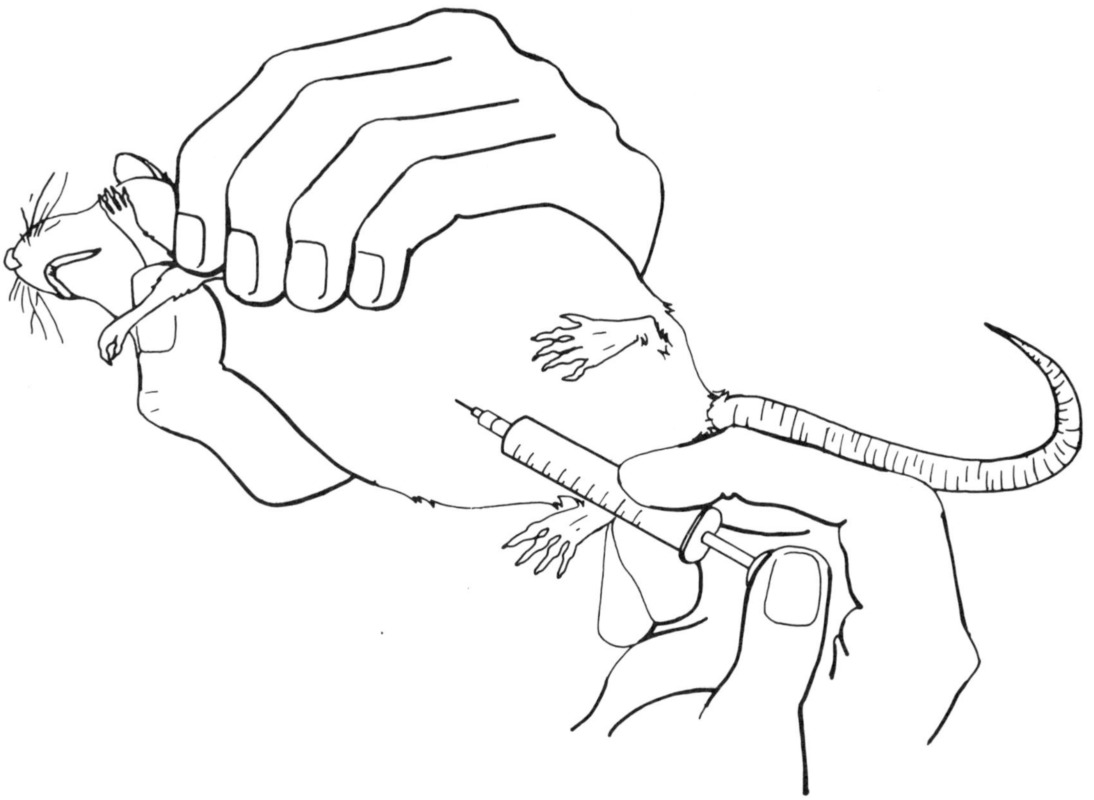

FIGURE 2.3. Method for Holding the Rat for Intraperitoneal (IP) Injection.

or oxygen under slight pressure into the oral cavity. Sometimes rhythmic compression of the chest area can restore breathing. Frequently, holding the rat by the hindquarters and jerking it up and down vigorously (so the viscera compress the lungs) can restore breathing (see Croft, 1960).

CAT

Ether can be used safely for short-term anesthesia, but it should be administered in an ether chamber to avoid the hazard of being clawed. Before administering ether, apply ointment to both eyes of the cat to prevent dryness and irritation. Excessive salivation during anesthesia can be checked by an ip or im injection of atropine sulfate (dosage is 1 cc/7 kg body weight of 1/120 grain/cc) prior to anesthesia.

Short-acting anesthesia (lasting approximately 15 to 20 minutes) can be induced by ip injection of thiopental sodium (Dipentol, Diamond). The suggested dose is 20 to 35 mg/kg body weight (Croft, 1960).

In order to take into account an idiosyncratic reaction, give Pentothal intravenously and administer it "to effect."

For a long-acting anesthesia, pentobarbital sodium (Nembutal) is most frequently used. The ip dosage is 30 to 35 mg/kg body weight, though whenever possible give intravenously and administer "to effect." To increase the safety margin, use a mixture of equal amounts of sterile physiological saline and Nembutal.

For iv injection, cephalic veins in the foreleg are quite satisfactory. Remove the hair over the intended site with clippers and scrub the skin with a disinfectant such as tincture of iodine. A 22- to 24-gauge needle from 1.9 cm to 2.5 cm long is commonly used for injection. An assistant immobilizes the cat on its side by holding the neck with one hand and the hindlegs with the other. The operator pulls the foreleg and, with the help of thumb and fingers, presses and stabilizes the cephalic vein (see Figure 2.4). If the cat is not extremely aggressive, the assistant may apply firm pressure above the elbow to raise the cephalic vein; otherwise, tie rubber tubing above the elbow as

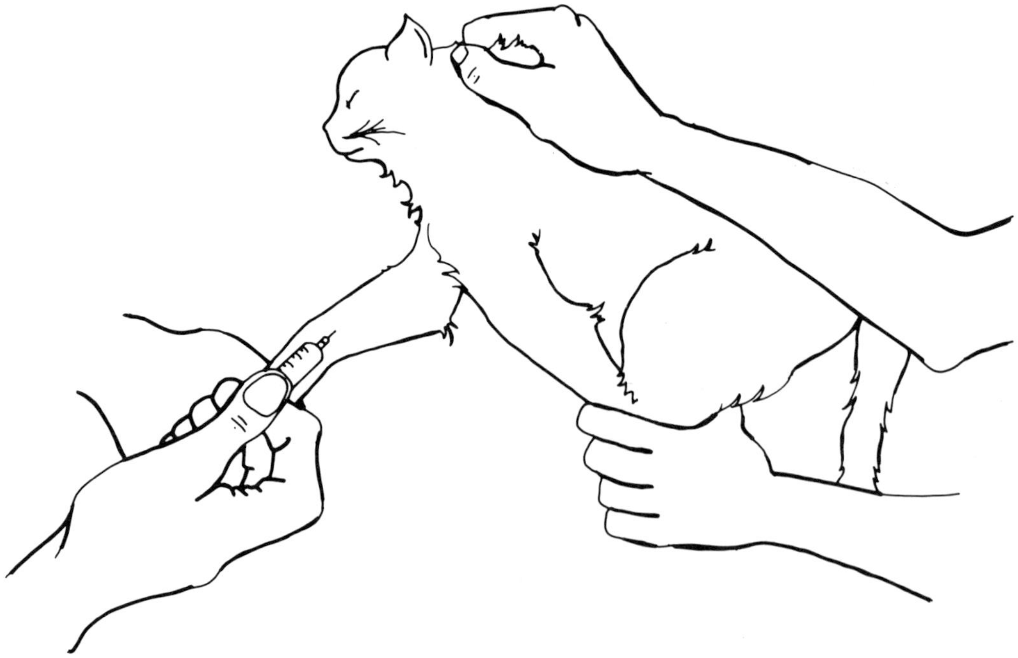

FIGURE 2.4. Method for Holding the Cat for Intravenous (IV) Injection. To stabilize the cephalic and prevent the vein from rolling, the operator places the thumb parallel and adjacent to the vein.

a tourniquet while the assistant holds the cat with both hands. Some investigators prefer wrapping the cat in a large towel and leaving one foreleg out for injection. A good policy is not to attempt insertion of both skin and vein in one thrust. Once the needle is inside the skin, it can easily be inserted into the vein. Moreover, the needle can more successfully penetrate the vein if it is inserted from the top rather than from the side. When the needle is in the vein, release the tourniquet (by either thumb pressure or tubing). Before injection pull the plunger back a little; if no blood appears, partially withdraw the needle and insert it again. Cats form hematomas (local swellings filled with effused blood) rather easily; therefore, if the needle is accidentally retracted, use a new site for further attempts.

For ip injection, an assistant keeps the cat in a vertical position by grabbing the loose skin behind the neck with one hand and both hindlegs by the other hand. Insert the needle at an angle lateral to the midline between the diaphragm and the pelvic area. After checking to make certain that the needle is not in the liver or bladder, expel the total amount with a quick thrust of the plunger to minimize discomfort.

Deep surgical anesthesia is accomplished if the corneal reflex (tested by blowing air on the eye or lightly touching it) and pedal reflex (foot retraction when the toe is pinched) are abolished.

Excessive saliva from the oral cavity should be removed whenever a gurgling or bubbling noise accompanies breathing. If breathing stops, it can sometimes be restored by rhythmic compression (20 to 30 times/min) of the chest. If the heart stops, epinephrine hydrochloride (adrenalin) should be injected intravenously (dosage is 0.3 to 1.0 ml of 1:10,000 epinephrine) within 3 to 4 minutes of cardiac arrest. Injection of Metrazol (Knoll) (6.7–7.1 mg/kg body weight) or Mikedimide (Panray) (16 to 20 mg/kg body weight), both of which are central nervous system stimulants, can also help restore respiration. In cases of barbiturate overdose, Mikedimide is preferred since it is a specific antidote to barbiturate.

MONKEY

If used for a short-acting anesthesia, ether should be administered in a chamber. Before administering ether, apply eye ointment to the animal's eyes to prevent irritation and dryness. Excessive saliva can be controlled by pretreating the animal with atropine sulfate (dosage is 1 cc/7 kg body weight of 1/120 grain/cc) one-half hour prior to surgery. Short-term anesthesia can be induced by pentothal sodium (12 to 16 mg/kg body weight). It should preferably be given intravenously and slowly "to effect." For long-acting anesthesia, pentobarbital sodium (Nembutal), administered intravenously, is commonly used (dosage is 20 mg/kg body weight).

For iv injection, monkeys can be restrained physically or in a squeeze cage. In order to restrain the monkey physically, capture it in a net and, if it is not too large or aggressive, one assistant can hold its arms behind the back with one hand and restrain the legs with another (see Figure 2.5). For larger and more aggressive monkeys, one assistant holds the arms and another holds the legs. Restraining the monkey in a squeeze cage is much easier and recommended especially for aggressive monkeys. Once the monkey is squeezed, pull a leg or arm through the bars of the cage for injection. Clip the hair on the site and apply a proper antiseptic. Use a 20- to 22-gauge needle, 1.9 cm to 2.5 cm long. The most frequently used site is the tarsal vein, or small saphenous vein. The iv injection procedure is identical to that reported for cats.

Give an ip injection at a point midway between the diaphragm and the pubic bone, lateral to the midline.

Deep surgical anesthesia is accomplished if the abdominal muscles are completely relaxed and pedal reflexes abolished.

If breathing stops, it sometimes can be restored by rhythmic compression (35 to 40 times/min) of the chest area. Mikedimide (16 to 20 mg/kg body weight) can be used as a respiratory stimulant. For cardiac arrest, give epinephrine (dosage is .5 to 1.0 ml of 1:10,000 epinephrine) intravenously within 3 to 4 minutes.

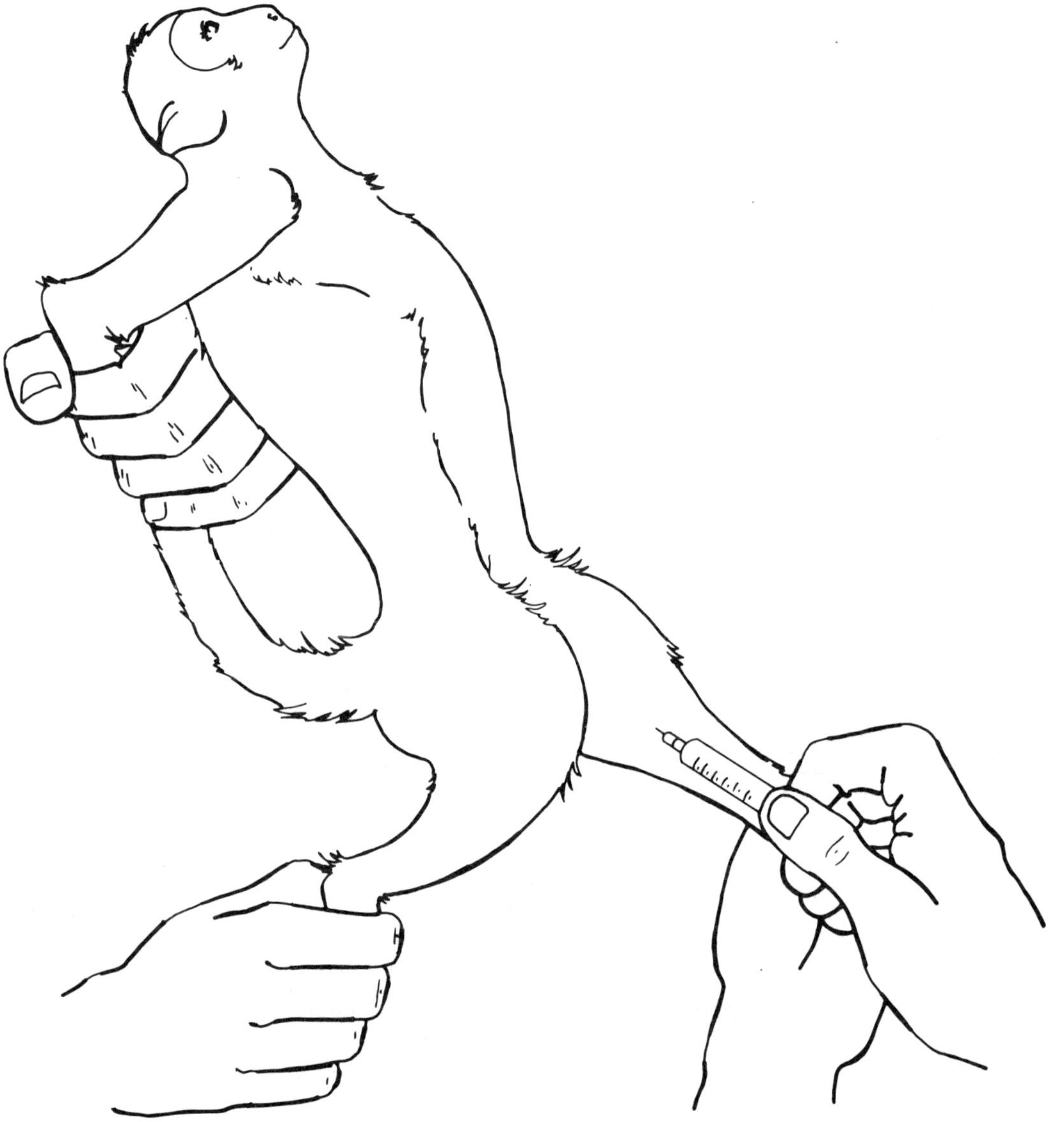

FIGURE 2.5. Method for Holding the Monkey for Intravenous (Saphenous Vein) Injection. The operator uses one hand to hold and rotate the leg laterally.

PREPARATION FOR ASEPTIC SURGERY

All animal surgery must be performed under aseptic conditions as rigorously observed as those in human surgery. It must be remembered that there is a direct relationship between position on the phylogenetic scale and susceptibility to postoperative infections; the higher an animal is on the phylogenetic scale, the greater the need for aseptic conditions. Animals used in behavioral research are usually trained preoperatively. Training often involves many months of work and hence the loss of such animals can be very costly. Furthermore, in behavioral research there are very few short-term experiments (those that terminate in a few days, for example); thus the unimpaired health of the operated animals over long periods of time is very important.

All instruments and materials to be used in surgery should be sterilized. Laboratories that work exclusively with rats need not purchase an autoclave. Sutures and related material can be purchased in sterilized packs, and most of the small instruments (forceps, hemostat, rongeur, and so on) can be sterilized in a three-quart pressure cooker. Make a rack from wire mesh by folding the mesh to fit the inside of the pressure cooker; the rack should be well above the water level. Place the instruments on the rack, thereby allowing them to be sterilized by steam rather than by boiling water. The instruments should be "cooked" for at least 30 minutes.

Another acceptable method of sterilization is the use of certain chemicals such as 70 percent ethyl alcohol or isopropyl alcohol. Isopropyl alcohol is recommended over ethyl alcohol since it is cheaper, has a slightly greater germicidal action, and is a better fat solvent than ethyl alcohol. If alcohol (either ethyl or isopropyl) is used to disinfect, the instrument should be wiped dry, since alcohol can cause metallic instruments to rust. Among the most effective and popular chemical sterilizing agents are Zephiran, Metaphen, and a borax-formalin mixture (100 cc 38 percent formaldehyde, 50 g borax, and 1000 cc distilled water), which are used for sterilizing sharp cutting instruments since steaming and boiling can dull the edges. The effectiveness of these chemicals as sterilizing agents increases if they are heated (37°C). If Zephiran chloride is used, metallic instruments should be immersed in a 1:750 aqueous solution for 30 minutes before surgery. The instruments should be cleaned, rinsed well, and dried before being placed in the solution, since Zephiran chloride is really effective only in the absence of soap or oils. To protect instruments from corrosion, antirust powder or tablets (containing sodium carbonate and sodium nitrate) should be added to the aqueous solution. Either four crushed tablets or two teaspoons of powder per gallon of Zephiran chloride solution are sufficient to retard corrosion. If instruments are to be stored in this solution for long periods of time, the liquid should be replaced at least once a week. Instruments containing zinc or aluminum should not be kept in Zephiran chloride, for these metals react with the alkali in the antirust compounds. Hypodermic syringes can be kept in Zephiran solution, but whenever possible the syringes should be cleaned first in acetic acid and then in 70 percent alcohol, and finally sterilized in steam. Use sterile long forceps to extract instruments from the pressure cooker or chemicals. Store the forceps in Zephiran solution. Permit all instruments to dry before use.

Packing the Autoclave

The method of packing the autoclave is based on two principles: (1) every article should be thoroughly sterilized; and (2) the articles should be wrapped in such a way as to minimize the possibility of contamination when the package is unwrapped. Establishment of a fixed procedure and some practice on the part of the user facilitate the proper packing of the autoclave.

The articles to be sterilized should be arranged into groups based on the order in which they will be used. For example, bundles containing gowns should also contain hand towels, since they will be used at the same time. A separate bundle should contain instruments, suture material, and sponges.

A double layer of muslin cloth is the best wrapping material not only because it is sturdy but also because it permits a uniform flow of steam. Commercial autoclave paper can also be used for wrapping material. All clothing items such as gowns, towels, and lap sheets should be laundered without starch before sterilization. Similarly, all instruments should be thoroughly cleaned with detergent and hot water. To prepare the bundles, spread the wrapping sheet into a diamond shape. Place a large hand towel on the wrap to serve as a table cover when the bundle is opened. Arrange the articles in the center of the towel. Pull the corners, one at a time, over the articles, turning back about 10 cm of the triangular corners; the final closing is performed by using masking tape (or Scotch autoclave tape, which has a temperature indicator) or straight pins. By lifting the folded triangular corners of a bundle prepared in this way, a nonsterile assistant can open the bundle without contaminating the inside contents. Indicate the contents of each wrapper in unwashable ink, and open the bundles only immediately before use.

The proper way to fold a gown is as follows: (1) fold the gown inside out with the sleeves back to back; (2) place the gown on the table and straighten it so that all the folds match evenly;

(3) fold it loosely from the underarm seam over toward the tie edge in a 10- or 12.5-cm roll; (4) place the open side down and, beginning at the hem, roll it up.

Make sure that all articles of clothing are free from holes or cuts, since their presence would defeat the purpose of sterilization. Test gloves for possible holes or leaks by filling them with water. The only items of clothing that need not be sterilized are caps and masks, though these should be clean.

For sterilization purposes, first pair gloves with palm up and thumb outside, dust with talc inside and out, and turn the cuffs back approximately 6.3 cm. Then, before placing in the autoclave, separate the gloves into two muslin envelopes marked "Right" and "Left" and numbered to indicate the size of the gloves.

All bundles should be packed so as to eliminate air pockets. Steam should be able to penetrate every layer of the cloth pack. Arrange the bundles in the autoclave in order of their use. Place a bundle containing towels, sponges, and a few scrub brushes on the front side of the autoclave, as these items will be the first to be used in preparing both the animal and the assistant for surgery. All items should be sterilized at 131°C and 15 lb pressure for 30 minutes if the bundles are not very large; increase the time for large bundles. Take care to release the steam before opening the autoclave door. Allow bundles to dry fully before removing, since bacterial infiltration can easily occur in wet material. Furthermore, sterilized bundles should not be used if they have been stored for over 24 hours. If sterile surgery is done only occasionally, it may be more convenient and less expensive to buy prepackaged sterile disposable gloves, towels, sheets, and drapes.

Preparation of the Animal

Animals should be anesthetized and hair removed from the incision area before the surgeon begins to prepare himself. For clean removal of hair, use clippers against the grain of the hair. Shave and clean an area slightly larger than the one to be used to facilitate extension of the incision should that be necessary. Once the animal is in the surgery room, position the head in the stereotaxic instrument if a lesion or aspiration technique is to be used. Since there is no reason to disinfect the whole head of the animal, place the head in the stereotaxic instrument before disinfecting the area of the incision. Clean the skin with tincture of iodine (Isoprep, Johnson) either by using surgical gauze or by spraying the tincture on the skin through a perfume atomizer. Because the same gauze should not be used twice, an atomizer has definite advantages. If using gauze, the best way is to start cleaning from the center and move outward to the periphery. Apply tincture of iodine at least four times; increase the number of applications if the skin is very unclean. A good indication of whether or not the skin is clean is that, once the tincture has been removed with a sterile gauze, a fresh gauze remains clean after it has been rubbed over the area. Next, clean the skin with isopropyl alcohol or 80 percent ethyl alcohol at least four times. Take strict precautions to avoid recleaning a spot with the same sponge. After drying, the animal is finally ready for the incision.

Preparation of Personnel

Surgery should not be done without an assistant. The operator and his assistant should both don caps and masks. The assistant should never touch the surgeon or any item that the surgeon is planning to use. The following steps are standard for "scrubbing."

Thoroughly wash the hands, arms, and elbows with soap, keeping the arms flexed so that the hands are above elbow level. Next rinse the hands with warm water, letting the water run off the elbow. Use a sterile brush to scrub the hands and arms, starting at the nails and progressing toward the body; the thorough and vigorous use of the brush assures better disinfection than many applications of soap. Use the brush for at least five minutes and clean the hands with warm running water. After scrubbing has started, never allow the hands and arms to fall below the waist or touch the body. The assistant then pours isopropyl alcohol on the surgeon's hands from a height so as not to risk touching him. Rub the palms together and wipe the hands with a sterile towel by using a towel for each hand or half of one towel for each hand.

The assistant then opens the bundle containing the gown, which he picks up at the seam to let the gown unfold. Then, holding the gown by the inside shoulder seams, the assistant extends it toward the surgeon. The surgeon inserts his arms halfway into the sleeves of the gown, raises his hands vertically, and allows the gown to slip onto his shoulders (see Figure 2.6). The assistant may help in tying the string of the gown but should be careful never to touch any part of the surgeon except the back of his shoulders. The assistant then opens the envelope containing gloves and places the envelope on the table. Commercially packaged sterile gloves should be opened according to the directions on the package. Put on the gloves without touching the outer part of the glove; slip four fingers into the fold and pull the glove over the hand (see Figure 2.7).

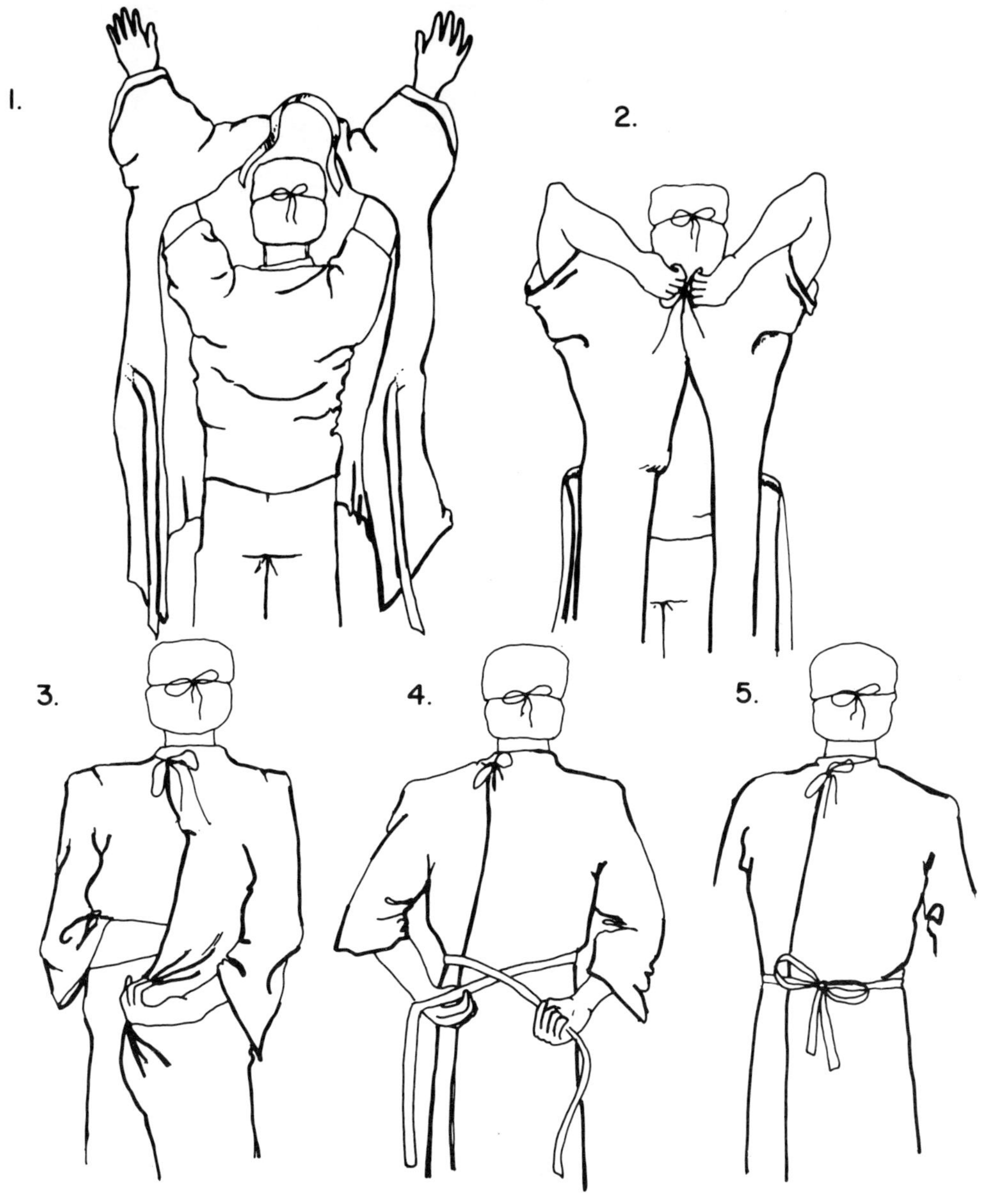

FIGURE 2.6. Procedure for Putting on a Gown.

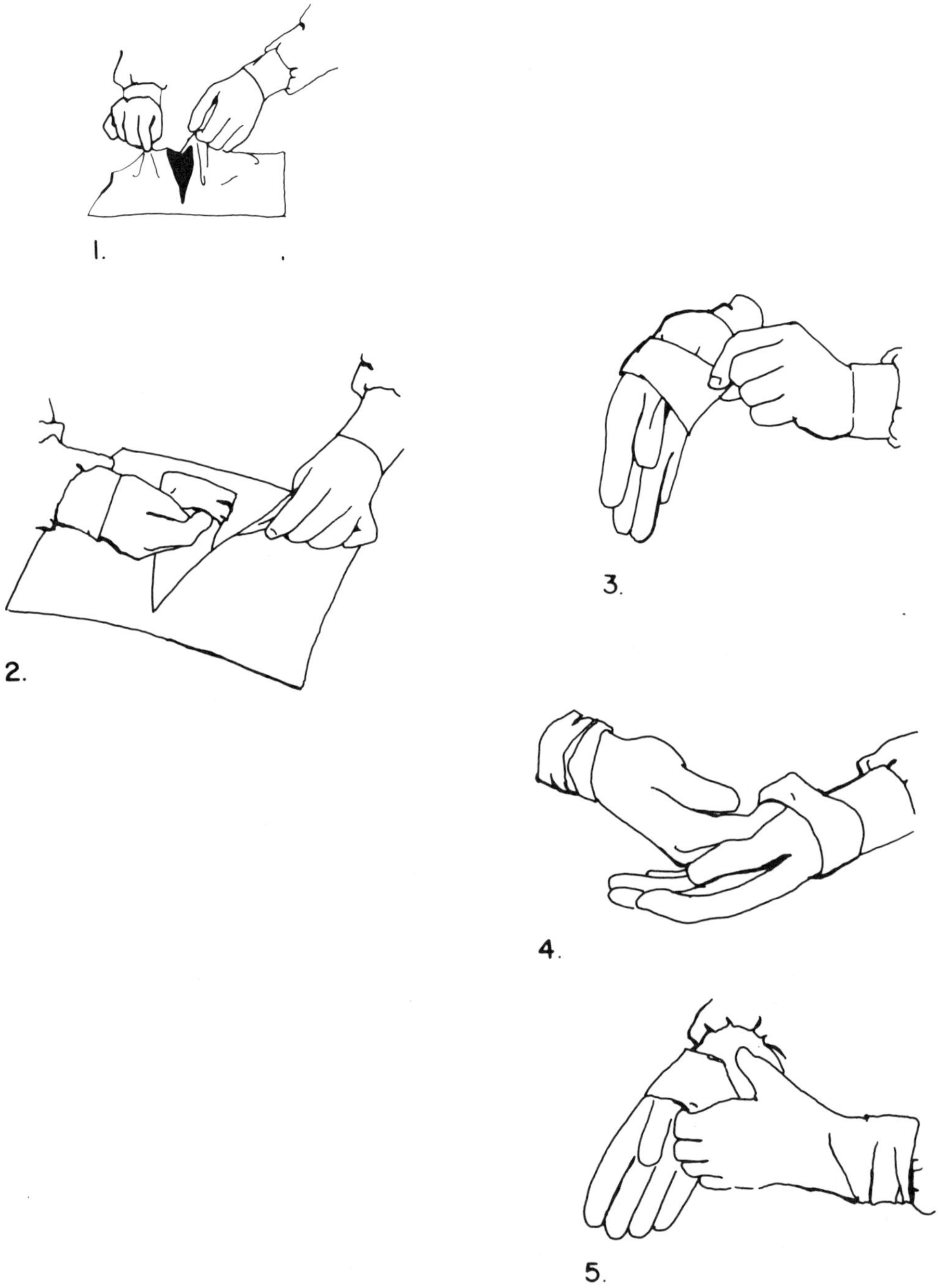

FIGURE 2.7. Procedure for Putting on Sterile Gloves.

The assistant should remain at least .6 m away from the surgeon, and, if he must help move the surgical table or instrument table, he should touch only the nonsterilized parts. If there is any contamination during preparation for surgery or during surgery, the surgeon must scrub again and use fresh drapes, towels, and so on. Thus a wise policy is to sterilize extra articles to meet such eventualities.

Suture

The purpose of suturing is to close an incision and provide support until the fibers have regenerated. There are two different types of suture material: (1) the absorbable type, which is absorbed by the tissues after some time (for example, surgical or cat gut, fascia lata); and (2) the nonabsorbable type, which is not absorbed by the tissues and must be removed before healing is complete (for example, silk, cotton, nylon, wound clip, stainless steel wire). The nonabsorbable sutures are either capillary or noncapillary. Capillary sutures absorb secretion, whereas noncapillary types perform support functions only. Note, however, that the strength of support is determined by the tissue itself and not the suture material. It is safe to say that surgery in behavioral research requires the noncapillary suture, except in the case of the installation of a stomach fistula, for which the absorbable type may be preferred.

The best material to use is silk, since it can be handled with ease, is well tolerated by the tissues, and is readily sterilized. Silk sutures come in different sizes ranging from very fine (0) to coarse (7). Use only finer varieties of silk, even in cats and monkeys. Though cotton is a capillary suture and without practice is rather difficult to work with, it is inexpensive and recommended for use with rats. For the rat, use common cotton thread (60) for suturing skin, but never use it on hollow organs such as the stomach.

Finally, the use of bone wax as a suture material should be noted. Bone wax is used to stop bleeding from the surface of severed bone. Store bone wax in sterile tubes, and, before using, place the sterile tube in warm sterile water for a few seconds to soften the wax. If the wax is too hard, it will crumble; if it is too soft, it will not adhere to the bony surface.

SUTURE PATTERNS AND KNOTS

One of the most important factors in surgery is proper suturing of the incision, which, to a large extent, determines whether or not the wound will heal properly. There are very few essential suture patterns and types of knots, but one should practice them thoroughly until all the movements become automatic. The different patterns and ways of tying knots can be practiced on a gauze sponge with the help of a good manual. Tauber (1965) provides many exercises that are generally helpful and include practically all suture patterns that may be used by behavioral researchers. Basically, most of the fancy patterns are not needed, and one needs to become familiar with only a few, such as the interrupted, continuous, and purse-string types (see Figure 2.8).

The most frequently used suture pattern is the interrupted type (see Figure 2.8A), which provides strength to the wound; if one knot slips, the others hold the wound edge together. The continuous pattern consists of running stitches that are tied only at the end of the incision (see Figure 2.8B). All skin suturing should be done with the interrupted pattern since it provides better support to tissues and is less likely to come out accidentally. The continuous pattern can be used for suturing incisions such as those in dura mater that would not be exposed to strain.

Another useful suture pattern is the purse-string type, which is used in holding a cannula in the stomach or esophagus or for holding an electrode implanted in the brain (see Figure 2.8C). Those who work with such devices in cats very frequently encounter what is known as a "weeping wound," where a discharge occurs that requires frequent cleaning and can be very irritating to the animal. The weeping wound can be avoided by using a noncapillary suture (especially the cardiovascular type coated with silicone) in a purse-string pattern around the electrode.

For proper regeneration, approximate the skin and tissues to their normal position and pick up as little tissue as possible with the needle. The needle will penetrate tissues (especially tough skin) easily if it is held steady; push the tissue against the needle rather than trying to push the needle through the tissues. It is wise to practice suturing with the help of a hemostat, since a hemostat can be very useful in performing a suture in a limited space or in an opening where hands cannot reach (see Figure 2.9). When using a hemostat or needle holder, place the holder on the flattened surface

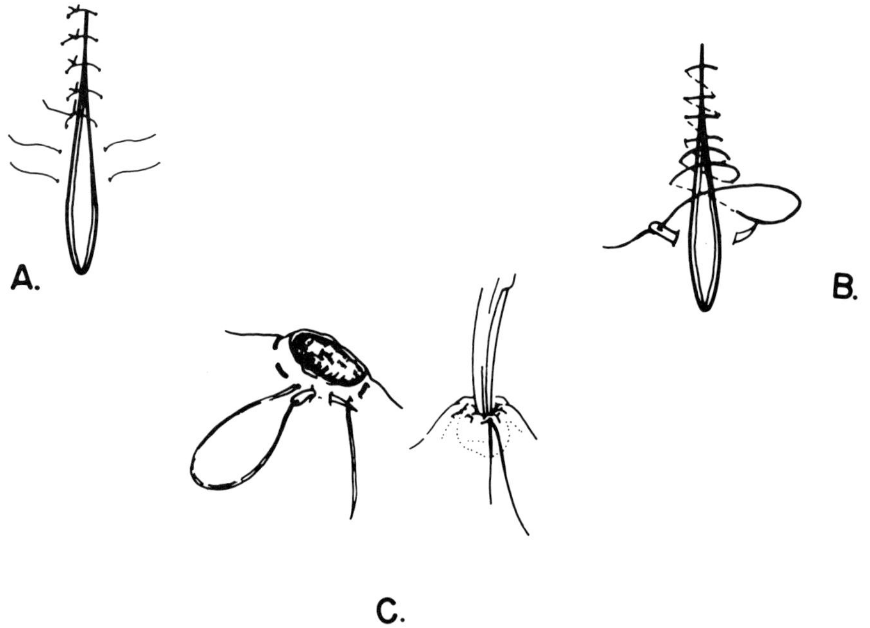

FIGURE 2.8. Suture. A. Simple Interrupted Sutures. B. Simple Continuous Sutures. C. Purse-String Suture.

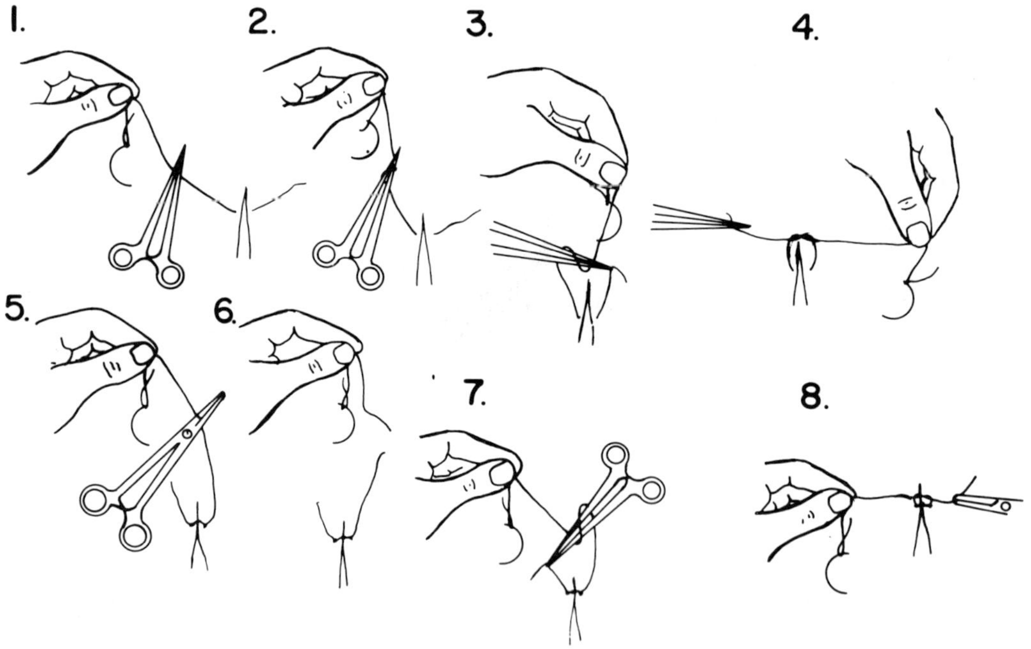

FIGURE 2.9. Tying Knots with the Aid of a Hemostat. From *Experimental Surgery* (5th ed.) by J. Markowitz, J. Archibald, & H. G. Downie. © 1964 by Williams & Wilkins Co., Baltimore, Md. 21202. Used by permission.

of the needle about 4 mm away from the eye of the needle; if the needle holder is clamped over the eye of the needle, the needle may weaken and break.

The most important factor in tying a knot is the amount of pressure on the suture. If suturing is done under pressure or tension, or if a coarse suture is used, the suture will penetrate the tissue and thus defeat the purpose for which suturing is intended—that is, to give support to the tissue until it regenerates. Tie the knot so that it cannot open; a square knot, if properly executed, will not slip open. Squeezing together and wiping the blood off the margins of the sutured skin serve as the best means of reducing the possibility of infection.

Postoperative Care

A systematic procedure should be developed for animal care during surgery and recuperation. The death of many animals during or after surgery is due mainly to loss of body heat (hypothermia), excessive hemorrhage, and respiratory complications. Frequently check the animals, especially cats and monkeys, for proper respiration, heart rate, and body temperature during surgery and recovery. During surgery, place the animal on a waterproof heating pad to compensate for heat loss. Occasionally, some procedure causes excessive loss of blood and the animal can be saved only by blood transfusion. Cold, pale extremities, rapid and shallow breathing, and a change in the color of the mucus membranes are sure signs of shock. In case of shock, give either blood or some plasma expander (for example, Dextran or a sterile physiological saline) intravenously.

Observe a recuperating animal until it regains consciousness, especially if it had any complications during surgery. Cats and monkeys should preferably be kept in an incubator during recovery. If such facilities are not available, place the animal on a heating pad or under an infrared lamp. During recovery, frequently turn the animal from one side to another to prevent hypostatic congestion. Turning is most important when the animal is placed on a heating pad; if the animal is left on the same side, excessive heat may cause skin burns.

Another complication that can arise is infection of the wound. A wise policy is to pretreat the animal with an antibiotic before surgery. The effectiveness of the antibiotic can be extended by injecting (im) an oil-base, or other long-acting, drug (for example, Bicillin SM, Wyath; dosage is 22,000 units/kg body weight). If the infection persists, repeat the antibiotic drugs.

REFERENCES

Croft, P. G. *An introduction to the anesthesia of laboratory animals*. London: The Universities Federation for Animal Welfare, 1960.

Farris, E. J., & Griffith, J. Q. *The rat in laboratory investigation*. Philadelphia: Lippincott, 1949.

Goodman, L. S., & Gilman, A. G. (Eds.) *The pharmacological basis of therapeutics*. (4th ed.) New York: Macmillan, 1970.

Jones, L. M. *Veterinary pharmacology and therapeutics*. Ames: Iowa State University Press, 1965.

Lumb, W. V. *Small animal anesthesia*. Philadelphia: Lea & Febiger, 1963.

Markowitz, J., Archibald, J., & Downie, H. G. *Experimental surgery*. Baltimore: Williams & Wilkins, 1964.

Schaffer, A. Anesthesia and sedation. In W. I. Gay (Ed.), *Methods of animal experimentation*. Vol. 1. New York: Academic Press, 1965.

Tauber, R. *Basic surgical skills*. New York: Ungar, 1965.

Valenstein, E. S. A note on anesthetizing rats and guinea pigs. *Journal of Experimental Analysis of Behavior*, 1961, **4**, 6.

Valenstein, T., Case, B., & Valenstein, E. S. Stereotaxic atlas of the infant rat hypothalamus. *Developmental Psychobiology*, 1969, **2**, 75–80.

SUGGESTED READINGS

Berry, E. C., & Kohn, M. L. *Introduction to operating-room technique*. New York: McGraw-Hill, 1972.

Lumb, W. V. *Small animal anesthesia*. Philadelphia: Lea & Febiger, 1963.

Schaffer, A. Anesthesia and sedation. In W. I. Gay (Ed.), *Methods of animal experimentation*. Vol. 1. New York: Academic Press, 1965.

Tauber, R. *Basic surgical skills*. New York: Ungar, 1965.

CHAPTER 3

Experimental Ablation

Devendra Singh
UNIVERSITY OF TEXAS AT AUSTIN

The earliest attempts to understand brain function consisted of observing behavior in the *absence* of certain brain structures or observing behavioral changes produced by removing parts of the brain. By comparing the behavior of an animal with brain damage with that of a normal animal or with its own behavior before brain damage, inferences about the functions of the damaged part of the brain could be made. Until the early seventeenth century, this strategy for inferring the relationship between brain and behavior could be used only when someone with a brain tumor or accidental brain damage could be found. However, after Flourens (Boring, 1950) successfully utilized the technique of surgical removal of restricted parts of the brain in animals, experimental ablation became the most frequently used tool for investigating localization of brain functions. As a matter of fact, before the discovery of electricity (and, therefore, the use of stimulation techniques) almost all information about cerebral localization of sensory functions was derived from ablation or mutilation of parts of the brain (Walker, 1957).

The greatest drawback of the early ablation techniques was that they were appropriate only for overlying cortical areas or areas that were readily accessible to surgery, as removal of deep subcortical structures required removal of overlying structures as well. The problem was resolved by the development of a stereotaxic instrument by Horsley and Clarke that permitted the destruction of discrete parts of subcortical structures with minimum damage to overlying cortical structures. The Horsley and Clarke technique (Carpenter & Whittier, 1952), broadly speaking, consists of a rigid metal headholder in which three-dimensional coordinates spatially locate a brain structure. Once a brain structure is located, it can be destroyed by a variety of means. Horsley and Clarke used electrical current to destroy subcortical structures by lowering an electrode insulated except at the tip to the target area and passing an electrical current of measured strength for a predetermined duration. The brain consistency is such that passage of the electrode produces very restricted damage; therefore, subsequent changes observed in the animal can be attributed to the damage produced in the subcortical area.

Modern stereotaxic instruments, still designed on the principles proposed by Horsley and Clarke, are much more precise and sophisticated than their early counterparts. Technological advances have made available a wide variety of methods, including temperature, electricity, ultrasound waves, and radioactive isotopes, for destroying neural tissue. It is now also possible to destroy subcortical structures with especially constructed fine knives without producing a great deal of damage to the cortex. Finally, with chemical agents, it is possible to make a brain structure nonfunctional only for a certain time to investigate the behavior of an animal in the presence and absence of a specific brain function. Functional damage, or reversible lesion, is a great methodological improvement for certain investigations.

Frequently, psychological research requires localization of some specific cortical and subcortical structure. Most of the surface structures of the cortex can be approached by using various anatomical landmarks; however, localization of deeper subcortical structures invariably requires the use of brain atlases and stereotaxic instruments. The first sections of this chapter describe the use of stereotaxic instruments. The latter sections deal with mechanical, electrical, and chemical methods of destroying neural tissues in animals.

STEREOTAXIC SURGERY

Stereotaxic Instruments

The decision to buy a specific type of stereotaxic instrument should be dictated by the nature of intended research. A wide variety of instruments, some of which are extremely sophisticated (such as those with a multiple electrode holder, which are for single cell recording) and expensive, are available. Unless very specialized research is intended, any ruggedly built stereotaxic instrument with interchangeable headholders (Baltimore) for different animals or ear bar and mouth adapters (Kopf) is suitable (see Figure 3.1). An added advantage is that adapters can be purchased later for

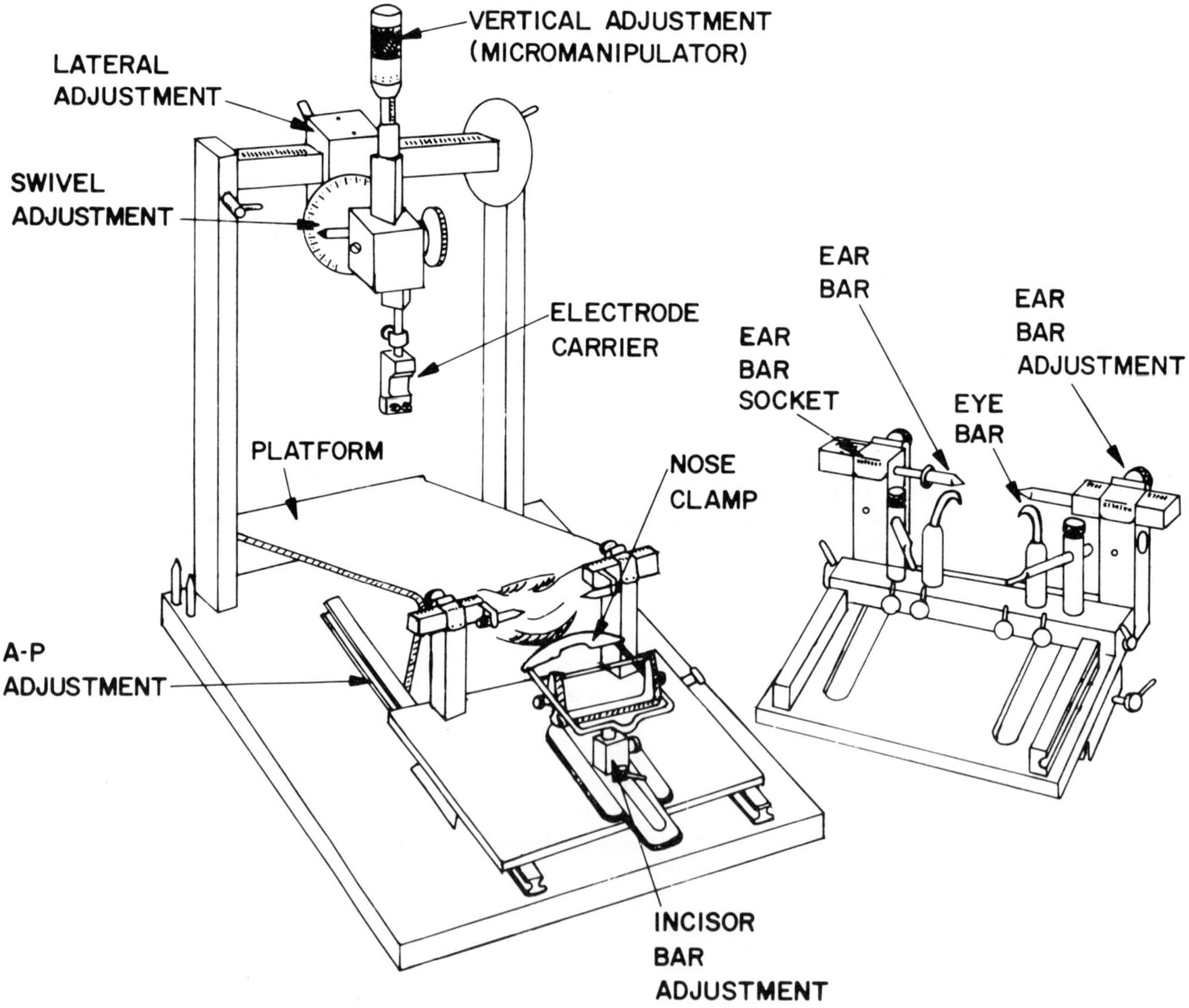

FIGURE 3.1. A Stereotaxic Instrument (Baltimore) with Interchangeable Headholders for Rats and Cats.

other animals as needs arise. Stereotaxic instruments usually do not have any device to support the body of the animal and, therefore, a plastic or wooden platform should be constructed for this purpose.

Whenever possible, purchase a stereotaxic instrument that permits angular as well as perpendicular insertion of electrodes (Baltimore; Kopf). Angular insertion has two distinct advantages over perpendicular insertion. First, in structures very close to the midsagittal sinus, angular insertion of electrodes eliminates the risk of damage to the sinus and resulting bleeding. Second, that the same target areas can be approached from so many different angles obviates the objection that some damage was produced to overlying structures and that the observed deficit is due to specific damage to the site as well as to the damage produced by the electrode track. The methodological objection that damage was produced by electrode penetration can be quite cogent in studies that require electrode implantation for some duration; Collias and Manuelidis (1957) have demonstrated that electrode implants produce neural injury even without the passage of any electric current. However, angular insertion permits the investigator to prepare control animals in which the target site is approached from different angles (hence different overlying structures are damaged). The angle for electrode insertion can be computed by using either simple trigonometry or an angle calibrator (Baltimore).

If cannula implants are planned, the electrode holder must be modified to hold the cannula. Attach a holder to the commercial electrode holder or order a cannula holder from the stereotaxic supplier.

The stereotaxic instrument should be carefully maintained. When the horizontal, or anterior-posterior, bars are moved, the thumb screw should be loose and the bars should easily slide out. The thumb screw should never be tightened with force, since to do so may damage the thread on the screw. Rough handling can cause play in the bars and reduce accuracy. After each use, clean the ear bars and head holder and wipe with 70 percent alcohol.

Stereotaxic Atlases

Many stereotaxic atlases are available for rat, cat, and monkey brains (for example, Pellegrino & Cushman, 1967, for rats; Snider & Niemer, 1961, for cats; Snider & Lee, 1961, for *Macaca mulatta* monkeys).

Almost all stereotaxic atlases provide a system of coordinates that permit localization of the brain structures with reference to three standard planes (see Figure 3.2): (1) a line between the center of two ears (that is, a line connecting the two auditory meatuses); (2) a line connecting the external auditory meatuses with the upper incisor teeth (rat) or the infraorbital ridge (cats or monkeys); and (3) a line bisecting the cranium. Thus the reference points provide the horizontal, vertical, and lateral planes. The zero points for different planes are, conventionally, defined on the basis of the interaural midline (that is, the point where the line between the two external auditory meatuses and the horizontal and vertical, or frontal, lines meet). The lateral plane is defined from the center of the interaural line. The horizontal zero plane in all the brain atlases is almost always arbitrarily defined. In order to approximate the atlas horizontal zero plane, the head of the animal on the incisor bar has to be adjusted to be a certain distance either above or below the interaural line. For example, for use of the de Groot (1959) and Pellegrino and Cushman (1967) atlases, the upper incisor bar for the rat has to be adjusted to 5.0 mm above the interaural line, whereas, for use of the Konig and Klippel atlas (1963), the incisor bar should be 2.4 mm below the interaural line to create horizontal plane zero.

Almost all stereotaxic atlases give distances in millimeters from the interaural line for anterior-posterior, vertical, and lateral planes. Thus any brain structure can be described as some distance anterior or posterior from the midpoint of the interaural line, above or below it, and some distance lateral. Most of the atlases provide coronal sections of the brain from the most anterior to the most posterior ends; some atlases also provide parasagittal (dividing brain into right and left parts) sections of the brain (Konig & Klippel, 1963).

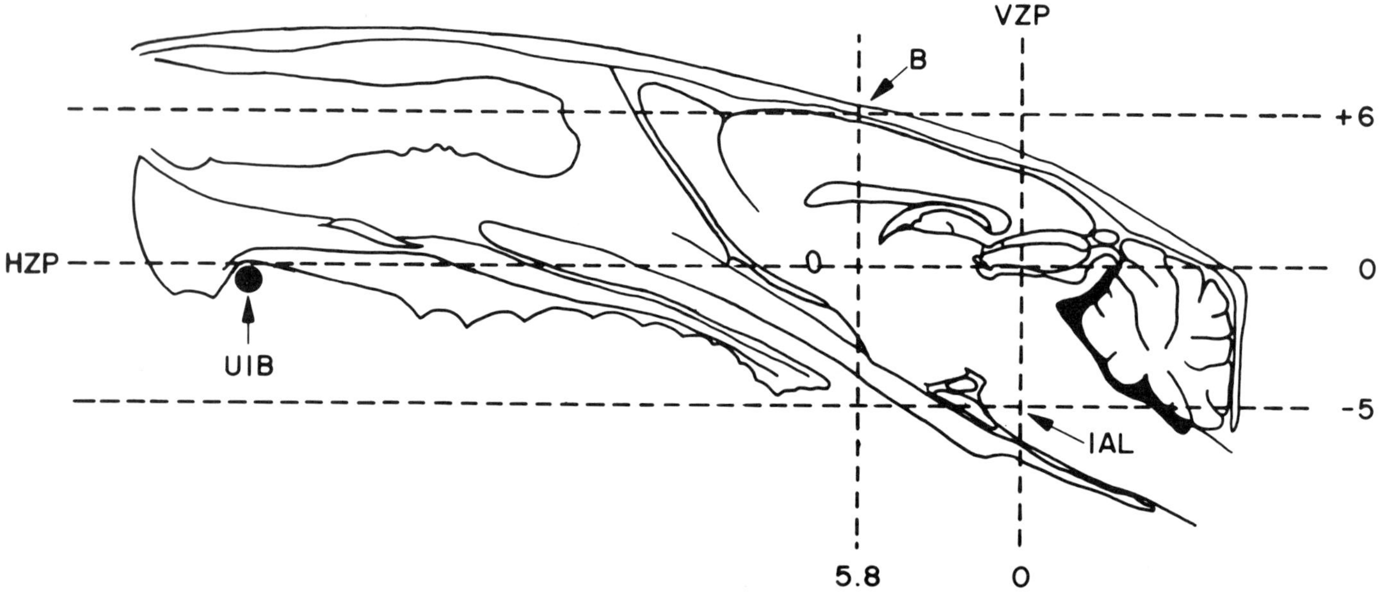

FIGURE 3.2. Midsagittal Section of a Rat's Head Illustrating the Position of the Head in the Stereotaxic Instrument for Developing the Coordinate Systems of de Groot (1959) and Pellegrino and Cushman (1967). Abbreviations: B—bregma; HZP—horizontal zero plane; IAL—interaural line; UIB—upper incisor bar; VZP—vertical zero plane. From *A Stereotaxic Atlas of the Rat Brain,* by L. Pellegrino & A. J. Cushman. © 1965 by Appleton-Century-Crofts. Reproduced by permission.

Estimation of Stereotaxic Coordinates

Each brain atlas provides coordinates for three dimensions: anterior-posterior (A-P); lateral (L); and horizontal (H), or dorso-ventral (D-V). The accuracy of these coordinates depends on strictly adhering to and producing reference points identical to those used in preparing the atlas. Furthermore, since brain size may differ in animals of different ages, using animals of the same age as those used for developing the atlas ensures greater precision of localization of a particular structure.

There are two ways to determine the stereotaxic coordinates for a given brain structure. The first method uses the midpoint of the interaural line as the reference point (interaural stereotaxic zero reference), whereas the other method uses external bony landmarks as reference points (skull reference). The most commonly used external landmarks are lambda and bregma points on the skull. The lambda is the midline intersection of the transverse and sagittal sutures; the bregma is the midline intersection of the coronal and sagittal sutures (see Figure 3.3). A few rat-brain atlases give coordinates for both the bregma and the interaural reference point (for example, de Groot, 1959; Pellegrino & Cushman, 1967) so that either method can be used.

To determine coordinates for a particular structure—for example, the ventromedial hypothalamic nucleus (VMH) in a rat—first locate the structure in the atlas (see Figure 3.4). For the interaural system, the following coordinates for VMH could be used: 5.6 mm A-P (upper right, Figure 3.4), 0.8 mm L (calculated from bottom scale, Figure 3.4), and −3.5 mm H (right-hand side, Figure 3.4; minus sign indicates that the structure is located below the horizontal zero of the atlas). Unlike the use of the bregma as the reference point, use of the interaural system permits the investigator to calculate the coordinates for a brain structure independent of the animal. Thus, after obtaining coordinates from the atlas, the next step is to determine the stereotaxic, or instrument, zero.

To determine the instrument zero, push the ear bars together symmetrically so that the tips of the bars are only 1 mm apart. Then lower the electrode and center the tip of the electrode

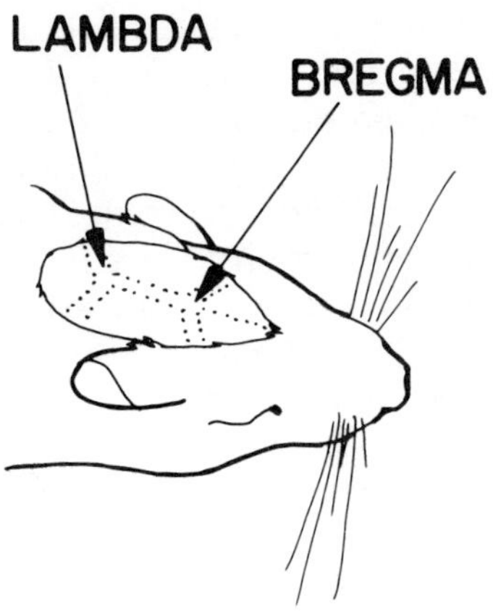

FIGURE 3.3. Lambda and Bregma Landmarks on the Skull of the Rat.

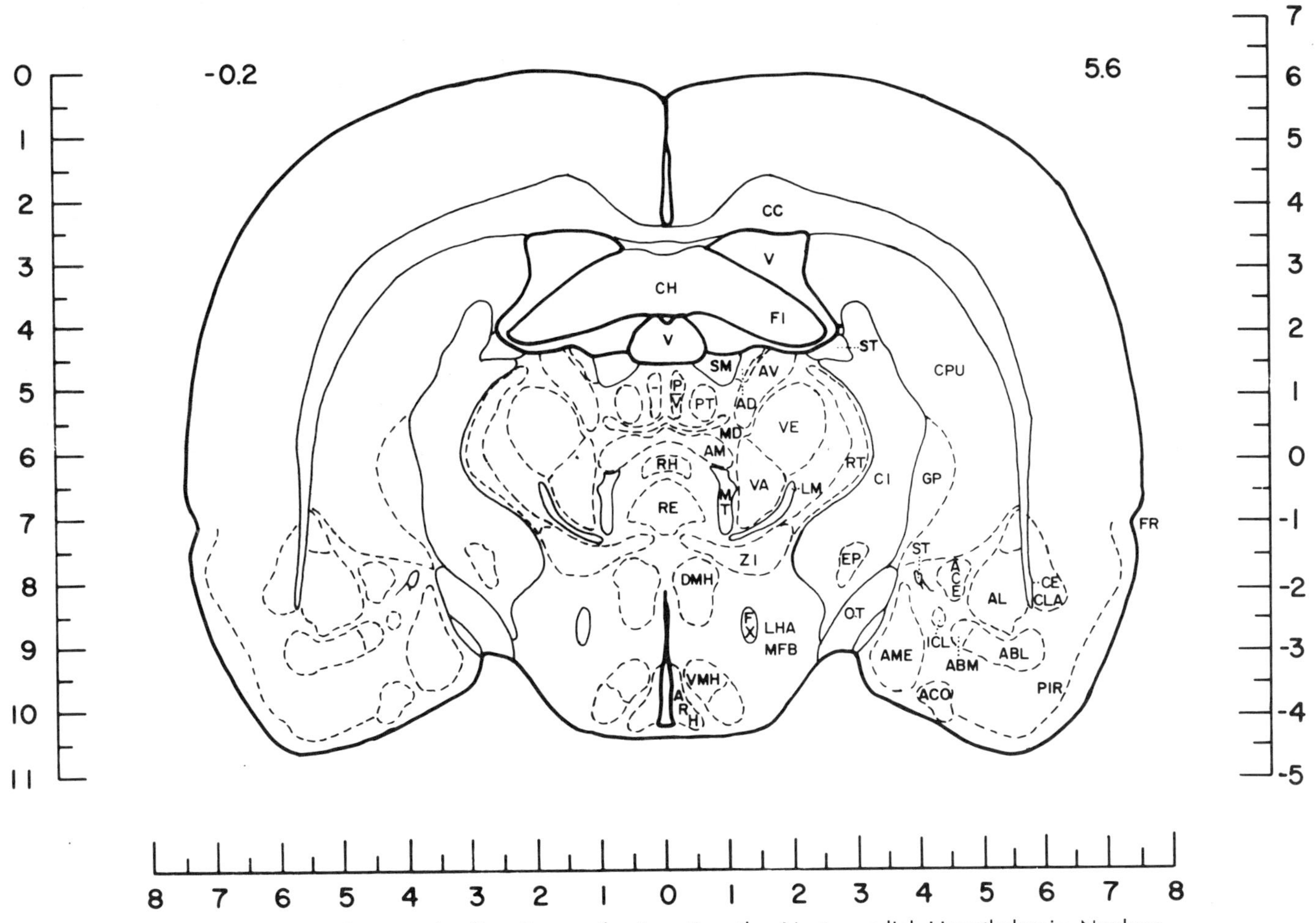

FIGURE 3.4. Stereotaxic Coordinates for Locating the Ventromedial Hypothalamic Nucleus. The number in the upper-right corner of the figure is the A-P coordinate using the interaural reference point; the number in the upper-left corner of the figure is the bregma reference (the minus reading indicates that the structure is posterior to the bregma). The horizontal coordinate is on the right side of the figure (the minus sign indicates that the structure is located below the horizontal zero of the atlas). The scale on the left is used to calculate horizontal coordinates when the distance from the dura mater is used. From *A Stereotaxic Atlas of the Rat Brain,* by L. Pellegrino & A. J. Cushman. © 1965 by Appleton-Century-Crofts. Reproduced by permission.

between the space of the ear bars. The readings on the A-P, L, and H scales of the instrument indicate the instrument zero. Either add or subtract the instrument readings from the A-P, L, and H obtained from the atlas. Thus, if the instrument-zero readings are 5.0 mm A-P, .5 mm L, and 6.2 mm H, the final coordinates are 10.6 mm A-P, 1.3 mm L, and 7.7 mm H (for the Pellegrino and Cushman atlas, adjustment of H requires adding 5.0 mm to the instrument H reading and then subtracting 3.5 mm, since it is below horizontal zero). Use of bregma reference points is justified mainly by the argument that, even in animals of the same age, enough variability exists in brain so that external landmarks should be used to correct for variability in each animal. For example, Skinner (1971) has shown that variability of bregma with respect to the rat brain is much less than that of external auditory meatuses that are used for defining interaural line. This finding suggests that the accuracy of localization is greater when the bregma is used as a reference point than when the interaural midline is used. For the Pellegrino and Cushman atlas, the coordinates for VMH with the bregma as the reference point would be as follows: −0.2 mm posterior to bregma (upper left, Figure 3.4), 0.8 mm L (bottom scale, Figure 3.4), and 9.5 mm H (left scale, Figure 3.4; distance from the dura mater). When the bregma is used as the reference point, unlike the procedure followed when the interaural midpoint is used, instrument readings are taken after the animal has been mounted in the instrument and the skull is exposed (see next section). Lower and center the electrode on the bregma so that they are touching. Add or subtract the readings on the scale of the instrument from the readings obtained from the atlas.

The use of the bregma as a landmark also facilitates the correction of lateral and horizontal coordinates. Because the measurements are obtained after the head has been mounted, proper mounting of the animal is not as critical as it is when the interaural reference point is used. The lateral coordinates can be corrected by using the center of the midline cranial (longitudinal) suture or the underlying superior sagittal sinus. However, the suture may not be at the exact midpoint of the brain, and removing the piece of bone over the superior sagittal sinus to use that as a reference point is worth the extra trouble. The horizontal coordinates also can be corrected by using the dura mater as the point to determine depth.

Mounting the Animal

The first step in mounting the animal is the insertion of the ear bar, which often is a difficult task. Note that inserting ear bars is easier in monkeys than in cats and rats. There are many ways to insert ear bars, and only repeated attempts and practice enable one to perform the task quickly. One way to insert the bar into rats is as follows: Place the head on the incisor bar; with one hand, keep the head steady with the fingers and push the ear laterally against the skull with the thumb to get a clear view of the meatus. With the other hand, insert the bar by gently moving it up and down while pushing (see Figure 3.5); when the bar no longer moves up and down, it is in the external meatus. Now tighten the set screw on the bar. Maintain firm pressure of the thumb on the head and start inserting the other bar; inserting from an angle sometimes helps. When the bar is in the meatus, push it down in the socket and tighten the set screw. If both ear bars are locked in position, the head should move only up and down, not sideways. Setting the ear bars properly is critical. If they are not set properly, pulling them out and starting all over again are easier than trying to correct.

For monkeys and cats it is best to have two people for inserting ear bars. The technique is very much like that described for rats. With two people, one can keep the head steady and firm after the first bar is inserted while the other person inserts the other bar. Again, if the ear bars are set properly, the head should move only vertically, not laterally.

Some stereotaxic instruments (for example, Kopf) come with ear plugs that are first inserted into the ears. Then bars are inserted into the ear plugs. Many investigators feel that ear plugs offer no great advantage for setting ear bars properly; the effort and skill are about the same as that required with ear bars alone. Furthermore, the tips of ear plugs, which are quite sharp, often damage the eardrums. If ear plugs are used, also using a control group of animals to ascertain the effect of ear damage, if any, is advisable.

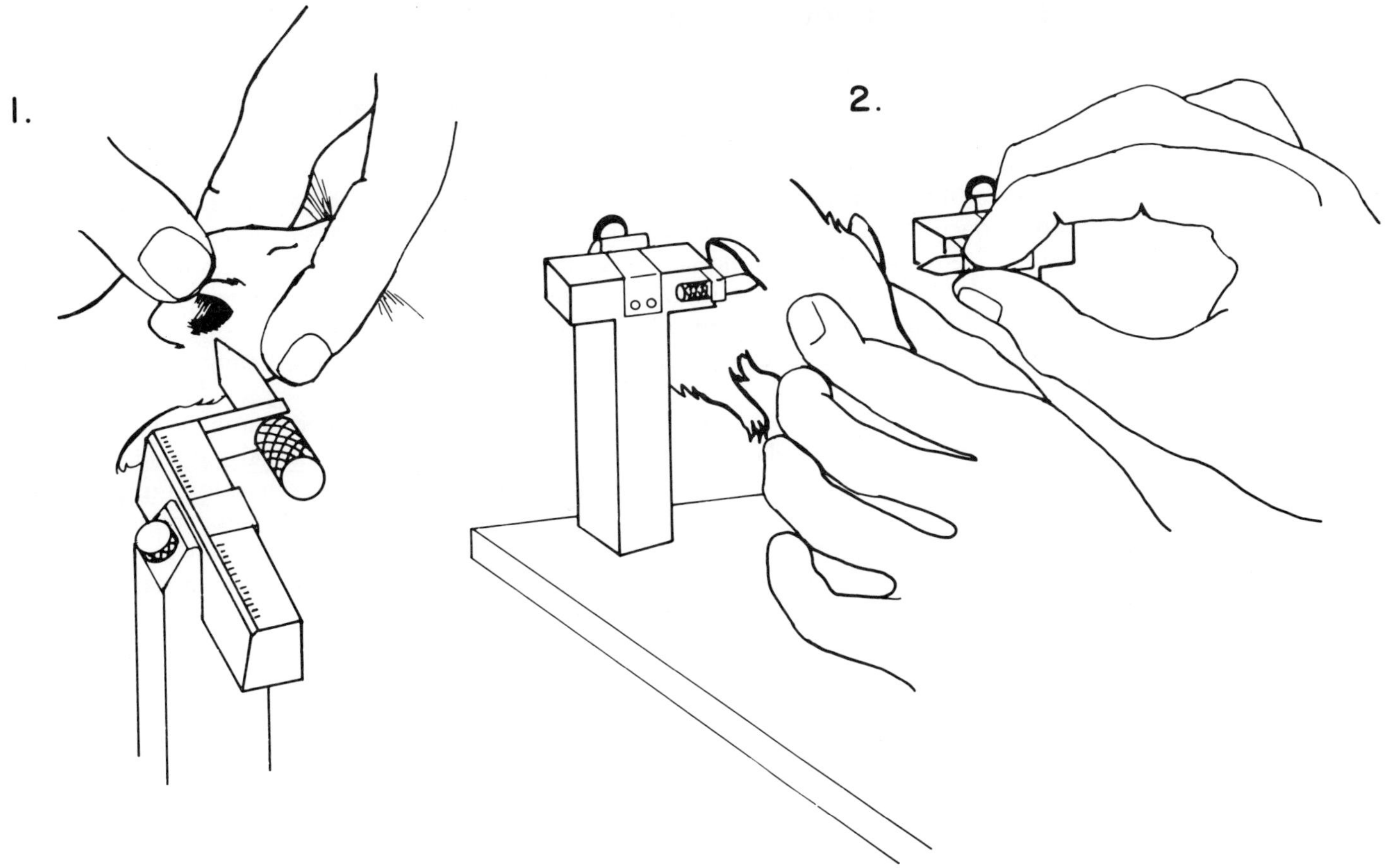

FIGURE 3.5. A Procedure for Inserting Ear Bars in a Rat. 1. Firmly hold the head with the fingers, and, with the thumb, move the ear laterally so as to get a clear view of meatus. 2. When one bar is inserted, keep the head in place with one hand and then insert the other ear bar.

When the ear bars are in place, they must be centered. The easiest way is to unlock the set screws on the ear bar slightly and push the bar with the palm of the hand until the readings on the scales of both bars are identical. Then, in the monkey or cat, place the eye bars on the infraorbital ridge; in the rat, tighten the nose clamp over the incisor bar.

The head-mounting technique described above can be used with mature or fairly mature animals in which facial bone structure is strong. However, in working with infant animals (especially 1- to 14-day-old rats), the standard head-mounting procedure for stereotaxic surgery is not possible. Valenstein, Case, and Valenstein (1969) describe a technique for mounting the head of infant rats: Place the anesthetized infant rat in a tray filled with Plasticine (mud putty) that is depressed to conform to the shape of the animal's body. To keep the animal's head and body immobile, place strips of clay on limbs, back, and neck. Place the tray in the fixed position, on a tilt table on which the U-frame of the stereotaxic instrument (Kopf) is attached; the tilt table permits movement in anterior-posterior and medial-lateral planes. Then expose the skull of the animal and level the head by lowering an electrode carrier with 2 rows of 3 pins each in which the two center pins are slightly raised to conform to the skull curvature. Lower the pins onto the skull along the midline, and adjust the tilt table to match the set of 6 pins positioned over the skull. The authors have prepared a stereotaxic atlas for the hypothalamus of infant rats (1 to 14 days old) that uses this method for head mounting.

Scalp Incision and Drilling

After anesthetizing the animal, shave the head. Any electrical hair clipper performs satisfactorily. For a close shave, move the hair clippers against the grain of the hair. Then place the animal in the instrument and prepare the incision sites while the surgeon and assistant scrub (see Chapter 2). To make a clean incision, pull the skin with the thumb. To start the incision, use the point of the scalpel blade (10) to pierce the skin; after piercing, move the blade parallel to the skull so that the whole cutting surface of the blade is used. Make the incision with one firm stroke; cut to the skull with firm pressure. A properly executed incision very rarely causes any bleeding unless the animal is poorly anesthetized. Making a longer incision than is necessary permits greater freedom to work. After making the incision, pull the skin downward laterally and hold it down with the help of a curved mosquito hemostat. In cats and monkeys the subcutaneous fascia must be cut before the skin is pulled down.

If sterile surgery is planned, the head of the animal should be draped before the incision is made. To drape the monkey or cat, place sterile towels around the area to be incised and hold them in place by inserting towel clamps through the towels and the underlying skin. Thus, for a midline incision, place two towels parallel to the intended site of incision and two towels perpendicular to them at the extreme ends of the intended length of the incision. This arrangement leaves a square, open area, and the four towel clamps, one at each point in the fold where the two towels meet, keep the towels in place.

After making the incision, the next step is to scrape away connective tissue that covers the skull. In rats the connective tissues can be scraped with a Q-tip without causing bleeding. In monkeys and cats, after the skin has been detached and pulled downward laterally, muscle can be retracted with the help of the back of the knife handle. Push aside the muscle over the intended area by bringing the back of the knife handle as close to the bone as possible. In some instances, cutting the muscle fibers, which invariably leads to bleeding, may be necessary. The bleeding can be stopped by placing on the site pellets of fibrin foam (Gelfoam) soaked in a solution of thrombin.

When the skull is exposed, dry it thoroughly with a cotton sponge and mark the intended site for drilling thc hole. In rats a dental drill or hobby drill with a foot-controlled rheostat works quite satisfactorily. An electrical drill can be used also for monkeys and cats, but some investigators prefer a manual drill, which generates less heat and gives better control. Depending on the size of the intended hole, use either a burr or a trephine. For smaller holes, use a burr, since it chips away the bone underneath it. A trephine, on the other hand, cuts a circular bone plate, which then is lifted out of the skull. Therefore, if the hole is to be large, a trephine is better than a burr, since after surgery the bone plate can be replaced in the hole.

A steady pressure on the drill held at a right angle to the skull increases the possibility of damaging the underlying dura mater. Only practice reduces this possibility. After some practice, one can feel the bone giving in, especially when steady and gentle pressure is maintained on the drill. Developing the feel by drilling holes in a few dead animals is a good idea. To minimize the risk of damaging the dura, allow the drill to extend out of the holder only up to the thickness of the bone, whereby one can feel as well as see that the hole is drilled. If funds are available, one can buy drills that stop automatically after the bone is drilled away (Smith, 1950). In rats very little bleeding from the bone occurs; however, in cats and monkeys the bleeding can be excessive, depending on the drilling site. If bleeding takes place, dry the site with cotton and apply bone wax.

MECHANICAL NECROSIS

Various methods of destroying neural tissues exist; each has its advantages and disadvantages. A wide variety of electrical, thermal, and other means are frequently used to destroy subcortical structures. However, since cortex is readily exposed after removing the bone, the oldest and most common technique used by psychologists is extripation, or aspiration. Mechanical cutting of subcortical fibers, or isolating structure, has recently become popular. Therefore, this section describes two methods—aspiration and knife cut—of mechanical necrosis.

Aspiration

Broadly speaking, aspiration entails removing neural tissues by suction. Aspiration is most frequently used to remove parts of the neocortex, though it has been used also for removal of subcortical structures such as the hippocampus (Gol, Kellaway, Shapiro, & Hurst, 1963). The aspiration technique is visually guided—that is, the surgeon must be able to define areas and decide whether or not, for example, all the layers of the neocortex have been removed. Proper aspiration is a skill that is acquired gradually. The removal of frontal neocortex in rats and monkeys, as described in this section, illustrates the technique, which is essentially the same as that employed at the Physiological Psychology Laboratory, Ohio State University.

The essential tools required for aspiration are the aspirator and the vacuum pump, in which pressure can be regulated. The aspirator is attached to rubber tubing, which is connected to the vacuum pump. The aspirator can be made from a 20- or 22-gauge hypodermic needle or from fine glass tubing. Bend the aspirator at a slight angle so that it can be held like a pencil parallel to the surface of the brain. To make a glass aspirator, draw the glass tube under heat to make a fine pipette (approximately $^1/_2$ mm). Some investigators (see, for example, Meyer & Meyer, 1971) prefer an L-shaped glass aspirator to the metal aspirator, since the glass type allows the surgeon to see the amount of tissue taken out. To connect the aspirator to the vacuum pump, rubber tubing containing a thumbhole opening is preferred. When pressure is required, the surgeon places his thumb on the hole. However, removal of the thumb from the hole instantly reduces pressure at the tip end.

The surgical steps are mounting the head of the animal, drilling the skull hole and enlarging it, aspiration, and closure of the wound. These steps differ considerably in rats and monkeys; hence the following sections describe the technique as used for each species.

SURGICAL PROCEDURE FOR RATS

After anesthetizing the animal and shaving the head, mount the head in a headholder. Any type of headholder can be used, since the only requirement is that the head be held firmly so that the skull can be drilled. If a stereotaxic instrument is available, mount the head in the stereotaxic instrument. After making the skin incision, scrape connective tissue. Drill two burr or trephine holes, one on each side of the midsagittal suture. These holes should be large enough (about 4 mm) to be enlarged with the help of rongeurs. To minimize damage to the brain, the rongeur jaws should grasp a small portion of bone and cut the bone without inward pressure toward the brain. Because the thickness of the skull toward the most anterior part is much greater than elsewhere, more care should be taken to remove the anterior part of the skull. Another difficult area is the bone overlying the midsagittal sinus, the removal of which frequently causes bleeding. One approach is to drill two holes, one on each side of the sinus, and sweep the drill to join the holes. However, if bleeding occurs, stop it by placing Gelfoam over the area. Some investigators leave a thin plate over the sinus. After removing the bone, remove all bone chips. Then cut and push aside the dura mater. Remove the neocortex under 6 to 7 pounds of negative pressure. If using an L-shaped aspirator, hold it parallel to the surface of the brain and move it slowly in an anterior-posterior direction. Only a small area should be worked on at a time. Invariably, bleeding occurs, and thus using the color of neocortex as a cue to determine the depth of aspiration is difficult. As neocortical tissue comes off much easier than subcortical tissue, however, after some practice the surgeon can, in most instances, succeed in removing only the neocortex. Another indication of depth of aspiration is the color (glossy white) of subcortical tissue.

After aspirating, suture the skin (interrupted suture) and administer an antibiotic.

SURGICAL PROCEDURE FOR MONKEYS

The surgical procedure for monkeys is much more difficult than that for rats, mainly because (a) aseptic surgery is required, (b) a bone flap or replacement is sometimes required, (c) muscle and dura flaps are required, (d) a greater amount of tissues is removed, and (e) more bleeding may occur.

As in the case of rats, the first step is to mount the head of the animal. Again, a stereotaxic instrument can be used for this purpose. Drape the animal and prepare the site of the incision. After removing the subcutaneous fascia, pull the skin downward laterally and hold it in place with towel clamps or retractors. Separate the muscles from the bone; with the back of a knife handle, detach the muscle from the skull at its insertion. Once the muscle is detached, retract it laterally and clamp it. Place a cotton gauze soaked in physiological saline on the muscle to prevent drying.

The type and number of holes to be drilled in the skull depend on whether or not the surgeon chooses to create a bone flap or to use a substitute for it (such as stainless steel wire mesh or a plate of dental cement) that would be replaced after surgery. There is no hard and fast rule about when to use a bone flap or a substitute. A simple principle to remember is that, if the bone is removed from a region that will have adequate postoperative protection (for example, the temporal region), a bone flap or substitute can be dispensed with. The use of a bone flap is a tedious technique that requires outlining the flap with a series of burr holes (usually 5 or 6), then, by means of a saw (Gigli), connecting the burr holes by sawing between them (except at one segment, where the bone would be cracked by elevating the bone flap). Meyer and Meyer (1971) describe the details for creating a bone flap. However, the use of a bone flap provides no added advantage (to justify the tremendous effort and the risk of damaging brain tissues) over substitutes such as a dental cement plate or wire mesh. When these substitutes are used, the surgeon can remove bone piecemeal with rongeurs.

The procedure to remove bone is similar to that described for rats. First, drill trephine or burr holes (8 mm) in the anterior portion of the skull. Then enlarge the holes with rongeurs. The technique of using rongeurs is the same as that described for rats, except that the skull is much thicker in monkeys. Furthermore, in monkeys sometimes dura mater sticks to the skull. Thus, after drilling holes and before rongeuring, separating the dura from the skull with a dural elevator may be necessary. Gradually chip the bone over the intended area and, whenever bleeding from bone occurs, apply bone wax after drying the bleeding site. Before cutting the dura, remove all bone chips. Dura can be lifted with a dural hook and cut with a knife blade. Take care to cut only the dura mater and not the pia mater. Do not cut dura close to the bone edge, since to do so makes suturing more difficult. Depending on the location, cutting the dura mater may cause bleeding, which can be stopped by placing with light pressure a pellet of Gelfoam over the area and then applying a wet, folded sponge, the weight of which usually controls bleeding.

Expose the cortex by making knife cuts in the pia-arachnoid in a small area at a time (about 4 to 6 mm), starting with the most lateral gyrus. Ablating the cortex in this manner has two distinct advantages: first, starting with the most lateral gyrus and moving medially keeps the surgical field free of blood (starting with medial and going to lateral covers the cortex with blood); and, second, working in one small area at a time permits the ablation of another area while bleeding (if bleeding occurs) in the first area is being stopped. Stop bleeding by rolling a small ball of cotton over the area with the tip of the aspirator. Remove the cortex under 6 to 7 pounds of pressure. Move the aspirator slowly in an anterior-posterior direction. Aspirate the cortical tissue close to the bone by bringing the tip of the aspirator as close to the bone as possible and moving it back and forth.

After aspiration, and before closure of the wound, bleeding from all points must be stopped. Then the dura can be sutured. It is not necessary to match dura, and two or three interrupted sutures (silk 00) can be used to loosely close the dura. After closing the dura, replace the bone flap or some substitute for it. One of the easiest methods is to pack the bone defect with Gelfoam and pour dental cement over it. When the cement is dry (4 to 6 min), suture the muscle flap over it. If frontal cortex is removed in a cat, the frontal sinus should be plugged with dental cement before the wound is closed to prevent infection. Match muscle before suturing. Use interrupted sutures again for suturing muscle. Finally, suture the skin. In monkeys use a continuous suture, which should lie in the subcutaneous layer, or else the monkeys invariably pull the sutures out before healing. For suturing skin use a half-circle cutting needle (6 or 7) with silk (0) thread. Fortunately, cats are not as active with their paws as monkeys are, so that the interrupted suture on the dermal layer can be used. Before returning the animal to its cage, administer antibiotics.

Mechanical Knife Cut

Mechanically produced lesions have a long history (first used in 1874, as reported by Carpenter and Whittier, 1952), although they were never very popular until recently. The recent interest in mechanical means of producing neural damage is, to a great extent, due to certain distinct advantages that this method offers over the electrolytic method. First, the knife permits disruption of fiber connection between two structures; discrete lesions that are restricted to small, interconnecting fibers between two structures are very difficult to produce electrolytically. Second, the introduction of the knife to cut fibers or to isolate a subcortical structure does not leave metal ion deposits, as can happen with the electrolytic method. Reynolds (1965) argues that the electrolytic method leaves metal deposits in the brain; hence observed behavioral deficits could be due to the irritation caused by metal ions rather than to brain damage. Although the possibility of ionic deposit can be reduced by using an electrode made of noble metals (platinum or iridium), the mechanical means apparently solves the problem of irritation caused by metal deposits. However, the mere insertion of a metal knife may also leave enough metal ions for irritation (Gold, 1970).

The basic approach throughout most of the knife-cut procedure is to determine the location of the structure and then lower the knife, or the cannula containing the knife, to the structure. If a cannula is used, a projecting knife or wire is passed through it and rotated. Of many different types of knives, only two are discussed in detail here. Gold (1970) describes a knife that is made by breaking an edge of a razor blade (see Figure 3.7A). After the tip is sharpened, the razor blade knife is mounted in a stereotaxic holder and lowered vertically into the brain. This knife can be used, for example, for cutting interconnecting fibers between the ventromedial hypothalamic and lateral hypothalamic areas. However, two problems are associated with this knife: (1) the cut extends to the surface of the brain; and (2) cuts in the horizontal plane are not practical. To produce horizontal cuts, many different types of rotating knives have been developed (Ellison, 1968; Halasz & Pupp, 1965), but these knives also produce a cut that extends from the surface of the brain to the target area.

The problems just described are solved, however, in those knives in which a retracting blade or wire is lowered through a fine guide shaft. Interestingly, the retracting knife, inserted through a fine cannula, was developed and used as early as the 1920s (Carpenter & Whittier, 1952). However, Caruthers (1968) reports one of the most versatile retractable rotating knives, which is capable of making planar cuts as well as hemispheric, or circular, lesions. The basic assembly consists of two stainless steel hypodermic tubings (see Figure 3.6). The two tubes fit into each other, the outer one serving as a guide shaft for the inner one. The inner tube can move freely inside the outer shaft. A phosphor-bronze wire, approximately .10 to .25 mm thick, is mounted in the inner tube. The collapse of the two tubes upon one another expands the wire into a cutting loop. A device built on the outer shaft stops rotation. The marking on the inner shaft, containing the wire, can be used to determine the depth and extension of the loop. A standard stereotaxic electrode clamp supports the whole assembly.

Gold, Kapatos, and Carey (1973) describe another knife, which can be adapted from a microliter syringe (Hamilton 7101). The syringe comes with a tungsten plunger wire (.015 mm diam) that extends to the tip of the needle (.04 mm) when the plunger is fully depressed. The essential step is to bend (45°) the needle and cut away all but the beginning of the bend. When the needle is in the brain and the plunger is depressed, the wire retains the bend as it exits the needle tip (see Figure 3.7). The calibration of the syringe barrel is used to determine the distance that the wire is extended. The addition of a Chaney adapter (7101 NCH), fitted with two stop-collars, makes presetting possible, to adjust the extension and retraction of the wire and to prevent the rotation of the wire plunger when the

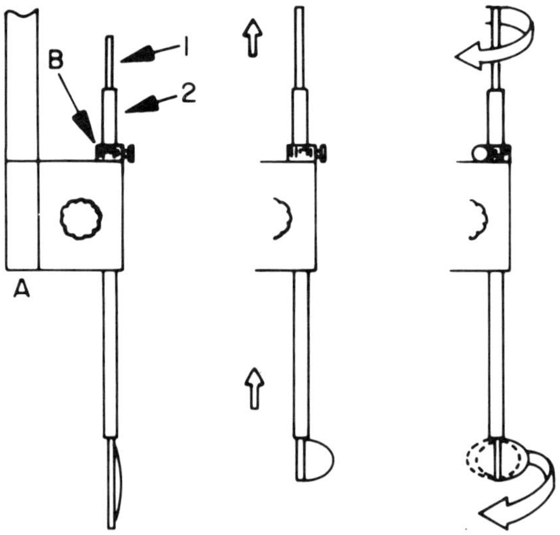

FIGURE 3.6. A Schematic of a Retractable Rotating Knife. Concentric shafts of hypodermic-type stainless steel tubing (1 and 2) are held in a standard stereotaxic electrode clamp. *Left.* The cutting loop is closed during insertion of the tome into the brain. *Center.* The cutting loop is expanded by a calibrated elevation of shaft 1 relative to shaft 2. *Right.* Procedure for making hemispherical or spherical cuts. The knurled nut on clamp A is unscrewed until the tome is free to rotate. Stop B prevents the tome from changing elevation. The retaining screw on B indicates the direction of the loop. From Caruthers, R. P., An expanding loop encephalotome for use in brain function research, *EEG & Clinical Neurophysiology,* 1968, **24,** 590–592. © 1968 by Elsevier Publishing Company. Reproduced by permission.

wire is retracted. The needle that originally comes with the unit is long and flexible; thus to stiffen the upper part of the needle, the part that never enters the brain, slip a 3- to 4-cm-long piece of 18-gauge hypodermic tubing over it (see Figure 3.7D). To make cuts in the frontal and sagittal planes, lower the syringe-knife, with wire retracted, to the desired depth and extend the wire by pressing on the plunger. Raise or lower the syringe-knife to make the cut; then retract the wire and withdraw the syringe-knife.

ELECTROLYTIC LESIONS

The use of electrical energy (direct current) to produce neural lesions in animals has been reported ever since 1895 (Carpenter & Whittier, 1952). The passage of direct current through neural tissue causes extensive biochemical changes (for example, hydrolysis, which changes the pH level), gas formation, and toxic metal deposit from the electrode that can produce localized lesions. The size and shape of electrolytic lesions depend on the diameter of the electrode, the size of the uninsulated tip of the electrode, the use of either monopolar or bipolar electrodes, and, finally, the use of either anodal or cathodal current. Although some investigators have in the past used bipolar electrodes to produce lesions, monopolar electrodes are now in general use, mainly because lesions produced by bipolar electrodes are larger and more irregular than those caused by monopolar electrodes. Also, a great majority of investigators prefer anodal lesions to cathodal lesions, primarily because the greater amount of gas formation at the cathode produces larger and more irregular lesions. This section, therefore, describes anodal electrolytic lesions produced by monopolar electrodes.

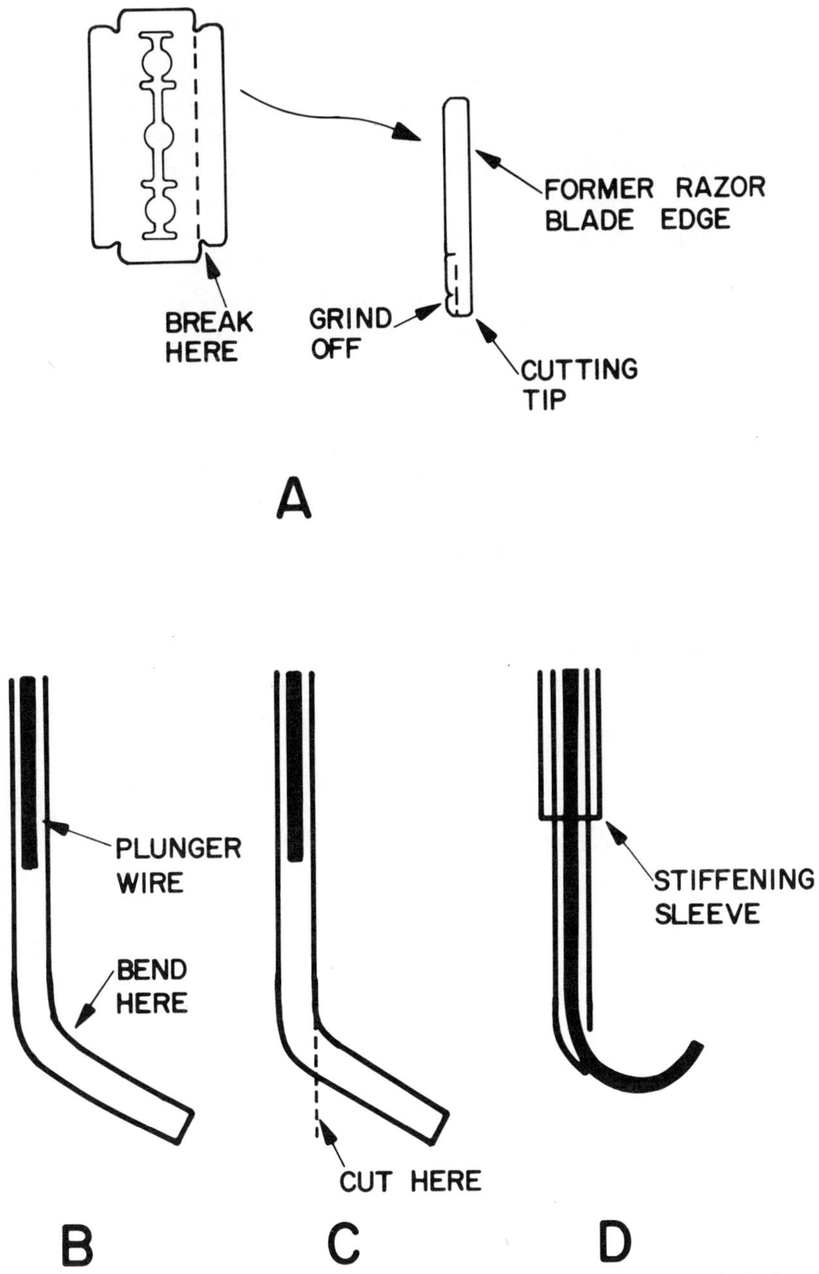

FIGURE 3.7. A Schematic of Two Types of Knives. A. The knife made by breaking an edge off a razor. B, C, and D. The technique for making a retracting-wire knife. The tip of microliter syringe is bent approximately 45° (B) and all except the beginning of the bend is cut away (C). A hypodermic tubing is slipped onto the needle shaft to stiffen the upper part of the needle (D). From Gold, R. M., Kapatos, G., & Carey, R. J., A retracting wire knife for stereotaxic brain surgery made from a microliter syringe, *Physiology & Behavior,* 1973, **10,** 814. © 1973 by Brain Research Publication, Inc. Reproduced by permission.

The Electrode

A variety of metals or alloys have been used to prepare electrodes. However, since passage of current leaves metal particles that are toxic to the neural tissue, electrodes made of platinum or iridium should be used whenever possible, as they are least reactive and leave very little metal deposit. The most commonly used metal, nonetheless, is stainless steel, which is very reactive, and the common source of supply is insect pins. The diameter of the electrode is determined by the structure to be destroyed. Electrodes for monkeys and cats can be made from a 20-gauge hypodermic needle or from stainless steel rods of .021 to .058 in. diam. If thicker electrodes are used, insertion alone produces greater injury to overlying structures than thin electrodes produce, and thus it is wise to use operated (that is, insertion of electrode but no passage of electric current) control animals to isolate the effect of the electrode penetration.

Electrodes, except for the tip from which the current is passed, must be insulated. They can be insulated with glass or plastic tubes, rubber varnish, cement, and so on. However, a heat-baked varnish coating (Epoxylite) is a durable and economical insulating material that can withstand steam or chemical sterilization. The insulating procedure is relatively simple. The electrode must be clean (washed with 70 percent alcohol) and dry. Immerse the electrode in a bottle or tube containing Epoxylite; to obtain a uniform coating on the electrode, gently and slowly lower it into and remove it from the bottle. Use an electrode holder made from an alligator clip, to prevent immersion of the upper tip (clip lead), to which the current leads will be attached. Follow the manufacturer's instructions for baking. Baking the electrodes for approximately one hour at 350° to 380°F is satisfactory. To ensure safety, apply one more coat of varnish and bake the electrode again.

The Lesion Maker

Many commercially produced lesion makers are available. All have dials for setting time and current intensity, and an amp meter that shows the current being passed between the negative and positive electrodes. Although not commercially manufactured, a lesion maker that includes a light that goes off when the electrode touches the animal and a circuit is completed can be made to order. The light provides the researcher a handy means to ascertain whether or not the electrodes are making proper contact to complete the circuit.

Procedure for Lesion Making

The procedure for lesion making can be divided into the following sequential steps: (1) checking the electrode for defects and leaks; (2) determining the current parameters to be used; (3) determining the stereotaxic coordinates; (4) surgery; and (5) postsurgical recovery.

CHECKING THE ELECTRODE

Because defects in the coating can develop during the insulation procedure or during storage, the electrode may contain electrical leaks. Check for leaks before using the electrode, since a lesion will occur at the point of a leak. Then determine the size of the tip of the electrode that is needed. For small lesions, scrape the insulation at the tip to expose .5 to 1 mm of metal; for larger lesions, scrape 2 to 3 mm of the tip. Scraping should be done very carefully with a scalpel blade under a low-power microscope. Check the electrode again for electrical leaks or incidental chipping caused by scraping the tip. Connect the uninsulated tip (clip lead) to the anode lead from the lesion maker. Lower the electrode into a beaker of physiological saline and attach the cathode lead to the tip to be used for lesion making. To test the electrode, pass through it a current of greater intensity than that used for lesion making. If the electrode is properly insulated, bubbles appear only at the tip. Use only those electrodes in which bubbles occur only at the tip. Note that anodal lesion making corrodes the metal; if the same electrode is to be used more than once, scraping the tip again may be necessary. Also, since new leaks may develop between uses, test the electrode for leaks before using it again.

DETERMINATION OF CURRENT AND TIME PARAMETERS

The size of the electrolytic lesion depends on current intensity (amperes) and duration (time)—that is, the quantity of electricity expressed in coulombs (ampere by time). The volume of destroyed neural tissue depends on the area in the brain (highly myelinated or vascularized areas in the brain require more current than other areas), the diameter of the electrode, the size of the tip of the electrode, and the coulomb units. Other factors being equal, the size of the lesion appears, at least for a few seconds, to be proportional to the coulomb units. For example, Carpenter and Whittier (1952) have shown that a 5-mA current passed through a monopolar electrode for 30 seconds produces a lesion of 2.0 mm diam. However, if the same current (5 mA) is passed for 60 seconds, the lesion diameter is about 2.6 mm. Thus, if larger lesions are desired, the current intensity rather than duration of current should be increased. However, the current and time parameters must be empirically determined. Some investigators (see, for example, Thompson, 1971) suggest application of different coulomb units in the albumin of raw egg to estimate the size of brain lesion that would be produced. However, Rowland (1966) demonstrated that in DC lesions coulombic effects (that is, electrolytic lesioning) appear first and mask heat effects (that is, thermal lesioning); hence gauging the lesion size by pretesting DC parameters in egg white is not valid. The best way to estimate the current and time parameters is to create the lesion and, histologically, confirm the size.

Finally, Rowland (1966) suggests that the anodal-lesion technique be employed only for lesions under 2 to 3 mm diam. If larger lesions are to be produced, one should either make them with multiple, smaller anodal lesions or use radio-frequency techniques (see below).

SURGICAL PROCEDURE

Before beginning surgery, determine the stereotaxic coordinates. If the interaural line is the reference point, record the instrument scale reading. If the bregma is the reference point, proceed with anesthetizing the animal (see Chapter 2). Shave the animal's head and mount the animal in the stereotaxic instrument. After preparing the skin, make the incision. For aseptic surgery, the surgeon and the assistant must scrub, and the animal's head must be draped (see Chapter 2). If the bregma is the reference point, thoroughly dry the skull after removing the connecting tissue to see the bregma more easily. After identifying the bregma, lower the electrode until it touches the bregma. Obtain readings from the instrument and make adjustments to the coordinates obtained from the atlas. Then use the corrected coordinates to move the electrode to the points where the holes are to be drilled in the skull. Mark the points with a hard pin or needle. Move the electrode carrier to the side to provide ready access for drilling the holes. Once the holes have been drilled, carefully remove all the bone chips. Then cut the dura mater under the drilled hole with the help of a dura knife. Cutting the dura mater before inserting the electrode is critical, especially in cats and monkeys; otherwise, the electrode may bend slightly. Now the animal is ready for making lesions. Double-check the coordinates before inserting the electrode. If the hole is slightly off the place where the electrode is to be lowered, increase the size of the hole with ronguers. If using the midsagittal sinus as a reference for the lateral coordinate, drill two holes, one on each side of the sinus, and then, with one sweep of the burr between the two holes, remove the bone. Sometimes the sinus breaks and bleeding ensues. Stop the bleeding by gently placing a pellet of Gelfoam over the bleeding point. When bleeding stops, use the sinus as the lateral reference point. Before inserting the electrode, it is wise to double-check that the time duration and current intensity are set at the desired level. Place the indifferent electrode in the anal sphincter and tape the wire from the electrode to the tail so that the electrode will not slide out. Clamp the active lead to the uninsulated head of the electrode. Then, lower the electrode to the desired depth and pass the current. If bilateral lesions are desired, repeat the process on the other side. After removing the electrode, place a piece of Gelfoam on the holes and thoroughly dry the skull. In rats suture the skin with an interrupted suture. In monkeys and cats suture the overlying muscle before suturing the skin. Before removing the animal from the apparatus, aspirate the accumulated saliva. If the animal has not been pretreated with an antibiotic, administer the antibiotic. After suturing, apply boric acid powder over the incision. Do not leave any food and water in the animal's cage, since the swallowing reflexes are not fully functional and the animal may choke while trying to eat.

RADIO-FREQUENCY LESIONS

General Information and Procedure

When a high-frequency alternating current (in the megacycle range) flows through a resistance, heat is generated in the resistance. Thus, during passage of high-frequency AC, heat or coagulation can kill brain tissue. The radio-frequency (RF) method, although using heat as the means of killing the neural tissue, is different from a cryoprobe, which involves heating the tip of a probe by some thermal means and then letting the tip impart heat to tissue by thermal conduction. In other words, the RF method converts energy into heat within the tissue, whereas in a cryoprobe, the cryoprobe tip imparts heat to the tissue. The problem with cryoprobe, or thermocautery, is that it is difficult to control and cannot be de-energized rapidly.

In the radio-frequency technique, a low-power, continuous-wave, radio-frequency current is passed between the electrodes. The volume of tissue destroyed is proportional to the electrical power used (Aronow, 1960). For a monopolar electrode of .021 in. diam and application of varying electrical power for 15 seconds, Aronow (1960) reports the following relationship between the area of damage and current intensity:

POWER (mA)	DIAMETER OF DAMAGED AREA (mm)
50	2.0
100	3.8
300	6.0
600	11.0

Note that equilibrium becomes established within 30 to 60 seconds (except in highly vascular sites), after which heat input and rate of heat conduction start away from the site. Therefore, to produce localized lesions, limiting exposure time to less than 60 seconds is advisable. To produce lesions of a larger diameter, increase electric power rather than extend exposure time.

A variety of inexpensive RF lesion makers are commercially available (Grass). Some slightly more expensive lesions makers incorporate on the tip of the electrode a temperature-sensing device (Radionics RFG-4), the output of which is shown on a meter. The temperature-sensing device permits a direct measure of maximum tissue heating and an objective measure of the time course of heat dissipation. Furthermore, since raising the temperature 10°C above the animal's body temperature for 15 seconds produces no significant neural tissue damage, the setup can be used for producing functional lesions of short duration.

To produce RF lesions, monopolar electrodes are most frequently used. The electrode for cats and monkeys can be made from stainless steel rods (.021 or .058 in.). The insulation procedure is the same as that described for electrolytic lesion making. Allow the clip lead of the electrode to remain uninsulated and scrape the tip of the electrode (about 1 to 2 mm). Because heat is the primary mechanism that produces lesions in the RF method, use egg white for checking the electrode as well as for estimating the size of the lesion. To test the electrode, attach the active lead to the uninsulated clip lead and place the indifferent electrode in a cup containing egg white. When the electrode is lowered into the egg white and the current is passed, only that portion of egg white that is in contact with the bare tip of the electrode is cooked.

Once the time and current parameters are estimated, the procedures for determining stereotaxic coordinates and for surgery are identical to those described for electrolytic lesions.

Some Limitations

The major disadvantage of the RF method is that it creates lesions of highly irregular shape in neural sites that contain a rich blood supply. Fluid channels make electrical properties of the medium nonhomogeneous, and, therefore, lesions in areas close to ventricles and blood vessels become irregular. Furthermore, the lesion size for identical time and current parameters may vary in different points of the brain because of differential resistance to heat.

The other disadvantage is that the RF method cannot reliably produce lesions smaller than 2 to 3 mm, since radio-frequency energy is difficult to adjust. A wise policy is to use the RF method only for producing lesions larger than 2 to 3 mm.

SPREADING DEPRESSION

In the early 1940s, Leao discovered that application of potassium chloride (KCl) on the cortex of a rabbit causes depression of normal electrical activity recorded from the cortex. Furthermore, because depression of electrical activity suggested inhibition of certain behavior normally regulated by the cortex, experimentally induced depression became a useful tool for investigating brain function. The spreading-depression (SD) method has been used extensively in learning and memory research, since it produces only functional loss during propagation and can be used for studying temporal, or time-dependent, functions of the cortex. The SD technique has also been used to study some of the subcortical structures.

Properties of Spreading Depression

When a KCl solution is topically applied to the exposed cortex of a rat or a rabbit, depression in electrical activity takes place. The spread of the depression typically is slow (2 to 3 mm/min) and exhibits little preference in path of propagation (Marshall, 1959). A slow change of potential, which is primarily negative, always accompanies the depression. The magnitude of the potential shift is reported to be in the range of −5 to −15 mV; the negative wave can last 40 to 60 seconds. The neuronal activity returns to normal in approximately 20 minutes to 3 hours, though the recovery time is variable. Evoked potentials recorded from the site become normal in about 24 hours after application of KCl. However, a great many metabolic and biochemical changes appear to take place after application. Krivanek (1969) reports that, after repeated application of 25 percent KCl, marked reduction occurs in brain protein synthesis and other metabolic changes, which outlast KCl application by days. The most reliable behavioral indicator of the efficacy of spreading depression is diminished sensibility (or hypesthesia). Rats under spreading depression do not exhibit placing responses; if a limb falls through a hole or between two spaced bars, the rat does not retract the limb. Except for the postural reflex loss, KCl-treated rats do not show any major motor impairment; bilaterally treated rats can learn different maze tasks and exhibit running speed and latencies similar to non-treated rats in a maze (Russell, Plotkin, & Kleinman, 1968). Note that depression of neuronal activity is not uniform throughout the depression period. It has been reported that every 6 to 10 minutes recurrent attenuation and recovery of electrical activity take place. Freedman (1969) reports similar cyclic bursts of activity followed by inactivity in behavioral tests such as licking a sweet solution and in spontaneous activity in the rat.

Some Qualifications

Before using the SD method, one should be aware of its limitations. First, species and ontogenetic differences greatly affect the ease with which spreading depression can be produced. Spreading depression can be easily produced in rats and mice but can be produced only with difficulty in cats and, especially, monkeys (Leao, 1963). Spreading depression appears to be much more easily elicited in those species that have relatively undifferentiated cortex. Although spreading depression has been produced in the squirrel monkey, the resultant amplitude of slow potential change is much smaller than that reported for rabbits and rats (Rebert, 1970). Similarly, spreading depression is difficult to produce in newborn animals—for example, in kittens before the age of 5 weeks (Leao, 1963) or in rats before the age of 12 days (Bures & Buresova, 1972).

Second, spreading depression does not always produce an inhibitory effect. In addition to cyclic bursts of activity and inactivity that occur during the depression period, some other, more specific excitatory effects have been reported. Huston and Bures (1970) have found that about 5 minutes after the initiation of a wave of spreading depression, rats eat and drink. Clemens, Waller, and Gorski (1967) have found spreading depression to facilitate mating behavior in female rats.

Third, electrical recovery and behavioral recovery from spreading depression do not always follow the same time course; many behaviors continue to be depressed after a full neural recovery. For example, animals exhibit hypesthesia long after the electrical function of the cortex has recovered (Carew, Crow, & Petrinovich, 1970). A single application of 25 percent KCl in the rat affects exploration of a novel environment for 3 to 5 days, although evoked responses recover after 24 hours (Buresova & Bures, 1969).

Fourth, repeated application of KCl (which may be necessary for certain experiments) can cause cortical lesion and complicate the interpretation of the data. Application of 25 percent KCl for 1 hour a day for 2 days can produce large lesions in the rat (Hamburg, Best, & Cholewiak, 1968). These findings imply that spreading depression is not a functional lesion in a true sense. Finally, propagation is problematic. Fifkova and Syka (1964) have shown that spreading depression interacts, both electrically and chemically, with subcortical structures, especially the thalamus and hypothalamus. The transcortical spread of the effect makes inferring whether a given behavioral manifestation is due to a cortical or to a subcortical system difficult.

The purpose of documenting the limitations of SD is not to imply that similar disadvantages are absent in other lesion techniques (see below). It is hoped that a realistic awareness of its limitations will enhance the use of the SD technique. However, its use with only mature rats (or rabbits) is advisable. Bures and Buresova (1972) suggest that rats weighing 180 to 200 g (approximately 3 months old) are the most suitable subjects for SD.

Surgical Procedure

After inducing anesthesia, shave the head of the animal and mount it in a stereotaxic headholder. Incise the skull and scrape the underlying connective tissue. Typically, in rats, holes are drilled midway between the bregma and the lambda, 1 to 2 mm lateral to the coronal suture. Holes should be large enough (about 4 mm) so that a filter paper soaked with physiological saline can be placed. Holes can be drilled with a trephine or a burr, but take extreme care not to break the dura mater; if the dura is ruptured, the animal should be discarded. Then pack the hole with a piece of cotton dipped in physiological saline and loosely suture the skin. Traditionally, a recovery period of 24 hours is given before the application of KCl, but 2 to 4 hours of recovery should be enough. For the application of the KCl, cut the skin sutures (preferably under novocain, powder or liquid local anesthetic) and remove the cotton piece with forceps. Place a circular filter paper or cotton gauze soaked in KCl in the hole. In behavioral research, the most frequently used KCl concentration is 25 percent. Following application of KCl, the tactile placing reflex (in the contralateral forelimb if unilateral SD is used) should be lost within 6 to 8 minutes.

Manual application requires picking up the animal and also replacing the KCl-dipped filters every hour or so to prevent evaporation. An alternative is to implant a capped cannula (0.5 mm i.d.) into the skull. The basic technique consists of attaching a polyethylene or metal tube with dental cement and holding the screws on the skull (for procedure see Chapter 4). The tube or the cannula can be filled with physiological saline and capped to prevent evaporation (if a cap is not available, use a piece of dental cement). In the method developed by Paolino and Levy (1970), the cannula assembly (see Figure 3.8) consists of the cannula base, mounted permanently on the rat's skull, and the cannula, which screws into the base. Make the cannula base from a $^6/_{32}$ threaded hexagonal nylon nut (Service), filed to a circular shape $^3/_{16}$ in. diam. Make the cannula from a 1.5-cm segment of $^6/_{32}$ threaded nylon rod through which two holes are longitudinally drilled with a drill jig and a No. 67 drill. Then, in each hole, force-fit a 3-cm segment of 22-gauge stainless steel tubing. A filed-down nylon nut on each cannula serves as a sleeve to ensure that, when screwed into the base, the cannula tip is positioned just above the dura.

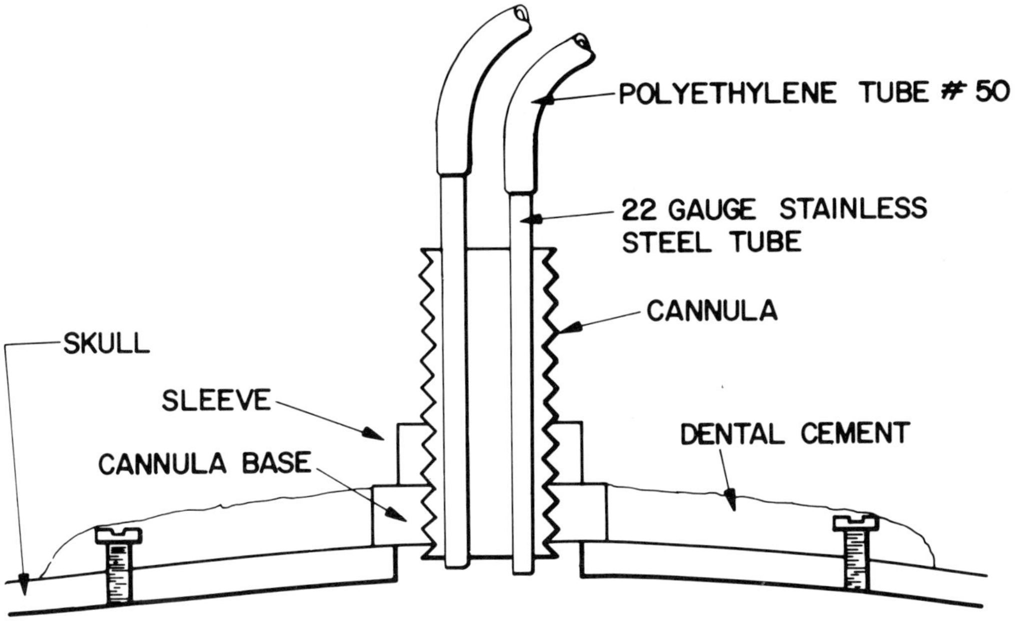

FIGURE 3.8. Diagram of a Cannula Assembly for Inducing Cortical Spreading Depression in the Freely Moving Rat. From Paolino, R. M., & Levy, H. M., A cannula assembly for inducing cortical depression in free moving animals, *Physiology & Behavior,* 1970, **5,** 1499–1500. © 1970 by Brain Research Publication, Inc. Reproduced by permission.

Permanently affix two cannula bases (one on each side of the midsagittal suture) to the skull. Trephine bilaterally two holes (3 mm) with centers 3 to 4 mm lateral to the sagittal suture and 3 to 4 mm posterior to the bregma. Position a cannula base over each trephined hole and secure it to the skull with dental cement and stainless steel screws (for technique see Chapter 4). Then screw each cannula into place. Administer KCl by means of polyethylene tubing fitted to one 22-gauge tubing in each cannula and connected to a syringe outside the test apparatus. Use the other 22-gauge tube in each cannula to contain the overflow.

If KCl is to be placed in some subcortical structure, use a double cannula (for preparation and implanting a double cannula, see Chapter 4). Tap the tip of the inner cannula against crystal KCl to pack a small amount of KCl into the tip of the cannula. Insert the cannula through the outer guide shaft to the desired neural structure.

Dose and Determination of Onset

Traditionally, 25 percent KCl is used in SD. Russell, Plotkin, and Kleinman (1968) report that a microinjection of 0.008 cc of 25 percent KCl to the surface of the dura produces a mean depression time of 90 minutes in the rat. However, an empirical determination of the time course of the depression is advisable. The placing reflex can be tested behaviorally. Carew, Crow, and Petrinovich (1970) report a novel method that uses a Plexiglas chamber with floor bars 2.8 cm diam spaced 2 cm apart (center to center). The spacing requires a fair amount of postural tonus; thus when hypesthesia sets in, the forelimb (contralateral to the depressed hemisphere) falls through the bar. Failure to retract the limb indicates onset of depression.

If precise duration of depression is critical, the electrical activity from the cortex must be recorded. When the electroencephalographic (EEG) amplitude is reduced to one-third the base line amplitude, the animal can be considered under depression. However, reduction in EEG amplitude may or may not correlate with behavioral depression. For example, an application of 1 percent KCl readily evokes neural depression without any sign of behavioral depression (Buresova & Bures, 1969).

OTHER TECHNIQUES

Many other techniques for producing permanent lesions in the brain have been reported but, invariably, they are expensive and require a special setup. For example, the use of ultrasound waves, although reported to produce precise lesions without the need for major surgery, requires an expensive setup. Some investigators have used beta and gamma radioactive pellets, which are implanted in the target area and which, after some time, produce localized lesions. At present, these methods do not represent a great enough improvement over other methods to justify the expense.

The most promising methods are those capable of producing accurate reversible lesions. One of the least expensive techniques is to introduce a local anesthesia to render a given part nonfunctional for a certain time. For example, 2 percent procaine hydrochloride mixed in .54 percent saline produces a functional loss in subcortical areas (Madryga & Albert, 1971).

Another such technique is localized cooling (Skinner & Lindsley, 1968), which, broadly, requires a cannula (cryogenic probe), the tip of which can be cooled. A functional blocking or physiological inhibition, obtained when the temperature of the probe is lowered between the range of +10°C to 0°C, has been demonstrated. Skinner and Lindsley (1968) report that a tip temperature of 0°C produces a functional blockage in tissues in an area of approximately 3 mm circumvolving the surface of the probe in the thalamic area of the cat. When the cooling is stopped, disrupted learned behavioral tasks and electrophysiological activity return to the precooling level within 3 minutes. Lowering the temperature below 0°C produces a permanent lesion that is caused primarily by crystalization of water and rupture of cellular membrane. Using a probe of 2 mm diam, Cooper (1962) has shown that maintaining a temperature of −40°C for 3 minutes produces a lesion of 6 mm; lowering the temperature to −50°C increases the size of the lesion to 8 mm. Skinner (1971) gives necessary details for making a cryogenic device that is quite suitable.

GENERAL CONSIDERATION

Although experimental ablation has been used extensively to study the relationship of brain structure and function, it has a few drawbacks. Many investigators (see, for example, Rowland, 1966) maintain that the major problem is to make accurate inferences about localization of functions. Apparently, no way exists to ascertain whether a particular postoperative behavior (for example, hyperemotionality) is due to the removal of a part or to the remaining functional tissues. Quite possibly, postoperative behavior reflects some compensatory reaction of the remaining neural tissues to the damage; if so, then damage to an area essentially produces effects that are not regulated by that area. A related problem is that a particular area may contain more than one functional system; because the damage cannot be produced in just one functional system, no meaningful inference about localization of function can be made.

Furthermore, even restricted lesions may have impact beyond the desired boundary of the intended lesions by destroying capillaries and by producing scars and edema. Finally, because of the irreversibility of lesions, the normal function of the destroyed part can be observed only in other, intact animals. Spreading depression overcomes some of the problems of irreversibility, but, as pointed out, it has other limitations such as species differences and the fact that certain parts of the brain do not demonstrate spreading depression (Leao, 1963).

The most promising technique for producing reversible lesions appears to be the use of local anesthesia such as procaine hydrochloride. The use of local anesthesia may be suitable for at least those experiments that do not require observations to be recorded over an extended period of time. The demonstration that a particular local anesthetic is not species-specific in its effects and that renders with equal facility most, if not all, parts of the brain nonfunctional would be a great methodological advance in understanding the relationship of brain structure to functions.

Finally, the complexity of the brain suggests that no one technique may ever succeed in unraveling its mystery. The most profitable strategy for understanding the function of the brain is the concurrent use of a variety of techniques such as ablation, chemical and electrical stimulation, and electrical recording.

REFERENCES

Aronow, S. The use of radio-frequency power in making lesions in the brain. *Journal of Neurosurgery,* 1960, **17,** 431–438.

Boring, E. G. *A history of experimental psychology.* (2nd ed.) New York: Appleton-Century-Crofts, 1950.

Bures, J., & Buresova, O. Inducing cortical spreading depression. In R. D. Myers (Ed.), *Methods in psychobiology,* Vol. 2. New York: Academic Press, 1972.

Buresova, O., & Bures, J. The effect of prolonged cortical spreading depression of learning and memory in rats. *Journal of Neurobiology,* 1969, **2,** 135–146.

Carew, J. T., Crow, T. J., & Petrinovich, L. F. Lack of coincidence between neural and behavioral manifestations of cortical spreading depression. *Science,* 1970, **169,** 1339–1342.

Carpenter, M. B., & Whittier, J. R. A study of the methods for producing experimental lesions of the central nervous system with special reference to stereotaxic techniques. *Journal of Comparative Neurology,* 1952, **97,** 73–131.

Caruthers, R. P. An expanding loop encephalotome for use in brain function research. *Electroencephalography and Clinical Neurophysiology,* 1968, **24,** 590–592.

Clemens, L. G., Waller, K., & Gorski, R. A. Mating behavior: Facilitation in the female rats after cortical application of potassium chloride. *Science,* 1967, **157,** 1208–1209.

Collias, J. C., & Manuelidis, E. E. Histopathological changes produced by implanted electrodes in cat brains: Comparison with histopathological changes in human and experimental puncture wounds. *Journal of Neurosurgery,* 1957, **14,** 302–328.

Cooper, I. S. A cryogenic method for physiologic inhibition and production of lesions in the brain. *Journal of Neurosurgery,* 1962, **19,** 853–858.

Ellison, G. D. Appetitive behavior in rats after circumsection of the hypothalamus. *Physiology and Behavior,* 1968, **3,** 221–226.

Fifkova, E., & Syka, J. Relationship between cortical and striatal spreading depression in rat. *Experimental Neurology,* 1964, **9,** 355–366.

Freedman, N. L. Recurrent behavioral recovery during spreading depression. *Journal of Comparative and Physiological Psychology,* 1969, **68,** 210–214.

Gol, A., Kellaway, P., Shapiro, M., & Hurst, C. M. Studies of hippocampectomy in the monkey, baboon, and cat. *Neurology,* 1963, **12,** 1031–1041.

Gold, R. M. Hypothalamic hyperphagia: Males get just as fat as females. *Journal of Comparative and Physiological Psychology,* 1970, **71,** 347–356.

Gold, R. M., Kapatos, G., & Carey, R. J. A retracting wire knife for stereotaxic brain surgery made from a microliter syringe. *Physiology and Behavior,* 1973, **10,** 813–815.

de Groot, J. *The rat forebrain in stereotaxic coordinate.* Amsterdam: Noord-Hollandsche Uitgevers Maatschappiz, 1959.
Halasz, B., & Pupp, L. Hormone secretion of the anterior pituitary gland after physical interruption of all nervous pathways to the hypophysiotrophic area. *Endocrinology,* 1965, **77,** 553–562.
Hamburg, M. D., Best, P. J., & Cholewiak, R. W. Cortical lesions resulting from chemically induced spreading depression. *Journal of Comparative and Physiological Psychology,* 1968, **66,** 492–494.
Huston, J. P., & Bures, J. Drinking and eating elicited by cortical spreading depression. *Science,* 1970, **169,** 702–704.
Konig, J. F. R., & Klippel, R. A. *The rat brain: A stereotaxic atlas of the forebrain and lower parts of the brain stem.* Baltimore: Williams and Wilkins, 1963.
Krivanek, J. Changes in protein, electrolyte and water metabolism caused by prolonged cortical depression in the rat. *Journal of Neurobiology,* 1969, **1**(2), 147–154.
Leao, A. A. P. On the spread of spreading depression. In M. A. B. Brazier (Ed.), *Brain function.* Vol. 1. Berkeley and Los Angeles: University of California Press, 1963.
Madryga, F. J., & Albert, D. J. Procaine injections into MFB-LHA during septal and preoptic self-stimulation. *Physiology and Behavior,* 1971, **6,** 695–701.
Marshall, W. H. On cortical spreading depression of Leao. *Physiological Review,* 1959, **39,** 239–279.
Meyer, R. M., & Meyer, D. R. Neurosurgical procedures with special reference to aspiration lesions. In R. D. Myers (Ed.), *Methods in psychobiology.* Vol. 1. New York: Academic Press, 1971.
Paolino, R. M., & Levy, H. M. A cannula assembly for inducing cortical depression in free-moving animals. *Physiology and Behavior,* 1970, **5,** 1499–1500.
Pellegrino, L. J., & Cushman, A. J. *A stereotaxic atlas of the rat brain.* New York: Appleton-Century-Crofts, 1967.
Reynolds, R. W. An irritative hypothesis concerning the hypothalamic regulation of food intake. *Psychological Review,* 1965, **72,** 105–116.
Rebert, C. S. Spreading depression in squirrel monkey lissen cephalic cortex. *Physiology and Behavior,* 1970, **5,** 239–241.
Rowland, V. Stereotaxic techniques and the production of lesions. In L. Martini and W. F. Ganong (Eds.), *Neuroendocrinology.* Vol. 1. New York: Academic Press, 1966.
Russell, I. S., Plotkin, H. C., & Kleinman, D. Cortical spreading depression and the problem of motor impairment. *Physiology and Behavior,* 1968, **3,** 849–855.
Skinner, J. E. *Neuroscience: A laboratory manual.* Philadelphia: Saunders, 1971.
Skinner, J. E., & Lindsley, D. B. Reversible cryogenic blockage of neural function in the brain of unrestrained animals. *Science,* 1968, **161,** 595–597.
Smith, G. W. An automatic drill for craniotomy. *Journal of Neurosurgery,* 1950, **7,** 285–286.
Snider, R. S., & Lee, J. C. *Stereotaxic atlas of the monkey brain (Macaca mulatta).* Chicago: University of Chicago Press, 1961.
Snider, R. S., & Niemer, W. T. *Stereotaxic atlas of the cat brain.* Chicago: University of Chicago Press, 1961.
Thompson, R. Introducing subcortical lesions by electrolytic methods. In R. D. Myers (Ed.), *Methods in psychobiology.* Vol. 1. New York: Academic Press, 1971.
Valenstein, T., Case, B., & Valenstein, E. S. Stereotaxic atlas of the infant rat hypothalamus. *Developmental Psychobiology,* 1969, **2,** 75–80.
Walker, A. E. Stimulation and ablation: Their role in the history of cerebral physiology. *Journal of Neurophysiology,* 1957, **20,** 435–449.
Waller, H., & Feldman, S. Somatosensory thalamic neurons: Effect of cortical depression. *Science,* 1967, **157,** 1074–1077.

SUGGESTED READINGS

Bures, J., & Buresova, O. Inducing cortical spreading depression. In R. D. Myers (Ed.), *Methods in psychobiology.* Vol. 2. New York: Academic Press, 1972.
Meyer, R. M., & Meyer, D. R. Neurosurgical procedures with special reference to aspiration lesions. In R. D. Myers (Ed.), *Methods in psychobiology.* Vol. 1. New York: Academic Press, 1971.
Rowland, V. Stereotaxic techniques and the production of lesions. In L. Martini and W. F. Ganong (Eds.), *Neuroendocrinology.* Vol. 1. New York: Academic Press, 1966.

Skinner, J. E. *Neuroscience: A laboratory manual*. Philadelphia: Saunders, 1971.
Thompson, R. Introducing subcortical lesions by electrolytic methods. In R. D. Myers (Ed.), *Methods in psychobiology*. Vol. 1. New York: Academic Press, 1971.

CHAPTER 4

Intracranial Chemical Stimulation

David D. Avery
COLORADO STATE UNIVERSITY

INTRODUCTION

Although techniques for injecting substances directly into the brains of animals were used as early as fifty years ago, only during the last decade has brain chemical stimulation assumed major importance as an investigatory tool for the study of brain mechanisms. Andersson (1952) reported the first studies directly dependent on chemical applications through indwelling cannulae implanted chronically in deep brain structures of animals. He injected hypertonic saline solutions into the brain through modified hypodermic needles cemented to the skulls of unanesthetized goats. Andersson observed that injections into hypothalamic regions led to immediate resumption of drinking in a completely water-satiated animal. These results, which Miller (1965) replicated in the cat, are presumably a function of the action of sodium chloride on osmoreceptors in the brain. Also in the 1950s, Feldberg and his colleagues (1954), working in Great Britain, initiated their inquiries into the effects on body temperature of injecting various drugs into the cerebral ventricles; and Fisher (1956) reported his observation of the effects on sexual behavior of injecting hormones into the hypothalamus of the rat.

The great importance of brain chemical-stimulation techniques for the behavioral sciences was not firmly established, however, until the publication of Grossman's (1962a, 1962b) extensive work on hypothalamic neurochemical mediation of feeding and drinking behavior. His experiments differed from the previous studies in that he injected substances thought to act as synaptic transmitters in the peripheral nervous system. His findings mark the beginning of a large number of experiments that strongly suggest that homeostatic mechanisms may be differentially coded in terms of brain neurohumors. (For a detailed review of this and subsequent work, see Grossman, 1967.)

Many investigators, encouraged by these results, began to use intracranial chemical-stimulation techniques in a wide variety of experiments. Studies of the neurochemical processes underlying hunger, thirst, sex, and temperature regulation have burgeoned. At present, experimenters are exploring the relationship of brain chemicals to sleep-arousal states, learning, memory, aggression, and various physiological mechanisms.

Thus in recent years chemical stimulation of the brain has assumed its rightful place as a powerful tool for discovering brain-behavior relationships. In view of the increasing use of the technique, this chapter introduces some of the technical considerations, problems, and theoretical implications of chemical stimulation of the brain to the investigator who has not had the opportunity to use this technique but would like to do so.

CONSTRUCTION OF CANNULAE

Cannulae suitable for stimulating with either liquids or crystals are commercially available for both large and small animals. However, cannulae comparable in quality to commercial cannulae can be constructed in the laboratory at reduced cost and with minimal effort. Following are the details for constructing an injection unit suitable for the rat or other small animals and one suitable for larger animals such as the cat or monkey. These cannulae are of the double-wall type, which allows repeated injections in chronic preparations. Each system consists of an outer guide cannula and an inner injection cannula (both of which are constructed from stainless steel hypodermic tubing), a dummy cannula, and a protective cap.

Small-Animal Cannula

The small-animal cannula is used for injecting liquids into either the ventricles or discrete brain loci of small mammals (see Figure 4.1). Construct the outer guide cannula from a 22-gauge hypodermic needle or from 22-gauge stainless steel tubing. Sweat the tubing into a piece of pre-threaded (6 to 32 threads) nylon bar stock 6 mm long and 3 mm diam, which has been drilled through the center with a $\frac{1}{32}$ in. drill. Before inserting the tubing, to ensure that the tubing does not become dislodged from the nylon hub, spread a small amount of epoxy cement on the part of the tubing that extends into the hub. Then, to construct a protective cap, machine and thread internally (6 to 32 threads) a nylon bar stock with dimensions of 4.8 mm o.d., 2.9 mm i.d., and 5.2 mm long. Construct the internal cannula from a 30-gauge hypodermic needle or hypodermic tubing. Cut the tubing so that the tip either extends 1 mm below or is flush with the guide cannula (some controversy exists as to which is the best technique; see Myers, 1971) and extends 10 mm above the top of the guide cannula. Cut a piece of 22-gauge tubing 10 mm long and glue it with epoxy cement to that

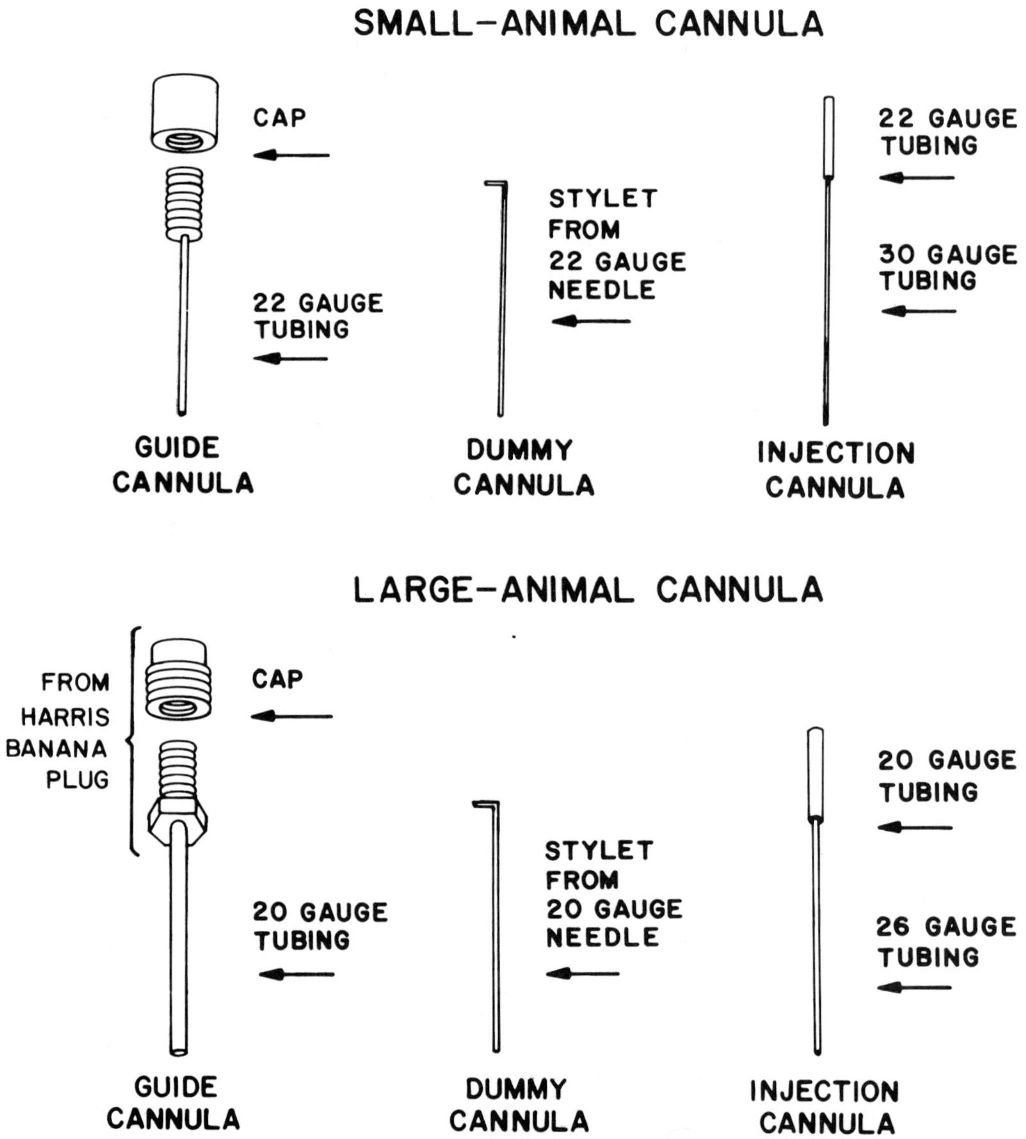

FIGURE 4.1. The Components of the Small- and Large-Animal Cannulae.

portion of the injection cannula extending above the guide cannula. The 22-gauge tubing serves as a stop for the injection cannula and facilitates attachment of polyethylene tubing from the injection syringe. When cutting hypodermic tubing, take care not to crimp the tubing at the cut. To avoid crimping, first fit the tubing with a stylet of appropriate size and cut the tubing with ordinary wire cutters. The stylet prevents the collapse of the tubing walls. A second satisfactory method is to cut the tubing with a diamond saw, which fits into the handpiece of a dental drill.

This injection cannula is suitable for applications of both crystalline and liquid substances. For crystalline injections, be sure that the injection cannula tip, when in place, is flush with the guide cannula tip. Clean the injection cannula with the aid of a stylet for a 30-gauge needle.

Construct a dummy injection cannula from the stylet for a 22-gauge needle. Crimp one end of the stylet to serve as a stop for the dummy cannula. Then cut the stylet with wire cutters or a diamond saw to the same length as the injection cannula. Keep the dummy cannula and the protective cap in place at all times except during stimulation to prevent the guide cannula from becoming obstructed and to ensure that the preparation remains aseptic.

Large-Animal Cannula

A simple and inexpensive cannula (see Figure 4.1) suitable for brain injections in larger animals, including the cat, rabbit, dog, and monkey, can be constructed from hypodermic tubing and components from a banana plug (Smith 211) as described by Decima and George (1964). First cut 20-gauge hypodermic tubing to the desired length and glue, using epoxy cement, or solder one end to the inside, brass component of the banana plug. Adapt the outer, chrome component of the plug to serve as a protective cap for the cannula assembly. Hacksaw the prong of the plug off at the base and file the rough edges. Construction of the internal injection cannula from 26-gauge hypodermic tubing is the same as that described for the injection component of the small-animal cannula (see above). A modified stylet for a 20-gauge hypodermic needle (see above) serves as a dummy cannula.

Both the small- and large-animal cannulae can be adapted easily to allow for either electrical recording or electrical stimulation concurrent with chemical injections (see Chapter 5). Briefly, adaption entails adhering preinsulated electrode wire to the outside of the external cannula. First stretch the wire to straighten it and then cut it to a length that extends 1 mm beyond the guide cannula and enough above the cannula to serve as a lead to the electrical hookup. Then place the wire alongside the guide cannula and, with insulating varnish, glue it to the guide shaft. If necessary for the particular recording or stimulation apparatus, then scrape the ends of the electrodes with a scalpel under a microscope (only the cross section of the electrode is suitable for stimulation and recording with most commercially available units).

CANNULA IMPLANT PROCEDURES

This section outlines procedures for the permanent implantation of double-wall cannulae into either discrete brain loci or the ventricular space. The techniques call for stereotaxic surgery and an anchoring procedure that uses stainless steel screws and dental acrylic. The discussion also touches on presurgical sterilization procedures, administration of anesthetic, and specific surgical techniques. (For a detailed discussion of anesthesia and basic surgery, see Chapter 2.)

Aseptic conditions must be adhered to if the animal is to remain healthy in a postoperative chronic preparation. All surgical instruments and materials should be sterilized either in an autoclave or in Zephiran chloride (see Chapter 2).

The following surgical details apply specifically to the rat; however, the same basic procedures and equipment apply also to other small animals and to larger species.

Prior to anesthetizing the animal, cut the external cannula so that its tip, when implanted, extends 1 mm above the desired brain site when the nylon hub is flush with the top of the skull at the point where the cannula enters the brain.

Most stereotaxic carriages come equipped with a holder suitable for electrode implantation. The holder is conducive also to cannula-implant procedures. One has only to substitute an appropriate stylet for the electrode and place the stylet in the holder according to the procedures for electrodes outlined by the stereotaxic instrument manufacturer. (Stylets from 22- or 20-gauge needles are appropriate for the small- and large-animal cannulae, respectively.) Position the stylet in the holder so that the stylet does not extend beyond the tip of the guide cannula during brain implantation; then slip the cannula onto the stylet. When the cannula is in place, calculate the stereotaxic coordinates (see Chapter 3).

The anesthetic typically employed in rat surgery is a combination of sodium pentobarbital (Nembutal) and chloral hydrate. Additionally, atropine sulfate (.05 ml of a .4 mg/ml solution) may be included in the anesthetic injection to relieve respiratory distress. The injection is typically administered intraperitoneally. Insert the needle 7 to 10 mm at a site 6 to 8 mm posterior to the rib cage and 1 to 3 mm lateral to the midline of the ventral surface of the animal. After inserting the needle, aspirate (withdraw the syringe plunger) before injecting to ensure that the tip of the needle is in the body cavity and not in a blood vessel or vital organ. If it is, the syringe draws blood. By 15 minutes after injection, the animal is usually sufficiently anesthetized for preparation for surgery. If the effects of the anesthesia begin to wear off during surgery, give a supplementary dose. Both sodium pentobarbitol and chloral hydrate should be one-fifth the initial dosage.

Closely cut the fur on top of the skull with animal clippers; scrub the underlying epidermis with Phisohex soap and then wipe with alcohol before placing the animal into the stereotaxic unit. Correctly positioning the animal depends on the type of instrument used and the particular stereotaxic atlas from which the coordinates for the implant are derived. Instructions are available with surgical units and in the atlas forewords (see also Chapter 3).

After positioning and firmly securing the animal in the stereotaxic instrument, make a midline incision through the skin on top of the skull, starting 1 mm posterior to the superior orbital ridge and extending approximately 20 mm posteriorly. Then retract the edges of the skin and underlying tissue laterally from the incision. Although commercial retractors are available, suitable ones can readily be made from stainless steel wire and rubber bands. Bend a small piece of wire 10 mm long at each end to grasp the edge of the incised skin. Tie one end of the rubber band to the middle of the wire and tie the other end to some part of the stereotaxic instrument. Adjust the tension so that the skull is sufficiently exposed for surgery. After retracting the skin, scrape the periosteum from the skull and thoroughly dry the exposed bone with gauze sponges and cotton. That the bone is completely dry is imperative; if it is not dry, the dental acrylic will not adhere well to the skull. Apply a 3 percent solution of hydrogen peroxide as an additional drying agent. The skull is then ready for marking and drilling.

Next, position the cannula tip at the desired location for entering the brain and mark the skull at this point. The holder can then be removed to allow sufficient space for drilling. Allowing a minimum of 2-mm clearance, mark for trephination three other sites, which are for the anchor screws to which the acrylic is secured. Drill the implant site with a No. 4 HP carbide dental burr. Utmost caution is necessary to avoid damage to the tissue below the skull. The three sites for anchor screws are drilled using a No. 35 HP dental burr. These sites are then threaded with a 0–80 bottoming tap. Place the tap perpendicular to the plane of the skull and make 1.5 clockwise turns; remove the tap by turning it counterclockwise. Exercise caution in this procedure, also, as too much pressure on the tap can fracture the skull, and too many turns of the tap lead to damage of the underlying meninges. Then, with 1.5 to 2.0 clockwise turns, screw 0–80 stainless steel screws $^{3}/_{16}$ in. long into the skull. (In larger animals, screws $^{5}/_{16}$ to $^{1}/_{2}$ in. long are preferred; they should be screwed 4.0 to 5.0 turns into the skull.) When all screws are in place, thoroughly dry the skull with cotton.

Bring the stereotaxic holder with cannula assembly into position again. Puncture the dura with a needle to avoid deflection of the cannula as it enters the brain. Now slowly lower the cannula to the desired depth. Apply dental acrylic to the bottom three threads of the cannula and to the anchor screws. After applying a small amount of acrylic and allowing it to dry (15 minutes), remove the stereotaxic holder. The acrylic should completely cover the anchor screws and leave no gaps be-

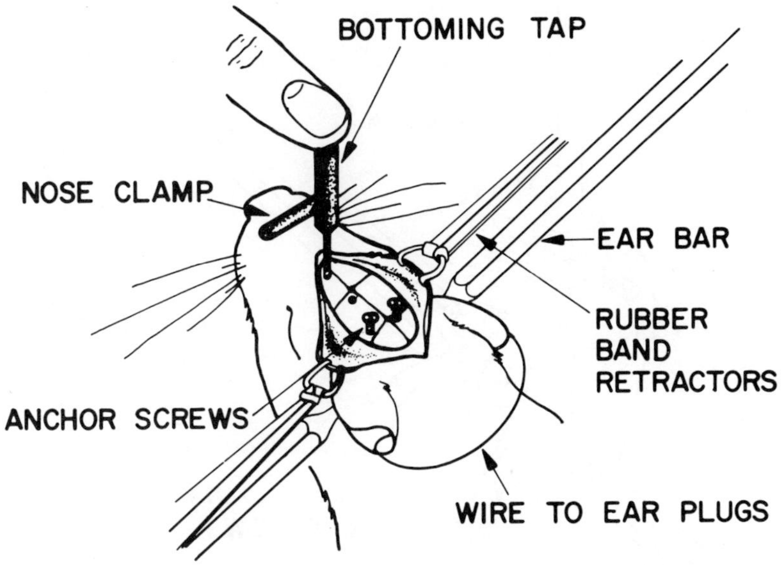

FIGURE 4.2. Proper Positioning of the Anchor Screws Showing Two Screws in Position and the Third Being Tapped.

tween the screws and the cannula. The edges of the acrylic must be smooth to prevent irritation of surrounding tissue. After the cement has dried completely (20 minutes), suture the incision anterior and posterior to the mound of acrylic. Usually 2 or 3 sutures at each end are sufficient. Many investigators prefer to use the purse-string suture (see Chapter 2) in larger animals.

The animal is ready to be removed from the instrument after the dummy cannula has been inserted and the protective cap has been put into place. Normal postoperative care procedures should be initiated. In addition to the normal postoperative care, the internal dummy cannula must be removed and cleaned with alcohol daily throughout the experimental life of the animal to protect against necrosis at the cannula tip.

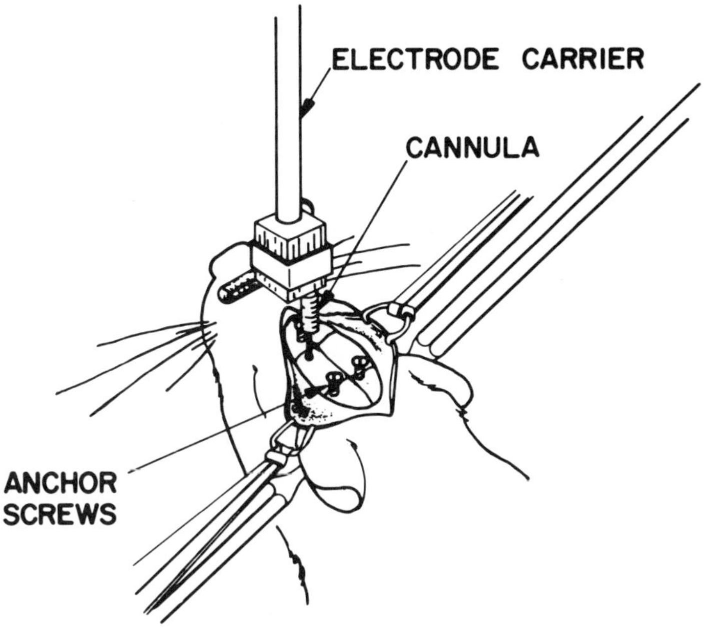

FIGURE 4.3. Insertion of a Cannula into the Brain with the Use of an Electrode Carrier.

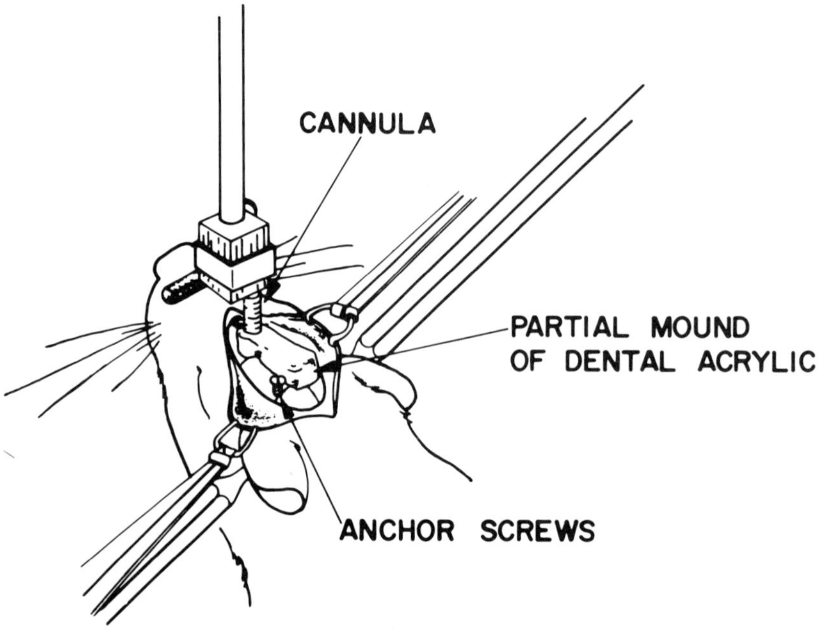

FIGURE 4.4. Early Stage of Dental Acrylic Application. At this stage the electrode carrier can be removed.

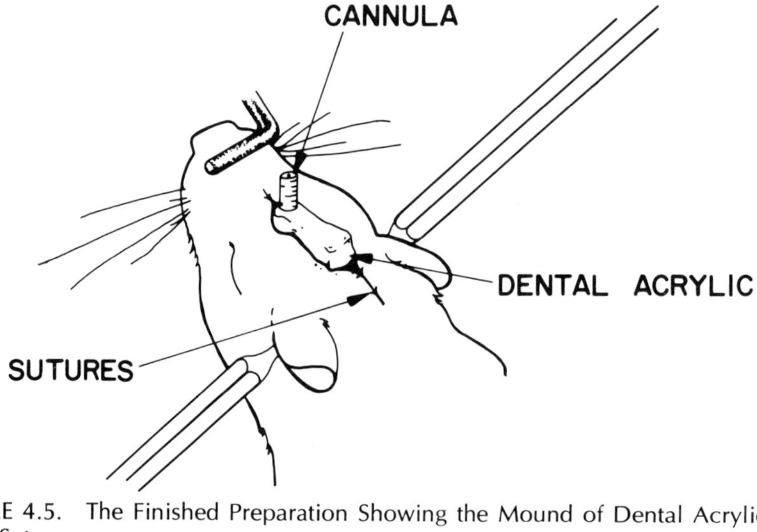

FIGURE 4.5. The Finished Preparation Showing the Mound of Dental Acrylic and the Location of the Sutures.

The procedures for implanting two cannulae in the same animal are basically the same as those for implanting only one. One necessary precaution is to avoid covering the skull with acrylic at the planned site of the second cannula. An additional problem arises if the two implant sites are close together. The distance between the two cannulae should be approximately two-thirds the diameter of the nylon protective cap of the small-animal cannula or of the chrome cap of the large-animal cannula; a smaller intercannula space makes removal and replacement of the caps difficult.

INJECTION PROCEDURES

This section outlines specific techniques for applying substances in either liquid or crystalline state to the brain. Before considering these techniques, some general comments with respect to injection procedures are in order.

Chemicals can be injected into the brain either into the ventricular space or into specific brain structures. The choice of the route of administration depends on the purpose of the experiment. Intraventricular injections are appropriate if one is interested in the general central effects of a drug as compared with effects observed after systemic administration. Many studies that have used this technique have amplified the importance of the blood-brain barrier. Thus this route of injection is particularly important for clarifying whether or not particular clinical drugs are affecting the peripheral and central nervous systems differentially.

In experimental work, direct brain placement is generally preferred to the ventricular route. Direct brain placement allows for exact histological verification of the cannula tip and a more precise identification of the neurological structures affected by the injections. However, caution is advised with respect to ascribing effects to specific neurological structures exclusively on the basis of cannula-tip localization. Identification of the exact location of the cannula tip is not necessarily evidence of the site of drug action; cannula-tip verification indicates only the site of drug application. Substances, whether injected in a liquid or the crystalline state, diffuse as a function of many factors, including volume injected, site of injection, and molecular weight. The site of action, therefore, may be some distance from the cannula tip.

The last section of the chapter discusses whether to use liquid or crystalline techniques. If one uses liquid injections, the choice of solvent is a prime consideration. Most substances, particularly neurotransmitters and their mimetics, metabolizers, and blocking agents, are water soluble. The two most commonly used solvents are physiologically neutral saline (.9 percent) and Locke-Ringer solution. If the solutions depart too much from endogenous pH levels (7.0), they may be buffered. If the solution is too acidic, sodium hydroxide may be used to bring pH back to the normal range; if too basic, hydrochloric acid may be used. One notable exception to those substances that are water soluble and thus conducive to liquid injection procedures is the relatively insoluble estrogenic steroid; with this and similar substances, crystalline techniques are mandatory.

Liquid Applications

The apparatus for microinjections of liquids into the brains of chronically implanted animals consists of the injection cannula, polyethylene tubing, a tubing adaptor, a microsyringe (Hamilton 710), a syringe holder, and a micromanipulator. Before filling the system, thoroughly clean and sterilize the injection cannula, tubing, and syringe. Use a 12-cc disposable syringe with a 22-gauge needle for cleaning. Fill the disposable syringe with a solution of warm water and detergent. Remove the injection cannula from the polyethylene tubing and extract the microsyringe plunger. Then, by back flushing, thoroughly clean the tubing and microsyringe. When the system is filled, reinsert the injection cannula and microsyringe plunger; flush the injection cannula by completely depressing the microsyringe plunger. Repeat the process several times with warm water. Dry the system by back flushing one time with acetone and by pumping air through the system several times with an empty 12-cc disposable syringe. To sterilize the system, place it in a drying oven at 300°F for one hour. The system can now be stored in an airtight, sterile container until use.

To fill the system for brain injections, follow the same basic procedure as that described for cleaning. However, after the system is filled, to avoid a dead space without fluid in the system, do not disengage the 12-cc syringe from the tubing until the plunger has been inserted. Take care also to avoid unwanted air bubbles in the liquid, as these can alter the volume injected. In addition, allow a substance that has been refrigerated to warm to room temperature before injecting it.

During injections, hold the experimental animal firmly, but gently, and support it underneath. Unscrew the protective cap and remove the dummy cannula. Then insert the injection cannula and force the solution out of the cannula by slowly turning the micromanipulator in a clockwise direction. If a 1-mm syringe is used, one complete turn of the micromanipulator injects one microliter of solution. Allow as much as 30 to 45 seconds to reduce the amount of mechanical stimulation. After the injection is completed, allow 45 seconds to 1 minute before removal of the injection cannula. If the cannula is removed too quickly, some of the solution may be drawn out with it. Clean and reinsert the dummy cannula and replace the protective cap. If external parts of the injection

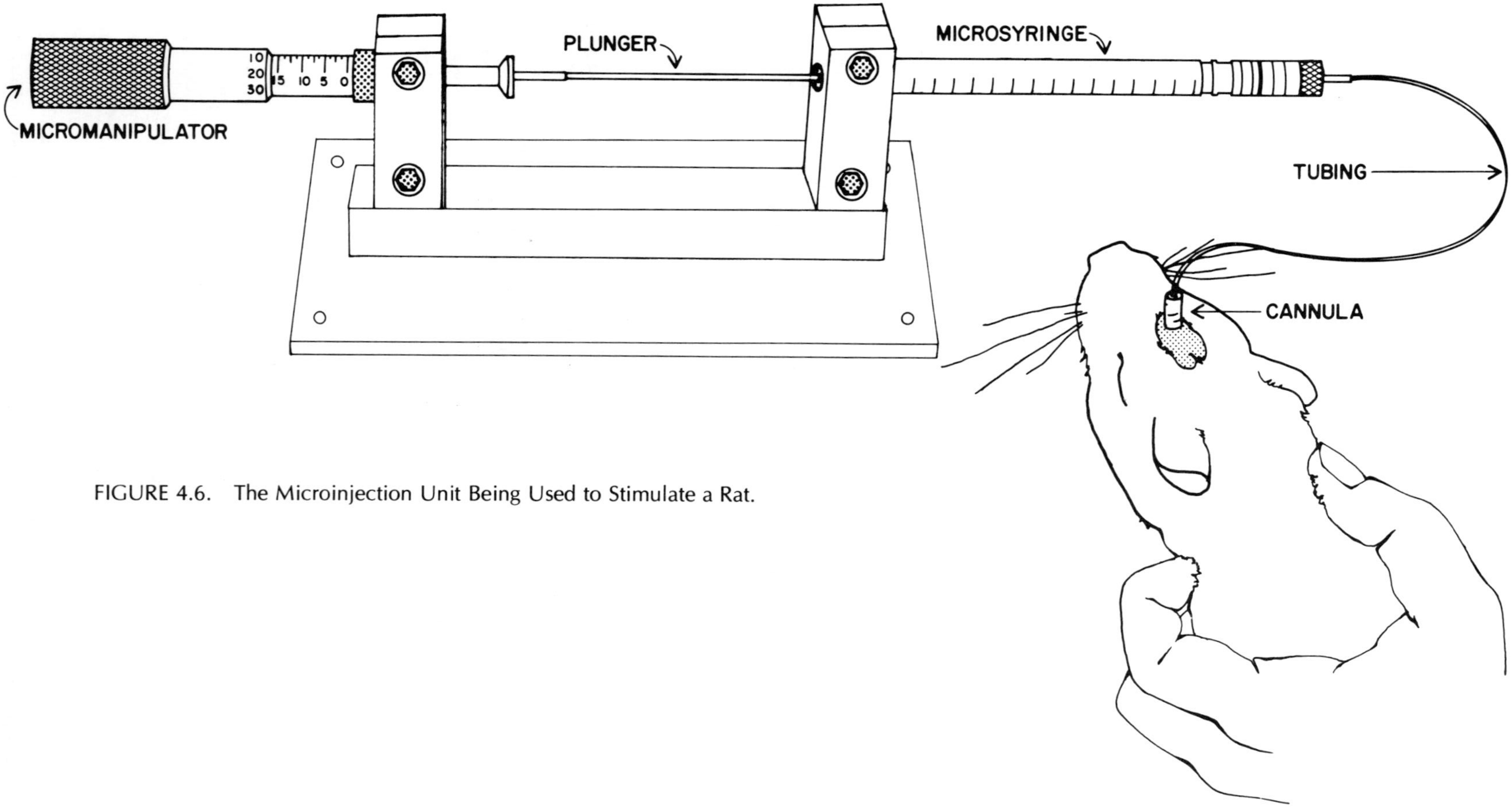

FIGURE 4.6. The Microinjection Unit Being Used to Stimulate a Rat.

cannula are thoroughly cleaned and sterilized between injections, two or more animals may be injected without refilling the system.

In addition to these hand-driven injection procedures, electrically driven pump devices are available for making microinjections. Although both procedures have been used successfully many times in experimentation, the automated pump has certain advantages. It can control more precisely the rate of injection and the volume of the substance. (For an excellent discussion of procedures with the automated pump, see Myers, 1971.)

Crystalline Applications

The injection cannula used for liquid applications can also be used for stimulation with crystalline substances. Tap minute amounts of crystals into the cannula by placing the crystals on a hard surface and repeatedly applying the tip of the cannula to these crystals. Estimate the amount of substance by weight or by volume based on the height of the column of crystals in the cannula. The latter measure can be determined by microscopic examination of the column height and calculations based on the molecular weight of the substance injected.

The injection procedure is essentially the same as that for liquids. Once in place, the loaded internal cannula is usually not removed until the experiment is completed. However, with most types of chemicals, the substance will diffuse from the cannula tip in 4 to 5 minutes, and, if desirable, the injection cannula can be replaced with the dummy cannula after this period of time. Procedures for cleaning and sterilizing the injection assembly after crystalline applications are the same as those described for liquid stimulation.

Other Techniques

Although the purpose of this chapter is to introduce the basic, simple chemical-stimulation techniques, another important procedure that should be mentioned is the push-pull cannula technique developed by Myers (1967, 1970). The basic unit consists of two cannula components, one that allows for the injection of specified amounts of solution to the ventricles or a specific brain site and a second component through which the same amount of solution can be collected. With this system one can, without changing total brain volume, manipulate brain chemistry and collect fluid samples for analysis of the effects of the manipulation in a chronic preparation. However, because of its complexity, the technique is not recommended for the beginning experimenter in brain chemical stimulation.

EXPERIMENTAL AND CONTROL PROCEDURES

In most experiments in which the independent variable is injections of substances directly into brain tissue, several important factors must be kept constant, or controlled for, if the results are to be exclusively attributable to the experimental manipulation. The latency from injection until the beginning of measurement and the elapse of time between successive injections are of utmost importance. Controls must be arranged for nonspecific drug factors such as pH, osmolarity, and vasomotor effects. If more than one substance is to be injected into a particular animal, appropriate controls must be used. The procedures discussed below should be of general benefit, though the consideration of each depends on the purposes of a particular experiment.

With injections of either liquids or crystals, most experimenters report that overt effects are observed after 4 to 8 minutes. Thus, in an experiment on the behavioral effects of intracranial chemical injections, measurement procedures should not be initiated until 10 minutes after injection. There are exceptions to this rule of thumb, however. For example, to observe the changes in core temperature induced by hypothalamic injections and the subsequent effects of these changes on behavioral thermoregulation, one would have to wait a longer period of time after injection, because significant changes in core temperature after intrahypothalamic injections occur from 15 to 45 minutes, depending on the substance injected (Avery & Penn, 1973).

In general, the effects of most centrally applied substances have dissipated by 24 hours after injection. Most experimenters, to be on the safe side, separate successive injections by at least 48 hours, and, in some instances, conditions warrant even longer periods.

To control for nonspecific activation of neural elements, substances such as strychnine sulfate should be injected as control drugs in a wide range of doses. The effects of these applications on the particular dependent variable under study can then be compared with the results observed after stimulation with the experimental drug; and the nonspecific effects, if any occur, can be assessed. Similarly, the influence of other properties (for example, pH and osmolarity) of the chemicals can be determined. Hypertonic, isotonic, and hypotonic solutions of sodium chloride (NaCl) should be injected to ensure that observed results are not due to osmotic stimulation. Acid-base effects can be determined by altering the pH of solutions if liquid injections are used or by introducing appropriate crystals if crystalline injections are used. Sodium hydroxide (NaOH) is generally used to make solutions more basic, and hydrochloric acid (HCl) is used to make solutions more acidic.

To determine whether the experimental drug is affecting vasomotor mechanisms, one can inject various control substances. Sodium nitrite and barium chloride are potent vasodilators, and posterior pituitary extract is a potent vasoconstrictor. Any of these control substances should be injected in amounts comparable to those of the experimental drugs. A sufficiently wide range of doses should be used to allay any misgivings that the observed results are due to influences not specific to the properties of a particular experimental drug.

In experiments that use more than one dose and more than one drug, the successive treatments should be counterbalanced in such a way that the order of drug treatments is systematically varied among subjects. Variation of order of treatment makes possible the statistical assessment of interaction effects among drugs, and, if these effects do occur, their influence on a particular treatment group of subjects can be kept at a minimum. A within-subjects design, in which every subject receives every treatment, reduces variability across subjects. (See Winer, 1962, for detailed discussions of experimental designs in drug research.)

Although the above considerations are by no means exhaustive, it is hoped that they will give the novice experimenter in brain chemical-stimulation research a healthy respect for the importance of adequate control procedures. Nothing can be more frustrating than to discover that one's results cannot be interpreted as exclusively attributable to the experimental manipulation.

GENERAL CONSIDERATIONS

As pointed out in the introduction to this chapter, brain chemical stimulation is a powerful technique for the exploration of brain mechanisms. As with other techniques, however, its use raises as many questions as it helps answer. Foremost among the questions are those concerning the desirability of one mode of chemical administration over the other; whereas one camp of experimenters espouses the virtues of liquid injections, the other camp swears by crystalline applications. At present, no clear-cut data exist for deciding which method is better; both have advantages and disadvantages. Robert Myers, the major proponent of liquid injection, criticizes stimulation with crystals on the basis of lack of control over pH, osmolarity, and local concentration; replication unreliability; and, most importantly, the fact that dose-response functions cannot be derived. On the other hand, Sebastian Grossman, the major user and supporter of crystalline stimulation, points out that the diffusion of even minute amounts of liquids injected into the brain is extensive and, furthermore, that the diffusion is different for various compounds and at different brain sites. He also objects to the possibility of mechanical stimulation when liquids are forced into the brain. As a reasonable solution to the dilemma, Alan Fisher (1969) suggests that the best procedure is to use both methods in a particular experiment if both are feasible in view of the experimental question and control needs.

Though brain chemical stimulation does not by itself elucidate completely the ways in which the brain functions to control bodily processes, the technique has already contributed considerably to our understanding of neurochemical processes in the central nervous system. The great value of the technique will not be fully appreciated until it is used in conjunction with other techniques. Alan Fisher (1969), in studies that combine electrical and chemical stimulation in the same animal and at the same site within a particular animal, has already indicated one direction that brain chemical stimulation can take. Obviously, combining techniques increases the difficulty of laboratory work in neural processes. However, this course must be followed to arrive at even first approximations to the answers to the many compelling questions about the role of the neural mechanisms that underlie bodily states and behavior.

REFERENCES

Andersson, B. Polydipsia caused by intrahypothalamic injections of hypertonic NaCl-solutions. *Experientia,* 1952, **8,** 157–158.

Annals of the New York Academy of Sciences, 1969, **157,** 894–984.

Avery, D. D., & Penn, P. E. Effects of intrahypothalamic injections of adrenergic and cholinergic substances on behavioral thermoregulation and associated skin temperature levels in rats. *Pharmacology, Biochemistry and Behavior,* 1973, **1,** 159–165.

Decima, E., & George, R. A simple cannula for intracerebral injections in chronic animals. *Electroencephalography and Clinical Neurophysiology,* 1964, **17,** 438–439.

Feldberg, W., & Sherwood, S. L. Injection of drugs into the lateral ventricles of the cat. *Journal of Physiology,* 1954, **123,** 148–167.

Fisher, A. E. Maternal and sexual behavior induced by intracranial chemical stimulation. *Science,* 1956, **124,** 228.

Fisher, A. E. The role of limbic structures in the central regulation of feeding and drinking behavior. *Annals of the New York Academy of Sciences,* 1969, **157,** 894–901.

Grossman, S. P. Direct adrenergic and cholinergic stimulation of hypothalamic mechanisms. *American Journal of Physiology,* 1962, **202,** 872–882. (a)

Grossman, S. P. Effects of adrenergic and cholinergic blocking agents on hypothalamic mechanisms. *American Journal of Physiology,* 1962, **202,** 1230–1236. (b)

Grossman, S. P. Neuropharmacology of central mechanisms contributing to control of food and water intake. In D. F. Code (Ed.), *Handbook of physiology.* Vol. 1. Section 6. *Alimentary canal.* Washington, D. C.: American Physiological Society, 1967.

Miller, N. E. Chemical coding of behavior in the brain. *Science,* 1965, **148,** 328–338.

Myers, R. D. Transfusion of cerebrospinal fluid and tissue bound chemical factors between the brains of conscious monkeys: A new neuro-biological assay. *Physiology and Behavior,* 1967, **2,** 373–377.

Myers, R. D. An improved push-pull cannula system for perfusing an isolated region of the brain. *Physiology and Behavior,* 1970, **5,** 243–246.

Myers, R. D. Methods for chemical stimulation of the brain. In R. D. Myers (Ed.), *Methods in psychobiology.* New York: Academic Press, 1971.

Winer, B. J. *Statistical principles in experimental design.* New York: McGraw-Hill, 1962.

SUGGESTED READINGS

Annals of the New York Academy of Sciences, 1969, **157,** 894–984.

Eccles, J. C. *The physiology of synapses.* New York: Academic Press, 1964.

Goodman, L. S., & Gilman, A. *The pharmacological basis of therapeutics.* (3rd ed.) New York: Macmillan, 1965.

Grossman, S. P. Neuropharmacology of central mechanisms contributing to control of food and water intake. In C. F. Code (Ed.), *Handbook of physiology.* Vol. 1. Section 6. *Alimentary canal.* Washington, D. C., American Physiological Society, 1967, 287–302.

McLennan, H. *Synaptic transmission.* Philadelphia: Saunders, 1963.

Miller, N. E. Chemical coding of behavior in the brain. *Science,* 1965, **148,** 328–338.

Myers, R. D. Methods for chemical stimulation of the brain. In R. D. Myers (Ed.), *Methods in psychobiology.* New York: Academic Press, 1971.

Myers, R. D., & Sharpe, L. G. Chemical activation of ingestive and other hypothalamic regulatory mechanisms. *Physiology and Behavior,* 1968, **3,** 987–995.

CHAPTER 5

Intracranial Electrical Stimulation

David D. Avery
COLORADO STATE UNIVERSITY

INTRODUCTION

Stimulation of the brain by directly applying a probe to the brain's surface and allowing electric current to pass from the probe to the brain dates back to the work of Fritz and Hitzig in the mid-1800s (Sheer, 1961). From that time on, physiologists have extensively used electrical stimulation as a tool for discovering the intricate relationship between brain and physiological process and for mapping the control of brain over motor functions. The real import of electrical stimulation for the behavioral sciences, however, was not evident until the near simultaneous discoveries of Olds and Milner and Miller in the early 1950s (Grossman, 1967). Olds and Milner observed that stimulation by electrodes chronically implanted in deep structures of the brain of the rat seemed to invoke pleasurable consequences and that, in fact, animals would learn to perform specified behavioral sequences on which the stimulation was contingent. Miller's experiments indicated that similar stimulation was aversive in some sites and could serve as an aversive control over specific behaviors. Beginning with these initial demonstrations, the reinforcing and motivational properties of electrical stimulation of the brain have continued to unravel the mysteries of the relationship between brain and behavior.

In more recent years a second, parallel research effort, centered largely in the work of Elliot Valenstein and his collaborators (1968, 1969, 1970), has evolved. It was observed that, besides having general reinforcement properties, certain parameters of stimulation in brain sites located mostly in the hypothalamus and related deep brain structures evoke a specific behavioral response having characteristics similar to motor components of normal, goal-oriented behaviors. For example, fully satiated animals, on receiving brain stimulation, eat, drink, or engage in other activities associated with basic homeostatic processes. Such behaviors are persistent, and, provided that stimulation conditions remain constant, the responses can be elicited repeatedly for hundreds of times. For a number of years, it was commonly thought that the consequences of electrical stimulation of the brain demonstrated the existence of fixed neural circuits that underlie basic drives. However, Valenstein et al. showed that, if the initial stimulus object to which the elicited behavior is directed (for example, a food pellet) is removed and if stimulation continues for a period of time, a new behavior emerges (for example, drinking). Thus the controversy over whether or not neural circuits that underlie certain specific motivated behaviors are fixed or plastic ensued and even now provides impetus to current research. (See Valenstein, 1973, for a thorough treatment of these topics.)

The inquiries into both reinforcing and motivational consequences of electrical stimulation of the brain represent the bulk of the experimental uses of the technique in psychology. In recent years, the work of Neal Miller (1969) on instrumental conditioning of components of the autonomic nervous system using brain electrical stimulation as a reinforcer exemplifies the importance of the technique as an investigatory tool with broad application. This chapter thus focuses on the implementation of the technique. As in the chapter on chemical stimulation of the brain, the intent is not to present a complete treatise on electrical brain stimulation and its many ramifications but rather to provide a methodology, including electrode construction, surgical procedures, stimulation procedures, and some theoretical considerations, that allows an unsophisticated investigator to conduct successful experiments.

Electrically stimulating the brain of any freely moving animal requires the following equipment and techniques: (1) electrodes for implanting in the brain; (2) a plug for connecting the electrode leads to the cable from the stimulator; (3) a sophisticated surgical technique that allows for accurate placement of the electrode; (4) a commutator, a device that allows the animal to move freely during electrical hookup; (5) a stimulator and methods for monitoring and controlling the parameters of stimulation; and (6) experimental procedures for observing and measuring the effects of stimulation. Adequate methodologies for each of these considerations are abundant. This chapter describes in detail only one or two that have been used successfully but, where appropriate, cites others.

CONSTRUCTION OF ELECTRODES

Many different types of electrodes, made from a variety of metals and insulated with a variety of materials, have been used to electrically stimulate, and to record electrophysiological potentials from, the brain. Two basic types of electrodes can be distinguished—monopolar and bipolar. A monopolar probe, as its name implies, consists of one pole situated in the brain and a reference lead placed at some other point on the animal. Because monopolar electrodes stimulate such a large area, they are rarely used in electrical-stimulation experiments.

All of the several types of bipolar electrodes have two leads with stimulating tips in close (usually less than 1 mm) proximity. The different spatial configurations of the electrode tips distinguish the different types of bipolar electrodes. The three most commonly used arrays are the following: (1) two side-by-side leads with exposed electrode tips in the same horizontal plane; (2) two side-by-side leads with the tips in different horizontal planes (one tip is generally 0.5 mm shorter than the other); and (3) concentric electrodes constructed by placing a small insulated wire inside an insulated hypodermic needle and extending the wire about 0.5 mm beyond the exposed area at the end of the needle.

Metals from which electrodes have been constructed include tungsten, stainless steel, platinum, and alloys such as nickel-chrome. The most commonly used insulating material is varnish,

FIGURE 5.1. Three Types of Stimulating Electrodes.

of which several types are available commercially. The choice of type of electrode and materials should be based on experimental requirements. However, the three types of electrodes described in the following pages accommodate the needs of investigations that use electrical stimulation of the brain. (For more detailed discussions of different types of electrodes and materials, see Sheer, 1961; Bures et al., 1967; Ervin & Kenney, 1971.)

Monopolar Electrode

Although monopolar electrodes are suitable only for very large areas of stimulation, they are constructed simply and form the basic components of the bipolar units. A highly suitable and nontoxic material for electrode construction is a nickel-chrome alloy wire (California Fine Wire) that, as a major advantage, is preinsulated with Formvar varnish. In addition, it has a small diameter (0.010 in.) and sufficiently low resistance (1000 ohms/ft). The first step in preparing the wire is to cut a length not to exceed approximately 2 feet and to stretch the wire by gripping each end with pliers and pulling gently (stretch to about 110 percent the original length). Stretching the wire, which both straightens it and increases its tension, minimizes the possibility of the electrode's bending during surgical implantation. Next, cut sections of the wire to correspond to the length of the electrode from the top of the skull to the intended site in the brain, to extend 2 to 3 mm above the top of the skull, and to extend to the connector (see the following section).

The nickel-chrome wire, because it is fine enough to serve as both electrode and lead wire, eliminates the need to solder additional wire to serve as a lead. Make a bend in the wire at the point where the electrode would extend 2 to 3 mm above the skull to permit the lead portion to extend to the connector. The only additional procedures are to ensure a square cut at the stimulating tip. Examine the electrode under a microscope and scrape off the insulation at the tip and at the lead ends for a good electrical contact with the connector. Buff the end gently on any motorized grinding wheel.

In most cases, just the cut end of the wire is sufficient stimulating-tip exposure; in other instances, scraping the insulation to provide a larger exposure for stimulating larger areas of the brain may be desirable. Mark the desired length of exposure on a piece of paper, make a comparison between this distance and the electrode tip under a microscope, and scrape off the desired amount of insulation with a surgical scalpel.

Bipolar (Side-by-Side) Electrode

The most easily constructed bipolar electrode is nothing more than two monopolar electrodes cemented together. If the tips are to be in the same horizontal plane, prepare two monopolar electrodes of the same desired length. Use either Insulx or Formvar to cement the two leads together. Insulx has the advantage of air drying, whereas Formvar must be baked to dry. With either substance, dip each monopolar lead into the insulating material up to the bend that separates the electrode proper from the lead portions. Slowly draw out each lead at approximately a 45° angle, which seems best for a proper coating of varnish. Then place the two wires together so that the tips are at the desired position (parallel or offset 0.5 to 1.0 mm). Hang the electrode by placing the lead end through a wire loop or through a drying rack in an oven (any of several laboratory ovens or an electric kitchen oven is suitable for baking on varnish). For Insulx, overnight air drying will suffice; for Formvar, bake at 300°F for 1.5 to 2 hours. If the electrode is to be placed in deep brain structures in a large animal (for example, a cat or monkey), a strut made from a piece of straightened electrode wire can be cemented to the two electrode wires to reduce the possibility of the electrode's bending during implantation. When dry, the electrode tips and lead ends must be scraped to remove insulating material; just the bare cross section of the tips is usually sufficient exposure for most experimental requirements. If additional wire exposure is necessary, scrape with a scalpel under a microscope;

make sure that sufficient insulation remains between the areas exposed on each tip (typically one should scrape approximately the outer half of the circumference of each tip).

Bipolar (Twisted-Wire) Electrode

A second, highly acceptable type of bipolar electrode is made by twisting two pieces of prestretched wire. Nickel-chrome wire is more than sufficient. The first step is to cut two pieces of prestretched wire to a length of 5 to 7 cm as determined by the required length of the electrode and lead portions (twisting reduces the overall length by less than 5 percent). To twist the wire, use either a variable speed drill or a small laboratory lathe. Place the two wires side by side, insert them into the drill or lathe chuck, and tighten. Grip the other end of the wires with pliers and apply tension by pulling firmly away from the chuck. Slowly engage the drill unit, allowing the two wires to be wound 7 to 10 revolutions/cm. To complete the construction of the electrode, follow the same tip- and lead-end-exposure procedures as those described for other types of electrodes. A major advantage that the twisted-wire unit has over the side-by-side unit is that the former electrode does not require cementing. The tips of the twisted-wire electrode can easily be separated if more intertip distance is desirable.

Chemode

The term "chemode," or "chemitrode," usually describes a combination package of an intracranial cannula and a bipolar electrode. Although many combinations are possible, a suitable unit can easily be constructed by cementing the side-by-side bipolar electrode to the outer guide shaft of either the small-animal or the large-animal cannula (see Chapter 4). After constructing the bipolar electrode, cut it to the same length as, or 1 mm longer than, the guide cannula. Determine the length on the basis of where the injection cannula tip will be located—either flush with or 1 mm beyond the tip of the guide cannula (see Chapter 4). Then dip the electrode into insulating varnish and place it alongside the cannula. Follow drying and tip-exposure procedures appropriate to the insulating material. Be sure that sufficient lead wire extends from the electrode to the connector to allow space for both the electrical and cannula connections.

Potential Problems

With any of the electrodes described, two potential problems, one structural and the other electrical, exist. The structural problem has been mentioned—electrodes may bend during surgery. Besides developing good surgical techniques, one may best avert the problem by prestretching the wire enough to ensure sufficient tension and, if the target area is deep within the brain, by cementing an additional strut wire to either the monopolar or the side-by-side bipolar unit. Add additional stability to the twisted-wire unit by increasing the number of revolutions per length. However, too much twisting can create the second (electrical) problem—a break in insulation.

The best solution to the electrical problem is to detect the insulation leakage and discard the electrode. Leaks can be detected easily with a standard ohmmeter. Connect the leads from the meter to the bare ends of the electrode leads. If there are no breaks between the two electrode poles, infinite resistance registers; less resistance indicates a short between the leads. To check for breaks at other points, moisten a small piece of cotton in saline. Attach one meter lead to one electrode lead and attach the other meter lead to the cotton. Run the cotton up and down the electrode; if a leak exists, resistance registers on the meter. Repeat the process with the other electrode lead. (For another good method for testing electrode insulation, see Ervin & Kenney, 1971.)

CONNECTORS

As is the case with electrodes, many different types of connectors for interfacing the implanted electrodes with the leads from the stimulator have been described in the literature. Connectors range from the sophisticated Sheatz plug (Sheatz, 1961) to one as simple as modified dress snaps (Miller et al., 1961). The major considerations in choosing a connector are the number of leads and the size of the animal. The three types of connectors described below take both considerations into account.

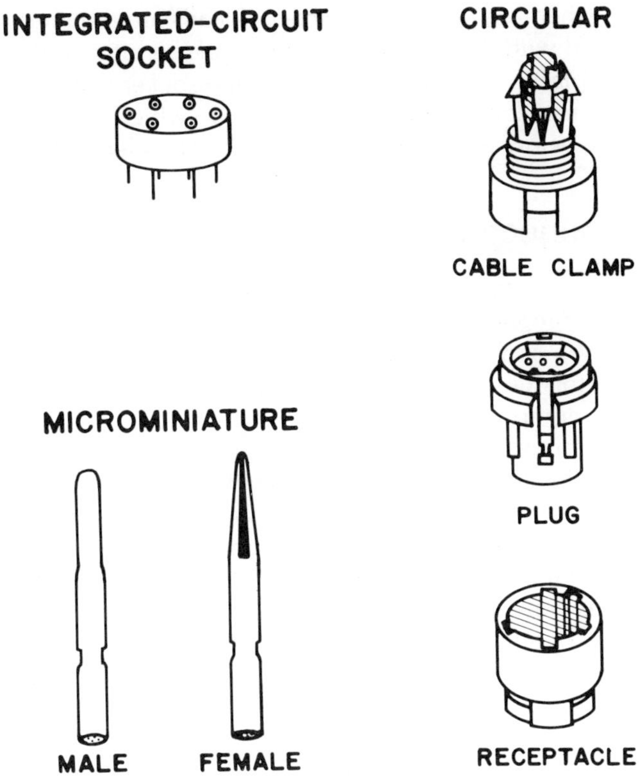

FIGURE 5.2. Three Types of Connectors Used for Interfacing the Electrode Leads with Leads from the Source of Electrical Stimulation.

Microminiature Connectors

Microminiature connectors manufactured by Amphenol are highly satisfactory for use with rats when no more than two bipolar electrodes (four leads) are implanted. The connectors are small pins with male (No. 220–P02) and female (No. 220–S02) components that, because they are manufactured from a gold alloy, have good conduction properties. No soldering is required to attach the pins to both electrode and stimulator leads. Attach the pins to the leads by using a hand crimp tool (Amphenol, No. 357–104) and by following the simple instructions that accompany the tool. Attach either the male or female to the electrode and attach its counterpart to the stimulator lead wire. However, one may find that hooking up the connection with the stimulator leads is easier when the male is crimped to the electrode. (Descriptions of how to firmly adhere the connector to the animal follows in the section on surgery.) Various types of wire are suitable for connecting to the stimulator. One can use single-strand wire (No. 8599–100) manufactured by Beldon, which is available at most electronics suppliers.

Integrated-Circuit Socket Connector

A second type of connector, which can be used for 6 to 12 leads, is an integrated-circuit socket (Series 8058) manufactured by Augat and available from Allied Electronics. The sockets range in size from approximately 10 mm diam (6-lead socket) to 15 mm diam (12-lead socket). The base in which the gold pins are pre-embedded is 4 mm thick. Thus these units can be used with either small rodents or larger animals when any of these numbers of leads are required. The pins on the bottom of one socket, when aligned with the receptacle portions of the pins on the top of a second socket, will plug in until the two plastic bases are flush. Thus the socket is used as a female receptacle to which the electrode leads are soldered and as a male plug to which the stimulator leads are soldered (see the section on surgery below for a description of soldering electrode leads).

Circular Connector

A third type of connector for up to 19 leads is the "Mighty Mite" circular connector series (No. 222) manufactured by Amphenol. The complete connector consists of plug (No. 222–11N19), receptacle (No. 222–12N19), and cable clamp (No. 222–518). The actual contacts are the micro-miniature gold pin connectors described above (male, No. 220–P02; female, No. 220–S02). After implanting the electrodes, crimp female pins onto the electrode leads and insert the pins into the receptacle with an Amphenol insertion tool (No. 356–200). Prepare the plug by first crimping male pins to the leads from the stimulator and placing the leads and pins through the cable clamp. Next, using the insertion tool, insert the pins into the pin holes on the back side of the plug. The plug, which is spring loaded, fits into the receptacle in only one position. The pin holes are numbered at the interfacing surfaces of both the receptacle and the plug; thus noting the electrode lead and stimulator lead origins eliminates confusion, even with as many as 19 leads. This connector is also quite satisfactory for electrical recording as described by Bennett (1973).

SURGERY

Initially, basic stereotaxic surgical procedures (see Chapter 3) and cannula implantation procedures (see Chapter 4) are also applicable to electrode implantation. The general preparations described here for the rat are essentially the same for both small and large animals. The following discussion also emphasizes specific procedures to be used with the electrodes and connectors described in this chapter.

General Procedures

The first step in the surgical procedure is the anesthetization of the animal. While waiting for the full effects of the anesthetic to occur, position the electrode in the stereotaxic holder and establish the stereotaxic coordinates. If more than one electrode is to be implanted and if other holders are available, establish coordinates for the additional electrodes (see Chapter 3). In each case make sure of the following: (1) that the electrode is parallel with the vertical plane of the holder; (2) that enough of the electrode will be exposed between the skull and the electrode holder after the electrode is in place in the brain to allow for cementing to the skull; and (3) that no insulation is scraped off during the mounting of the electrode in the holder. Prepare the animal and place it in the stereotaxic instrument (see Chapter 3). After incising the skin over the skull, retracting the superior temporal muscles, and scraping the surface of the skull, mark the position of entrance for each electrode to be implanted and determine the positions of the anchor screws. Allow sufficient space for the particular type of connector used. Now, trephine each implant site with a No. 4 HP dental burr and drill the screw sites (2 or 3 screws, depending on available space) with a No. 35 HP dental burr and thread them with a 0–80 bottoming tap. Next, in 1.5 to 2.0 clockwise turns, screw in the 0–80 stainless steel screws ($^3/_{16}$ in. long).

Before inserting an electrode, puncture the dura with the tip of a hypodermic needle to prevent the electrode from bending. After lowering the electrode to the desired depth, apply a small amount of dental acrylic to adhere the electrode to the skull. Allow approximately 5 minutes for the acrylic to harden; then carefully remove the holder. Repeat this process for each electrode. The next step is to attach the electrode leads to the connector.

Specific Procedures

MICROMINIATURE CONNECTOR

The male pin (Amphenol, No. 220–P02) can be crimped to the electrode lead either before surgery or after the electrode is in place and firmly adhered to the skull with dental acrylic. In either case, the lead wire should be long enough to allow the connectors to be positioned at the back quarter of the skull at a posterior angle of about 45° with the top plane of the skull. Such positioning keeps the lead wires away from the front visual plane of the animal and thus not only reduces the

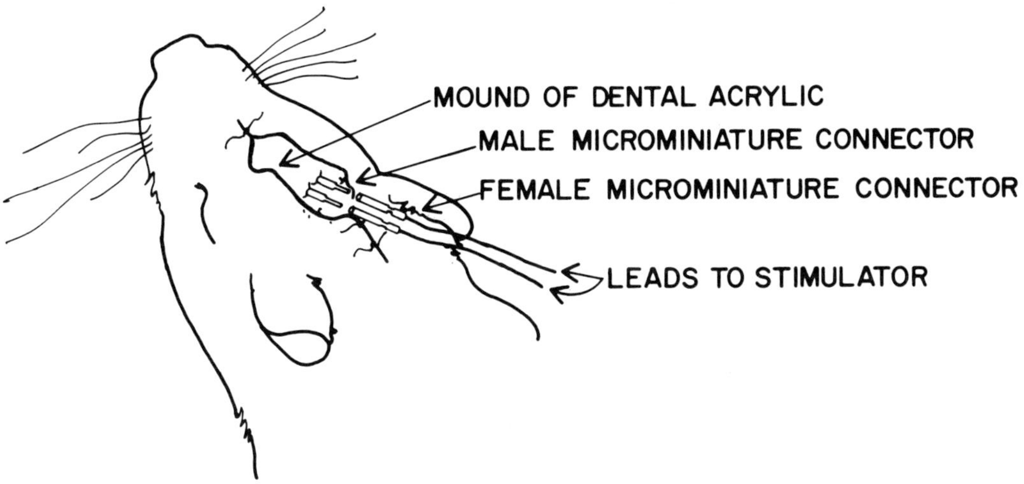

FIGURE 5.3. Male Microminiature Connectors Attached to Electrode Leads and Embedded in Dental Acrylic in the Rat. Female Microminiature Connectors Attached to Stimulator Leads and About to Be Connected to the Animal.

animal's distraction and irritation but also prevents entanglement with the front legs and paws. The pins should be cemented with dental acrylic to leave enough exposure to allow for a flush connection with the female pins (Amphenol, No. 220–S02) that were previously connected to the lead wires from the stimulator. Complete the preparation by building a smooth mound of dental acrylic over the electrode leads at the base of the connectors and the anchor screws. The last step is to suture the incision at the anterior and posterior ends with one or two sutures.

INTEGRATED-CIRCUIT SOCKET CONNECTOR

Two basic procedures can be used with this type of connector (Augat, Series 8058). The electrodes (usually when only two electrodes are implanted) can be soldered and the shafts can be positioned and aligned before surgery so that the socket is held in the electrode holder and the electrodes are lowered simultaneously into position. However, the more frequently used and generally more desirable procedure is to solder the electrode leads to the socket pins after the electrodes have been implanted and cemented to the skull. The first step is to position the socket so that it is centered over and parallel to the top plane of the skull. Next, bend and cut the electrode leads so that they are in close proximity to the socket pins and in a preconceived order (generally numbered clockwise or counterclockwise); make sure that the electrode leads correspond to appropriate stimulator leads. After the leads are positioned, if necessary, scrape off more insulation in order to make solder connections with the socket pins. Before actually soldering, tine the exposed lead ends

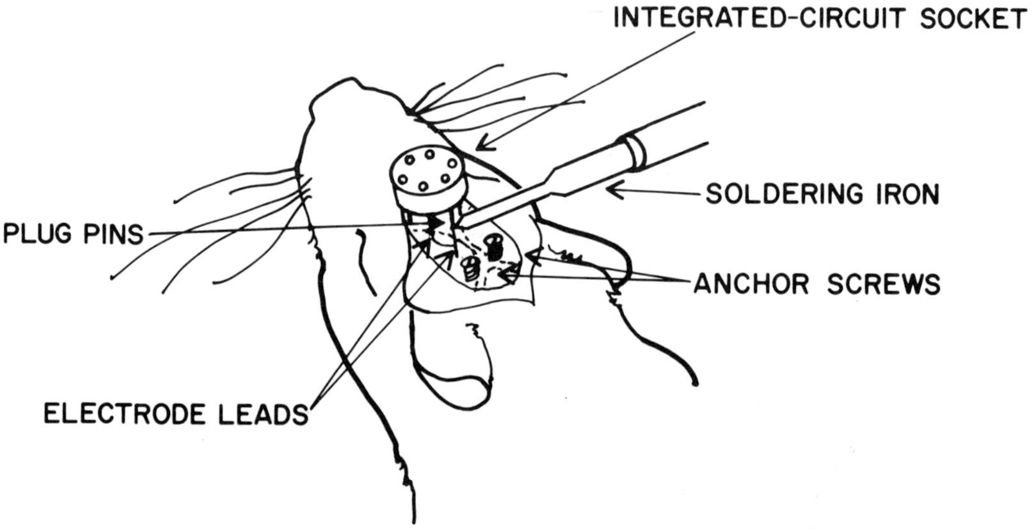

FIGURE 5.4. Soldering of Electrode Leads to Pins of the Integrated-Circuit Socket Connector.

and pin tips with silver solder by applying small amounts of melted solder to both portions. Solder each lead to its appropriate pin; take care not to burn the skull or surrounding tissue. In addition, provide a heat sink by gripping the electrode lead with small pliers or forceps to prevent the electrode tip from heating and causing cell damage. Finish the preparation by filling the spaces among the pins, leads, and anchor screws with dental acrylic, smoothing the edges around the connector with acrylic, and suturing the anterior and posterior extremities of the incision.

CIRCULAR CONNECTOR

The circular connector (Amphenol "Mighty Mite" receptacle, No. 222–12N19) is generally used with larger animals (cats and monkeys). The electrodes are prepared before surgery as previously described by crimping female microminiature connectors (Amphenol, No. 220–P02) to the electrode leads. When all electrodes are in place and cemented to the skull, insert the microminiature connectors into the numbered holes in the base of the receptacle. To make insertion easy, dip each connector in petroleum lubricant, place the pin in its appropriate hole in the receptacle, and gently push the pin in place with an insertion tool (Amphenol, No. 356–200). After inserting the pins, be sure to clean the lubricant from each pin to prevent interference with electrical contact. Add additional acrylic, smooth the edges, and cover all leads and screws. Make sure that the receptacle is firmly embedded in dental acrylic but not so far embedded as to retard connection with the plug (Amphenol, No. 222–11N19) that houses the leads from the stimulator. Complete the preparation by suturing the extremities of the incision.

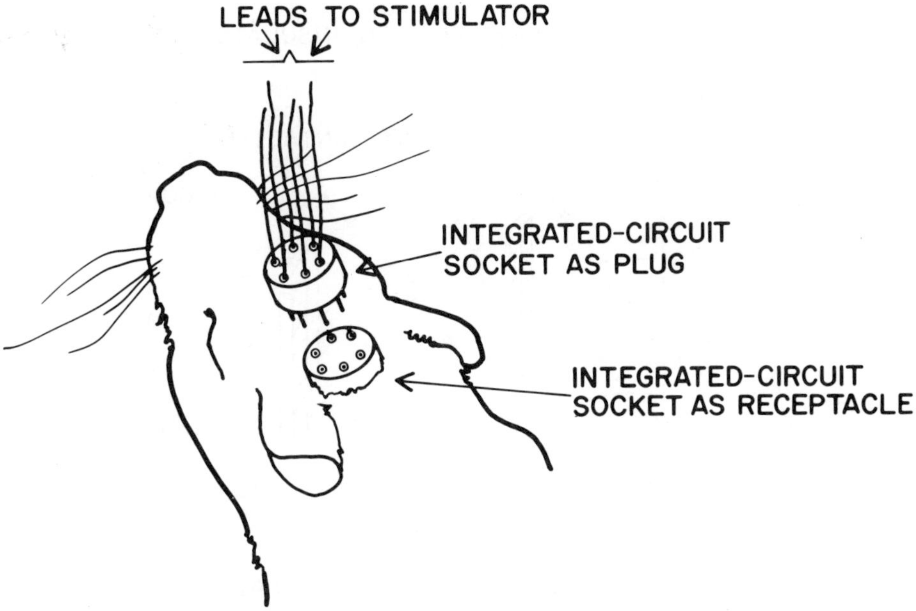

FIGURE 5.5 Integrated-Circuit Socket Connector with Electrode Leads Soldered and Embedded in Dental Acrylic. A Second Integrated-Circuit Socket Connector that Serves as a Plug from the Stimulator.

THE COMMUTATOR

A problem in any experiment that requires an electrical hookup between an animal and a stimulation or recording device is to allow the animal sufficient freedom of movement without disrupting the connection and without entanglement with lead wires. An inexpensive commutator that satisfactorily solves this problem (Moss & Avery, 1971) can easily be constructed. As an added advantage over commercially available units, this device can be programmed so that electrode pairs can be prescheduled. Use the following materials for construction: (1) an unsealed ball bearing with inside and outside diameters of 18 mm and 40 mm, respectively; (2) two conductor washers for each pair of conductors to be used (washers the size of a U.S. penny work fine); (3) Potter and Brumfield unenclosed two-contact relays (the coil should be operated by the same voltage as the program control equipment—for example, 28 volts DC); (4) 2 square feet of Plexiglas ($^1/_4$ in.); and (5) cement.

To construct the commutator, first assemble the rotating portion. Remove all packing grease from the bearing, clean thoroughly with a solvent, and oil with a lightweight machine oil. Next, cut circles of 18 mm diam from the Plexiglas; these, when stacked, must fit tightly in the center of the bearing. Drill the circles through the center to accommodate the lead wires from the animal (the size of the drilled holes depends on the number and total diameter of the leads). Cut enough circles to separate the conductor washers, to completely fill the inner space of the bearing, and to extend approximately 2 mm beyond one side of the bearing. Now solder the conductor washers, which must be 20 mm diam so that they extend beyond the edges of the Plexiglas circles when sandwiched between them, to the lead wires that will be connected to the animal. Make sure of the following: (1) that there is a washer for each lead; (2) that each lead is insulated from all other leads; and (3) that a Plexiglas ring is placed between all washers before soldering. After testing for conductance, glue the washers and rings with epoxy cement and stack them as shown in Figure 5.6. Take care to keep the column straight and at right angles with the bearing. Figure 5.6 shows the assembly of only one contact pair; however, additional contacts can be added by stacking additional rings and

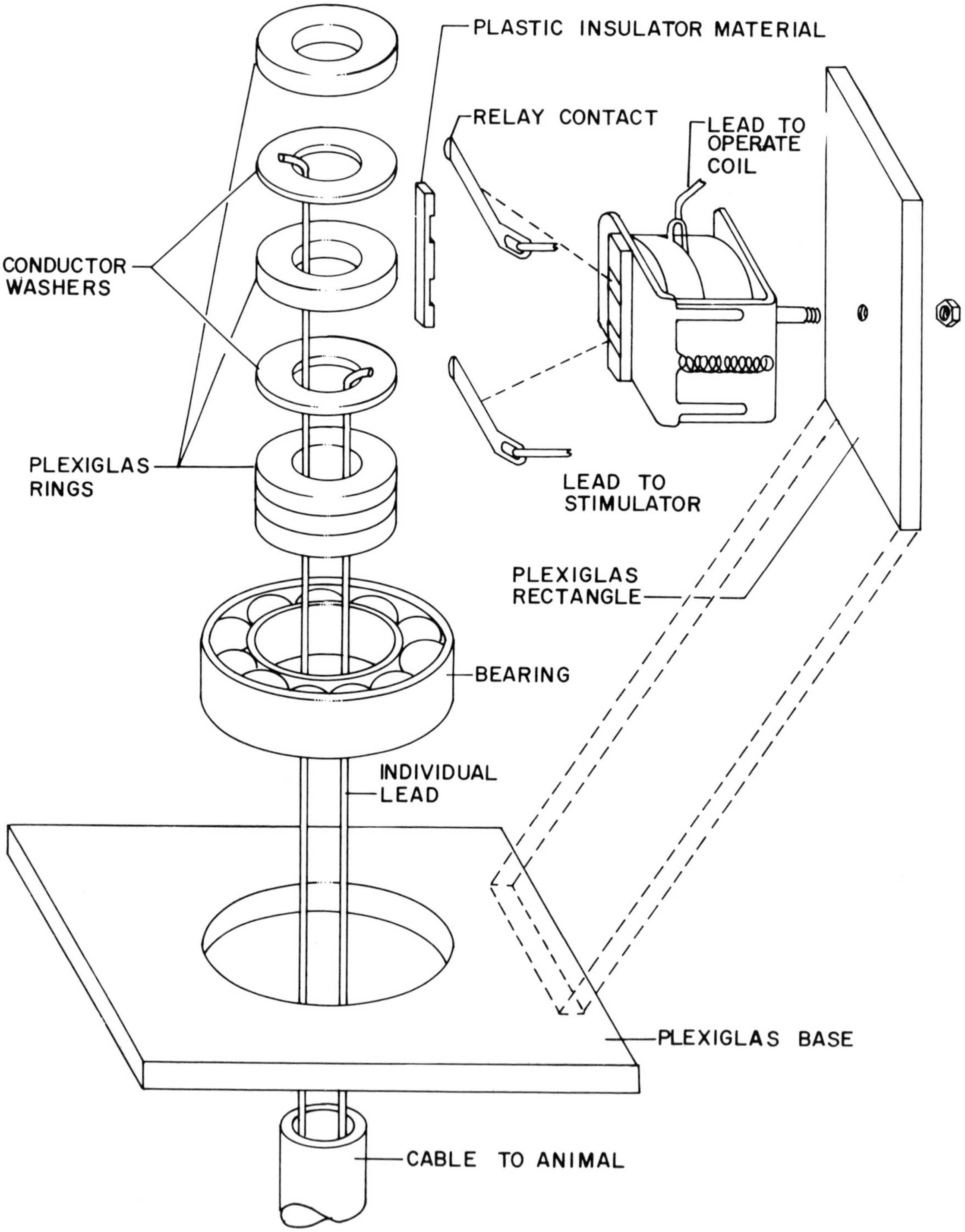

FIGURE 5.6. Exploded View of Commutator Showing One Contact Pair. From D. E. Moss and D. D. Avery, An inexpensive, programmable electromechanical commutator, *Physiology and Behavior,* 1971, **7,** 649–651. Reproduced by permission.

conductor washers. Fill the hollow center of the column with dental acrylic to further insulate and add stability. Recheck conductance. Now the rotating portion of the commutator is complete and can be mounted on a Plexiglas base. The base should be 15 cm by 15 cm to accommodate the relays and the rotating portion. Cut a hole in the center to accommodate the outer diameter (40 mm) of the bearing. Attach the bearing with metal clips and screws so that it can be removed for cleaning.

The second stage of construction is to prepare and mount the relays so that their contacts ride on the rotating conductor washers. First, remove all parts of the relay so that only the coil, the common (movable) contact, and the bracket that holds the common contact on the coil remain. Thus the normally open and normally closed contacts and all unnecessary bracket materials are removed; the conductor washers serve as normally closed contacts. Remove the plastic insulator material in

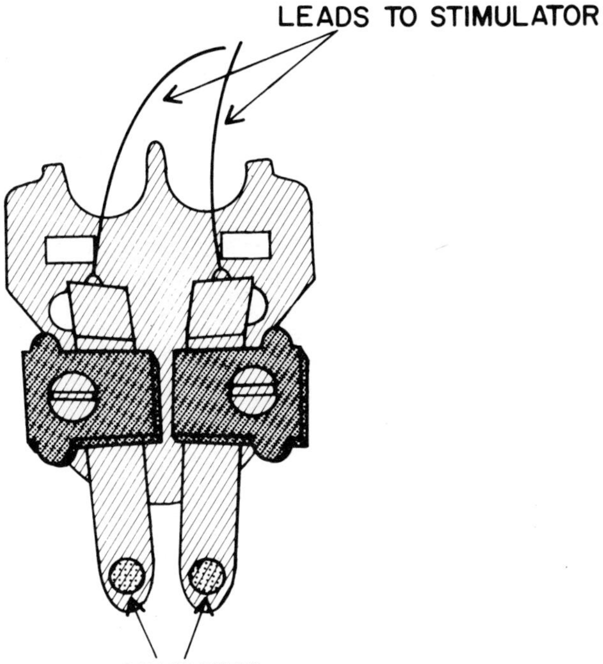

FIGURE 5.7. Relay Contacts After Removal of Unnecessary Portions.

which the common contacts are mounted from the metal support by drilling out the small rivets. Cut the plastic strip in half to allow separate adjustment of each contact so that it can be centered on the conductor washer. With the bolt that extends from the center of the coil, attach each relay to a small piece of Plexiglas. Cement the piece of Plexiglas to the Plexiglas base through which the rotating portion passes so that the contacts close on the conductor washers when the coil is unoperated but open when the coil is operated.

The following procedures complete the construction of the commutator: (1) attach leads from the stimulator to the relay contacts; (2) attach the leads from the conductor washers to the male plug (that is, integrated-circuit socket, microminiature connector, and so on); (3) connect the relay coils to the programming equipment; and (4) construct a Plexiglas cover to keep dust from the contact surfaces. During stimulation all relay coils except the one controlling the contacts through which the electrode receives current are operated; thus only two contacts ride on their appropriate washers. The resultant reduction of surface friction allows the rotating portion to move freely to allow, in turn, uninhibited animal movement. Moreover, the electrode that is to be stimulated can be preprogrammed and switched automatically.

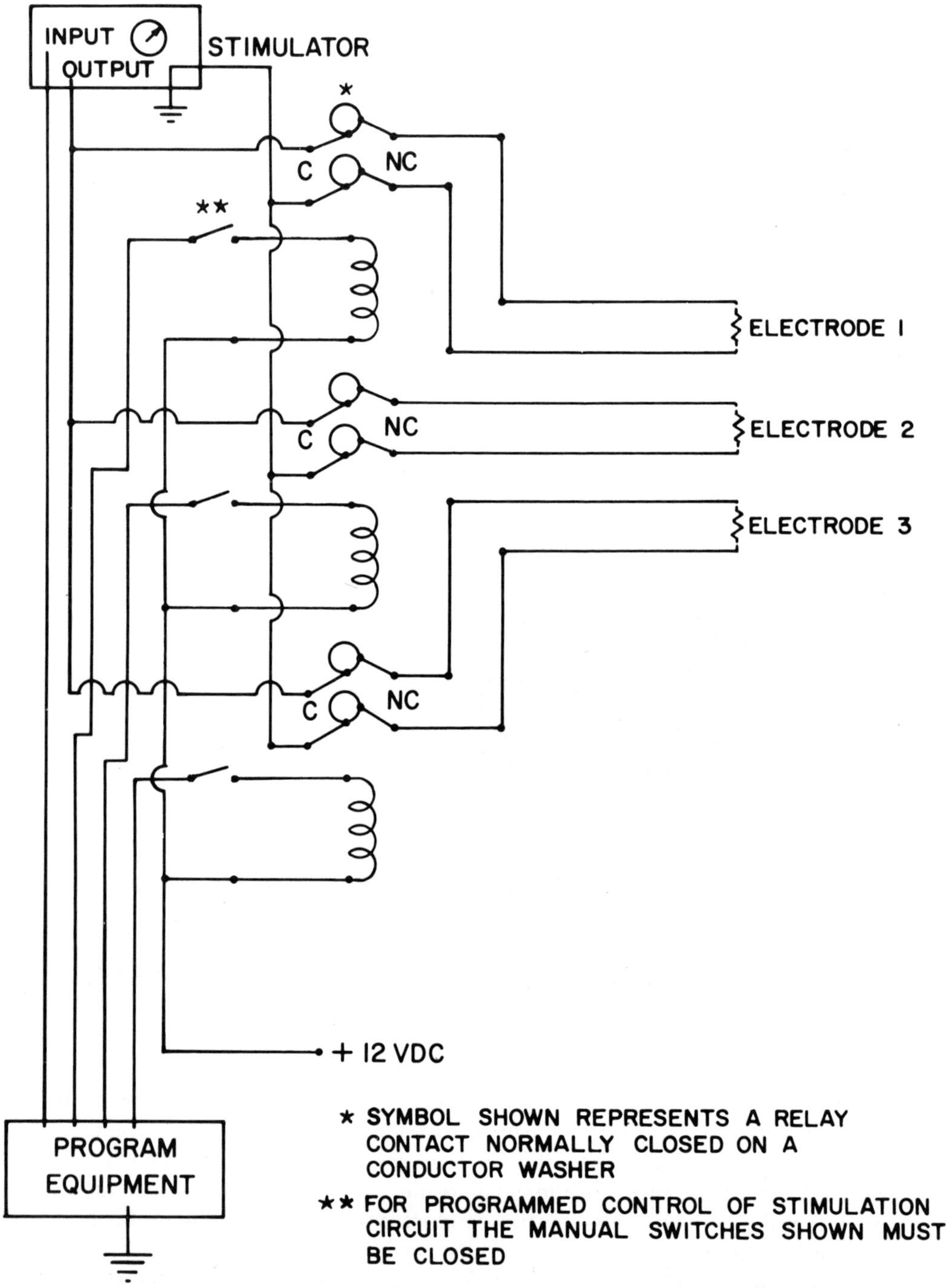

FIGURE 5.8. Wiring Schematic for the Commutator, Including Both Stimulating and Programming Circuitry. From D. E. Moss and D. D. Avery, An inexpensive, programmable electromechanical commutator, *Physiology and Behavior,* 1971, **7,** 649–651. Reproduced by permission.

The commutator can also be used satisfactorily for EEG recording. However, certain modifications are necessary to protect against noise if the unit is to be used for electrophysiological recording (see Moss & Avery, 1971).

STIMULATOR CONSIDERATIONS

Stimulator and Parameters of Stimulation

Of primary concern in experiments that involve electrical stimulation are the parameters of the stimulus. Many different forms of stimulation, including different waveforms, frequencies, voltages, pulse durations, stimulus train durations, and envelopes of train (rate of growth and decay) have been used and discussed in the literature. Except for the limitations imposed by the possibility of injurious stimulation, no clear-cut guidelines exist for determining which stimulation parameters are best for any particular experimental requirement. The choice is dictated by the limitations of the stimulator available to the investigator. These units, many of which are commercially available, range in price from several hundred to several thousand dollars. This section, in line with the utilitarian approach of the chapter, discusses these various parameters and certain avoidable difficulties in stimulation with little reference to the theoretical issues found throughout the literature. (For detailed discussions of these issues, see Ervin & Kenney, 1971; Fischer et al., 1961; Lilly, 1961; Miller, Jensen, & Myers, 1961; and Mickle, 1961.)

A stimulator that is typical of those found in behavioral research laboratories is the Grass S48 solid-state, square-wave stimulator. This stimulator (or any stimulator for that matter) has two major components: one that provides the electric current, the power source; and one that provides systematic variations in the time domain. The power supply of the S48 has a voltage range from 15 mV to 150 V continuously variable in 10 decades, a peak output current of 150 mA, an output impedance of 250 ohms on all voltage ranges, and a maximum power output of 22 W. The power supply is regulated so that current and voltage outputs are constant. Constant outputs are probably the most important characteristics of any stimulator; if forced to choose between constant voltage and constant current, however, one should choose the latter, as it is more critical. The output of the S48 is well above the requirements of experiments that utilize electrical brain stimulation; never do such requirements exceed 20 mA.

The timing parameters of the S48 allow for the following waveforms: DC, single pulses, repetitive pulses, trains of pulses, and trains of twin pulses. The pulse rate is continuously variable from 1 per 100 sec to 1000 pulses per sec, with a variable duration of 10 msec to 10 sec. The train rate is continuously variable from 1 per 100 sec to 1000 trains per sec, with a variable duration of 1 msec to 10 sec.

Stimulus Isolation and Monitoring

In addition to the stimulator, a stimulus isolation unit must be used to avoid current injury and stimulus artifact. A cathode ray oscilloscope (CRO) also should be included for monitoring stimulation parameters, particularly voltage and current. Stimulus isolation protects against unidirectional direct current and ground return circuits from the animal that can produce stimulation artifacts and, in extreme cases, electrocute the animal (Ervin & Kenney, 1971). One recommended stimulus isolation unit is the Grass SIU5, which is driven directly by the stimulator output and requires no other power source. It is a transistorized radio-frequency circuit that is connected in series with the stimulator output and the stimulating electrodes. The voltage output from the stimulator modulates the carrier frequency of the oscillator in the isolation unit, the secondary coil of which is isolated from ground, and thus isolates the animal from ground return loops. Additional circuitry, by rectifying and demodulating the signal, reproduces the original waveform from the stimulator. (For a detailed discussion of stimulus isolation and appropriate circuitry, see Mickle, 1961.)

Any CRO that can be synchronized with the stimulator is acceptable. For example, the Tektronix 5103N oscilloscope system has two channels; thus both voltage and current (with the use of a current probe) can be monitored simultaneously. However, as monitoring interrupts stimulus isolation, measures should be taken only periodically, not continuously. The importance of measuring both parameters throughout an experiment cannot be overemphasized. An exchange of ions, which takes place between chronically implanted electrodes and the brain medium, leads to a polarization of either or both the electrode and the surrounding tissue. Such changes alter waveform and intensity of stimulation so that frequent CRO monitoring (at least before and after each daily experimental session) is critical for proper experimental control. (For a more detailed discussion of these problems, see Ervin & Kenney, 1971.)

Overheating is another potential source of injury. High-frequency currents can cause the tissue surrounding the electrode to overheat. However, overheating is not a problem with most commercially available stimulators because their maximum-frequency ranges are relatively low.

STIMULATION PROCEDURES

There is no set rule for choosing the parameters of stimulation for any particular experiment. The best course is to search the literature concerning a particular species and brain area and obtain the parameters used by other investigators. Even after a thorough search, however, one may still be left with selecting among many possible parameters. In behavioral research, the usual procedure is to start with a low-current output (less than 50 μA) and systematically increase it until a behavioral response to the stimulation is observed. Then, if required by the experimental situation, take this level as a threshold value and increase the intensity until a particular behavior is reliably repeated with several subsequent stimulations.

Elicited Behaviors

An experiment performed in my laboratory may serve to illustrate both typical parameters of stimulation used in hypothalamic structures in the rat and a procedure for determining whether a reliably elicited behavior has occurred. In this experiment my colleagues and I were interested in what stimulus-bound behaviors—for example, eating, drinking, wood gnawing—would be elicited from two groups of adult animals that were treated differentially at an early developmental stage. (For a discussion of stimulus-bound behaviors, see Valenstein et al, 1968, 1969, 1970.) We used twisted-wire electrodes, either the integrated-circuit socket connector or the microminiature connectors, the commutator, the Grass S48 stimulator, and the Grass SIU5A stimulus isolation unit.

The test procedure consisted of placing a food- and water-sated albino rat into a small test chamber, which was constructed from Plexiglas (12 in. wide × 18 in. long × 18 in. high) and which contained food pellets, water, and a wooden block. After a 30-min adaptation period, each animal was screened by stimulating the lateral hypothalamus with 30-sec stimulus trains of biphasic rectangular pulses at 100 pulses per sec with a pulse duration of 0.2 msec followed by a 30-sec interstimulation period. Screening was started at one V and was increased by one V with each 30-sec stimulation period until 15 V was delivered; intensity was then increased up to 30 V in 2-V increments. Screening was terminated when the following occurred: (1) a reliable stimulus-bound behavior was observed; (2) a withdrawal or painful response was observed; or (3) an intensity of 30 V was reached. If a stimulus-bound behavior was observed, the interstimulus interval was increased to 60 sec and the animal was given 20 test stimulations at the voltage and corresponding current (both were monitored on an oscilloscope) at which the behavior first appeared. The 20 trials provided an index of the reliability of the behavioral observations. In this particular experiment we were able to identify specific behaviors elicited from over 75 percent of our electrodes with thresholds ranging from 200 to 700 μA.

The purpose of describing this procedure is not to indicate a general procedure that should always be used but rather to give the reader some guidelines, a place to start, in conducting his first experiment that uses electrical stimulation. Only through experience, which involves a great deal of trial and error, will any investigator arrive at a procedure that meets his particular experimental requirements.

Self-Stimulation

As was pointed out in the introduction to this chapter, animals will learn an instrumental response to receive electrical stimulation in certain brain sites. This phenomenon not only provides a fruitful research area but also can be used as a dramatic laboratory exercise or demonstration for students interested in the biological basis of behavior. The following describes a technique that is used with the rat and that frequently serves as a teaching tool.

The stimulation and monitoring equipment described in the previous section on elicited behaviors is used. The S48 stimulator has a modulation control receptacle that allows it to be externally programmed by connecting one side of a normally open switch to the tip of a phone plug that plugs into the modulation input receptacle and by connecting the other side of the normally open switch to the midterminal of the phone plug. When the normally open switch is closed, a continuous train of pulses is produced until the switch is opened.

Any operant chamber is a sufficient environment for demonstrating self-stimulation. The switch on the manipulandum serves as the normally open contacts through which stimulation is controlled. To shape an animal to press the bar for brain stimulation, successive approximation procedures similar to those used with more conventional reinforcers are appropriate. However, it must be determined first that a particular electrode is potentially reinforcing. Slowly increase the level of current until a behavioral change is observed and the animal engages in active searching behavior (nose in the air, sniffing, exploring the chamber) when the stimulation is terminated. When this level is reached, the animal can be trained to press a bar (or engage in other operant responses) by selectively reinforcing appropriate response changes. The parameters of stimulation, which have been observed to adequately maintain self-stimulation over long periods of time (up to three-hour sessions), are the same as those described in the section on elicited behavior.

CONCLUSION

A final consideration—interpretation of results—deserves brief comment. A frequently cited reason for stimulating the brain is to determine what part the stimulated region plays in governing some aspect of bodily function or behavior. However, no matter how obvious an interpretation of a particular result may seem, one must be very careful in drawing conclusions from observations following electrical brain stimulation. First of all, just because stimulation at a particular brain site causes an invariant observable change, it does not necessarily indicate that what was observed is the usual function of that part of the brain. Electrical stimulation is a highly artificial intrusion into the normal workings of the brain; electric flow is rarely accompanied by electron flow in living tissue but is a function of ion exchange across cell membranes (Ervin & Kenney, 1971). Another source of difficulty in interpretation is the problem of localization of function. We now know that distinctively definable brain loci that have a very specific function are rare at best and probably do not exist. Rather, we are faced with the difficult problem of determining whether the electrode, which when stimulated led to a measurable change, was located in the normal input (sensory), output (motor), or integrative part, or in some secondary aspect of the neural system underlying the observed change. Yet all too frequently we find elaborate theoretical discourses, based on all too few observations, that proclaim that a certain brain area is most assuredly the "head ganglion" for this function or that behavior. However, these and other limitations should not be taken as an indictment against electrical stimulation as an experimental tool; many very worthwhile results counter such a conclusion. Rather, one must be very careful in specifying the limitations of one's own interpretations that follow experiments involving electrical brain stimulation or any of the other techniques described in this book.

REFERENCES

Bennett, T. L. The effects of centrally blocking hippocampal theta activity on learning and retention. *Behavioral Biology,* 1973, **9,** 541–552.

Bures, J., Petran, M., & Zachar, J. *Electrophysiological methods in biological research.* New York: Academic Press, 1967.

Ervin, F. R., & Kenney, G. J. Electrical stimulation of the brain. In R. D. Myers (Ed.), *Methods in psychobiology.* New York: Academic Press, 1971.

Fischer, G., Sayre, G. P., & Bickford, R. G. Histological changes in the cat's brain after introduction of metallic and plastic coated wire. In D. E. Sheer (Ed.), *Electrical stimulation of the brain.* Austin: University of Texas Press, 1961.

Grossman, S. P. *A textbook of physiological psychology.* New York: Wiley, 1967.

Lilly, J. C. The balanced pulse-pair waveform. In D. E. Sheer (Ed.), *Electrical stimulation of the brain.* Austin: University of Texas Press, 1961.

Mickle, W. A. The problem of stimulation parameters. In D. E. Sheer (Ed.), *Electrical stimulation of the brain.* Austin: University of Texas Press, 1961.

Miller, N. E. Learning of visceral and glandular responses. *Science,* 1969, **163,** 434–445.

Miller, N. E., Coons, E. E., Lewis, M., & Jensen, D. D. Electrode holders in chronic preparations: B. A simple technique for use with the rat. In D. E. Sheer (Ed.), *Electrical stimulation of the brain.* Austin: University of Texas Press, 1961.

Miller, N. E., Jensen, D. D., & Myers, A. K. A comparison of the Lilly waveform and the sixty-cycle sine wave. In D. E. Sheer (Ed.), *Electrical stimulation of the brain.* Austin: University of Texas Press, 1961.

Moss, D. E., & Avery, D. D. An inexpensive, programmable, electromechanical commutator. *Physiology and Behavior,* 1971, **7,** 649–651.

Sheatz, G. C. Electrode holders in chronic preparations: A. Multilead techniques for large and small animals. In D. E. Sheer (Ed.), *Electrical stimulation of the brain.* Austin: University of Texas Press, 1961.

Sheer, D. E. *Electrical stimulation of the brain.* Austin: University of Texas Press, 1961.

Sheer, D. E. Brain and behavior: The background of interdisciplinary research. In D. E. Sheer (Ed.), *Electrical stimulation of the brain.* Austin: University of Texas Press, 1961.

Valenstein, E. S. *Brain stimulation and motivation.* Glenview, Ill.: Scott, Foresman, 1973.

Valenstein, E. S., Cox, V. C., & Kakolewski, J. W. The motivation underlying eating elicited by lateral hypothalamic stimulation. *Physiology and Behavior,* 1968, **3,** 969–971.

Valenstein, E. S., Cox, V. C., & Kakolewski, J. W. The hypothalamus and motivated behavior. In J. Tapp (Ed.), *Reinforcement and behavior.* New York: Academic Press, 1969.

Valenstein, E. S., Cox, V. C., & Kakolewski, J. W. Reexamination of the role of the hypothalamus in motivation. *Psychological Review,* 1970, **77,** 16–31.

SUGGESTED READINGS

Bures, J., Petran, M., & Zachar, J. *Electrophysiological methods in biological research.* New York: Academic Press, 1967.

Ervin, F. R., & Kenney, G. J. Electrical stimulation of the brain. In R. D. Myers (Ed.), *Methods in psychobiology.* New York: Academic Press, 1971.

Sem Jacobsen, C. W. *Depth-electrographic stimulation of the human brain and behavior.* Springfield, Ill.: Charles C Thomas, 1968.

Sheer, D. E. *Electrical stimulation of the brain.* Austin: University of Texas Press, 1961.

Suckling, E. E. *Bioelectricity.* New York: McGraw-Hill, 1961.

Valenstein, E. S. Stability and plasticity of motivational systems. In F. O. Schmitt (Ed.), *The neurosciences: Second study program*. New York: Rockefeller University Press, 1970.
Valenstein, E. S. *Brain stimulation and motivation*. Glenview, Ill.: Scott, Foresman, 1973.
Valenstein, E. S., Cox, F. C., & Kakolewski, J. W. The hypothalamus and motivated behavior. In J. Tapp (Ed.), *Reinforcement and behavior*. New York: Academic Press, 1969.

CHAPTER 6

- INTRODUCTION
- BASIC ELECTRICAL CONCEPTS
  - VOLTAGE
  - CURRENT
  - RESISTANCE
  - CAPACITANCE
  - INDUCTANCE
  - AC AND DC VOLTAGES AND CURRENTS
- IMPORTANT BASIC CIRCUITS IN ELECTROPHYSIOLOGY
  - CIRCUITS AFFECTING AC VOLTAGES OR CURRENTS
  - CAPACITIVE CIRCUITS
- GENERAL CONSIDERATIONS IN ELECTROPHYSIOLOGICAL RECORDING
- THE NATURE OF VOLTAGE SOURCES IN THE BRAIN
- GENERAL PROPERTIES OF ELECTRODES
- GENERAL PROPERTIES OF CONNECTIONS AND CABLES
- OTHER SOURCES OF NOISE IN RECORDING SITUATIONS
- GENERAL PROPERTIES OF AMPLIFIERS
- CONTROLS IN AN IDEALIZED AMPLIFYING SYSTEM
- CALIBRATION
- DATA DISPLAY AND STORAGE SYSTEMS
- ELECTROPHYSIOLOGICAL RECORDING SYSTEMS USED WITH BEHAVING ANIMALS
  - MULTIPLE UNIT RECORDINGS
    - ELECTRODES
    - CONNECTORS
    - CABLES
    - PREAMPLIFIERS
    - SHIELDING OF THE PREPARATION
    - FURTHER AMPLIFICATION AND TREATMENT
    - CALIBRATION
  - SINGLE UNIT RECORDING IN THE BEHAVING ANIMAL
  - EVOKED POTENTIAL RECORDING WITH IMPLANTED ELECTRODES
  - RECORDING OF EEG ACTIVITY
  - SLOW POTENTIAL AND DC RECORDINGS FROM BRAIN
    - ELECTRODES
    - CONNECTORS AND CABLES
    - AMPLIFIERS
    - DISPLAY
  - BRAIN IMPEDANCE RECORDING
- RECORDING EPs, SPCs, AND EEG FROM HUMANS
  - ELECTRODE LOCATIONS
  - PREPARATION OF SKIN SURFACE FOR ELECTRODE PLACEMENT
  - FIXING ELECTRODES TO THE SCALP
  - RECORDING OTHER ELECTRICAL EVENTS FROM HUMANS

Electrophysiological Recording in the Behavioral Laboratory

Donald A. Irwin
SOUTHERN ILLINOIS UNIVERSITY

INTRODUCTION

Electrophysiological recording can be approached in two ways: (1) recordings of physiological responses can be made in acutely prepared nonbehaving organisms and (2) recordings can be made in chronically prepared organisms where overt behavior can be observed and manipulated. This chapter deals with the latter.

The techniques of recording electrophysiological responses from behaving animals are among the most technically difficult techniques in physiological psychology. The goal of this chapter is to familiarize the novice with basic concepts and procedures necessary for successfully gathering electrophysiological data. Because the topic is difficult, this chapter cannot cover all the information necessary for successful data gathering. Additional reading will be needed, as will some hands-on experience with recording equipment.

Additional readings are listed at the end of this chapter; the beginning investigator will wish to refer to these as well as to readings in the experimental literature covering a specific technique or techniques. User's manuals provided by manufacturers of recording equipment are an invaluable source of knowledge, and it is essential to become familiar with these manuals for specific equipment.

Three basic issues concerning the interpretation of electrical recordings must be considered first. Strictly speaking, a physiological response is not recorded; rather, what is recorded is an electrical property or a change in an electrical property of a living organism. The recorded change in electrical property is a by-product of an indirect reflection of a physiological process, rather than the process itself. Second, a given type of electrical response may be the reflection of any number of different physiological processes; that is, there may be multiple sources for the electrical change. When an electrical change is recorded, the recorder can never be sure which of a number of processes or sources is responsible for the event without additional evidence.

Some electrical recording methods are less affected by the problem of multiple sources than others. The nerve cell action potential that occurs when a nerve cell undergoes a rapidly conducted change in its membrane structure is an example of one electrical response that distinctly and unambiguously reflects a physiological event. Its interpretation is clear. In contrast, such electrical responses as the more slowly changing voltages that can be recorded from the brain cannot be clearly interpreted. They may be produced by activity of glial cells, neurons, or blood vessels; these, as well as other sources, are capable of producing similar electrical events.

The third consideration regarding interpretation concerns the relationship of different electrical responses to behavior. Although the nerve cell action potential is well understood in terms of its physiological basis, the relationship of data on single cell action potential to behavior is obscure. On the other hand, slow potential recording from the human brain and scalp has been shown to be clearly related to various complex behaviors, although its physiological meaning is obscure. The appropriateness of a given type of electrical recording in behavioral experiments must be considered in terms of whether the data are likely to provide the type of answers needed.

Once the potential usefulness of a given type of electrophysiological data for a research program is determined, methodology must be examined. Methodology determines directly what the investigator sees. It is impossible to record a slowly changing voltage from the brain of an animal with certain types of amplifiers; however, even if an appropriate amplifier is used and used correctly, the investigator's records may be severely distorted by other components of the recording system such as electrodes or cables or even by the method of analyzing the data. Each component of a recording system has electrical properties of its own that may severely alter the expected electrical response or even generate spurious electrical responses that can be mistaken for an organism response. Knowledge of these properties is essential if the investigator is to obtain useful data.

In spite of difficulties in interpretation, many different electrophysiological responses have been extensively and gainfully studied. For central nervous system recording, they include:

1. Single cell (unit) recording
2. Multiple cell (unit) recordings (MUs)
3. Electroencephalography (EEG)
4. Evoked potentials (EPs)
5. Slow potential and DC recordings (SPCs)
6. Impedance recording.

For electrical recording of peripheral responses, they include:

1. Electrocardiography (EKG)
2. Eye movements
3. Electroretinogram (ERG)
4. Galvanic skin response (GSR)
5. Skin potential responses (SPs).

Each type of response depends to a large extent on a unique method of recording it. In other words, the method partially determines the type of response obtained. Nevertheless, the methodology or system for all recordings has features in common, such as:

1. Electrodes or transducers
2. Cables or other devices to transmit signals from the electrodes or transducers
3. Amplifiers to receive transmitted signals
4. Signal conditioners
5. Display devices
6. Data analysis systems.

Each of these basic components of a recording system is considered in this chapter, as is each electrophysiological response listed above. However, it is first necessary to discuss basic concepts in electricity, since even a rudimentary discussion of recording techniques requires some knowledge of electrical properties. The following is a brief presentation of basic electrical concepts. This discussion is intended only as an introduction to concepts essential to understanding basic recording methodologies.

BASIC ELECTRICAL CONCEPTS

The term "electricity" derives from the Greek name for "amber." The Greeks noted that when amber was rubbed by a piece of animal fur, the amber exhibited a force capable of attracting small objects. The property that the amber has to exert force is *electric charge*. Today, it is known that a body is charged because it has either more or fewer electrons than protons in its atomic structure. Since electrons are considered to have one unit of negative charge and protons one unit of positive charge, a charged body can have either a net negative or a net positive charge. The magnitude of a charge depends on how many more or fewer electrons there are than protons.

Two basic laws describe the behavior of charged bodies. The first is that like charges (either positive or negative) repel each other and unlike charges attract each other. The second law, called Coulomb's Law, states that the force between two charges is directly proportional to the product of the magnitudes of the two charges (Q_1Q_2) and inversely proportional to the square of the distance (d^2) between the charges times the dielectric constant (K) of the medium separating the two charges. Mathematically, Coulomb's Law is stated as follows:

$$F = \frac{Q_1Q_2}{d^2K}.$$

The unit of measurement of charge (Q) is the electrostatic unit. It is a charge that, when placed 1 cm from an equivalent charge, exerts on it 1 dyne of force. A dyne is a basic unit of force magnitude. The dielectric constant of the medium through which the force acts refers to a physical property of the medium; for example, a vacuum has a dielectric constant of 1.0 and glass has a dielectric constant of about 10. The unit of charge in the equation—the electrostatic unit—is too small to use in equations that will be examined later. A convenient unit of charge is the coulomb, which is defined as 3 billion electrostatic units.

A second kind of force, other than force caused by charge, that needs to be considered here is the force caused by magnetism. Magnetism is defined as the property of an object that enables it to attract pieces of iron. Magnets have poles designated as either north or south. As with Coulomb's Law for charged bodies, there is an analogous law for magnetized bodies. It is stated mathematically as:

$$F = \frac{M_1M_2}{d^2\mu}.$$

In this equation, M_1 is the strength of one magnetic pole, M_2 is the strength of another magnetic pole, μ is the magnetic permeability of the medium through which the force acts, and d^2 is the square of the distance between the magnetic poles. The concept of magnetic pole is analogous to the concept of charged bodies. As with charged bodies, unlike poles (north or south) attract each other and like poles repel each other.

A charged body has a charge force field around it that decreases as the square of the distance from the object, as given by Coulomb's Law. There is also a magnetic force field around a magnetic pole. A relationship exists between charges and magnetic fields in that, when a charge moves, it generates a magnetic field and, when a magnetic field moves, it induces nearby charges to move. Thus, when a magnetic field moves across a wire, electrons in the wire are induced to move and, when an electron moves down a wire, it generates a magnetic field radiating out at right angles to the wire.

Voltage

Whenever a force acts on a body to change its motion, work is performed. Work is the product of force times the distance through which the force acts. The unit of measurement of work is the joule.

When work is performed, energy is consumed. Energy is the ability to perform work. Work need not necessarily be performed for energy to exist in any system. For example, a battery contains energy, but work is not performed unless the battery is connected to an electronic circuit. The energy of the battery is said to be potential or potential energy. The term "potential" is conventionally used for potential energy in electricity and is represented by the symbol E. The unit of measurement of potential is the volt, which is work per unit charge. Mathematically, E can be stated as:

$$E = \text{joules/coulomb.}$$

Current

When a battery is connected in an electronic circuit, the potential energy of the battery performs work by moving electrons or charges through the circuit. The movement of charges is called *current* and is represented by the symbol I. The unit of current is the *ampere,* which is a measure of the number of coulombs moved per second. Mathematically, I can be stated as:

$$I = \text{coulombs/second.}$$

Resistance

Certain materials oppose the movement of charges or allow charges to move freely through them. These materials are said to possess the properties of electrical resistance and conductance. Electrical resistance is the property of a material that opposes current. Resistance, measured in ohms, is represented by the symbol R.

Conductance is the property of a material that allows current to flow. Conductance, measured in MHO, is represented by the symbol G. The relationship between resistance and conductance is obvious: they are reciprocals of each other.

One of the basic laws in electronics is called "Ohm's Law." This states the relationships among potential, current, and resistance. Mathematically, it can be stated as:

$$I = E/R.$$

Capacitance

Capacitance is another property that a material or device can display. Capacitance is the property of a material or device that opposes a change in voltage. Devices that display this property are called capacitors. Capacitance, measured in farads, is represented by the symbol C. Mathematically, C can be stated as:

$$C = I/\text{rate of change of } E.$$

One farad is equal to 1 ampere generated in a device by a change of 1 volt in 1 sec across the device. A convenient way of looking at this equation is to rearrange terms as follows:

$$I = C \times \text{rate of change of } E.$$

The current through a capacitor is directly proportional to the number of farads and to the rate of rise or fall of voltage. Two important relationships follow from this: (1) a capacitor strongly opposes current when slowly changing voltages occur across it but weakly opposes current when voltages change rapidly; and (2) the degree of opposition to current of a capacitor is inversely proportional to the size of the capacitor in farads.

A capacitor has another property that gives it its name—that is, the capacity to store a charge. The capacity in farads equals the number of coulombs stored per volt applied to capacitation. A capacitor has a capacity of 1 farad if it will store a charge of 1 coulomb for each 1 V applied. Mathematically, it can be stated as:

$$C = Q/E.$$

A device that has the property of capacitance usually has a highly specific physical structure. The structure includes two surfaces that are capable of storing a charge and that are separated by a short distance by some dielectric material. (A dielectric material is one that has a high opposition to current flow.) Although electrons (charges) cannot flow directly through the dielectric material, they flow onto the surface of one side of the capacitive device and build up a charge on that side. The force field of the charge acts through the dielectric material and by its repelling force on like charges moves electrons out of the material on the opposite surface of the capacitive device, thus giving the appearance that current is actually flowing through the capacitor. The behavior of a capacitor thus illustrates the operation of Coulomb's Law of charged bodies.

The term "reactance" rather than resistance is used to describe the opposition to currents by capacitors when voltages and currents are changing over time. It is represented by the symbol X_C:

$$X_C = I/C \times \text{rate of change of E.}$$

Like resistance, X_C or capacitive reactance is a measure of the degree of opposition to current and is expressed in ohms. It should be remembered that a resistor is a device that has a fixed opposition to current flow (resistance, expressed in ohms) regardless of whether the current is steady or changing over time. A capacitor has a variable opposition to current flow (capacitive reactance, also expressed in ohms); slowly changing currents are strongly opposed and rapidly changing currents are weakly opposed.

Inductance

Inductance is the property of a material or device that opposes a change in current. Devices that have the property of inductance are called "inductors." Inductance is represented by the symbol L and is measured in henries. L can be stated mathematically:

$$L = E/\text{rate of change of I.}$$

The opposition of an inductor to current, as with capacitors, is called reactance or inductive reactance and is represented by X_L. The degree of reactance is directly proportional to the inductance and the rate of change of current across the inductor.

An inductor acts in an opposite manner to a capacitor. Currents that change rapidly are strongly opposed by an inductor but weakly opposed by a capacitor. Currents that are steady or slowly changing are weakly opposed by an inductor but strongly opposed by a capacitor.

AC and DC Voltages and Currents

Currents that change over time are alternating currents or AC. A steady current is a direct current or DC. In electronics, the rate of change of a voltage or current is usually expressed with reference to a sine wave. The measurement of rate of change is in terms of the number of repetitions of the sine wave per unit of time or frequency represented by f. If the frequency is expressed in repetitions per second, it is expressed in terms of the symbol Hz. A voltage that is changing in a sine wave fashion and completing 100 sine wave cycles in 1 sec has a frequency (f) of 100 Hz. A voltage with a frequency of 100 Hz is considered to have a higher rate of change than a voltage at a frequency of 50 Hz.

The actual unit of rate of change is called omega (ω) or angular velocity. The value of omega is expressed mathematically as $\omega = 2\pi f$.

The word "frequency" has a highly specific meaning in electrical recording. It refers to the rate of repetition of sine waves. It does not refer to the repetition rate of wave forms that are not sine waves. Thus, if a nerve cell discharges an action potential ten times a second, it is not discharging at a frequency of 10 Hz because the nerve cell discharge voltage is not a sine wave of voltage.

IMPORTANT BASIC CIRCUITS IN ELECTROPHYSIOLOGY

Understanding the operation of electronic devices can be greatly simplified by the use of "circuit diagrams." This is a convenient method of symbolically representing the properties of electronic circuits and also for representing the electronic properties of neurons, the brain, and other tissues. A list of symbolic elements is presented in Figure 6.1.

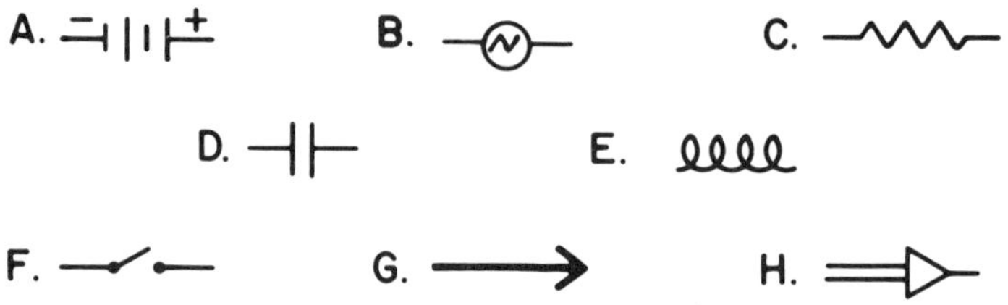

FIGURE 6.1. Common Symbols for Electronic Components: A. DC Voltage Source, B. AC Voltage Source, C. Resistor, D. Capacitor, E. Inductor, F. Open Switch, G. Direction of Current, H. Amplifier.

The simplest case for considering the behavior of an electronic circuit is when a direct current is applied through a resistor. Figure 6.2 illustrates such a circuit as well as the use of Ohm's Law. This is a circuit containing a DC voltage source, a switch, and a resistor. When the switch is open, as shown, no current flows through the circuit. When the switch is closed, current flows through the circuit. The magnitude of the current in amperes (I) is equal to the voltage divided by the resistance. Thus, with a 10-volt battery and a resistance of 100 ohms, the current is 1/10 of an ampere. A slightly more complex circuit and an important one is illustrated in Figure 6.3. It is called a "voltage divider."

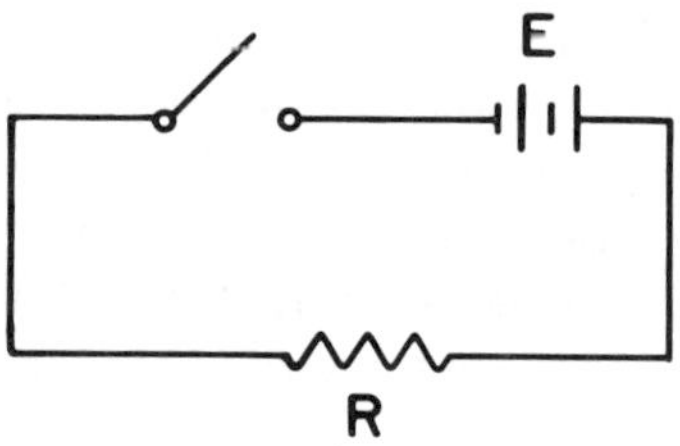

FIGURE 6.2. A Simple Resistance Circuit.

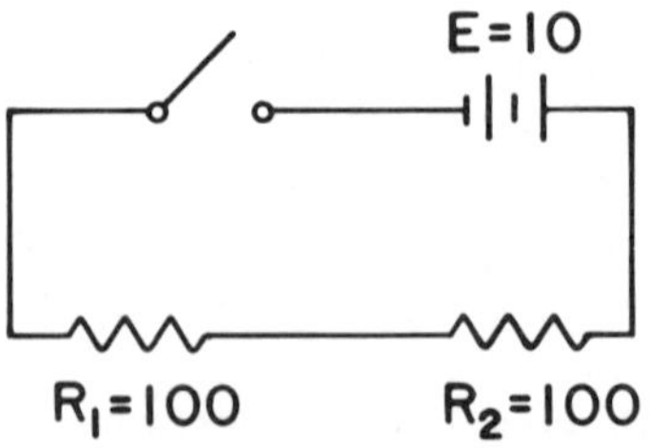

FIGURE 6.3. A Series Resistance Circuit.

As shown in Figure 6.3, there are two resistors in series with the battery. When the voltage is applied to the circuit by closing the switch, the current traveling through the circuit, given by Ohm's Law, is the voltage divided by the total resistance of the circuit. Resistors in series, as in this circuit, add together so that the total resistance is equal to the sum of $R_1 + R_2$. Hence, if $R_1 = 100$ ohms and $R_2 = 100$ ohms, $R_{total} = R_1 + R_2 = 200$ ohms. Since $R_1 = 100$ ohms and $I = 1/20$ amperes, the voltage measured across R_1 is $E = I \times R$ or $E = 100$ ohms $\times$ 1/20 amperes $= 5$ volts. One-half of the applied voltage appears across R_1, and one-half of the applied voltage appears across R_2. This circuit is called a "voltage divider circuit" because resistors in series have voltages across them in direct proportion to the fraction of the total resistance in a circuit they represent; in other words, they divide the voltage. In a circuit with two series resistors, the voltage across R_1 is equal to:

$$E_{R_1} = E_{source} \times R_{R_1+R_2}.$$

If the circuit has more than two series resistors, the voltage across any one of the resistors is the source voltage times the ratio of that resistance to the total resistance.

Voltage divider circuits are highly important in electrical recordings from the brain. The brain can be considered as a voltage source in series with a resistance. When one records, a circuit for current is provided by the electrodes and cables that run through an amplifier. The amplifier has some resistance to currents flowing through it. This situation can be depicted schematically as in Figure 6.4. The voltage that the amplifier "sees" or the voltage that appears across the amplifier is

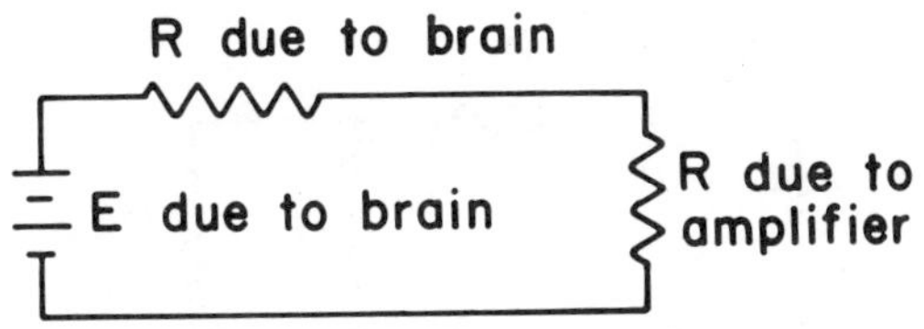

FIGURE 6.4. A Series Resistance Circuit in Which the Battery Is Considered the Voltage Source in the Brain and the Two Resistances Originate in the Brain and in the Amplifier.

a function of the proportion of resistance caused by the amplifier divided by the total resistance. Mathematically, this can be stated as:

$$E_{seen\ by\ amplifier} = E_{brain} \times \frac{R_{caused\ by\ amplifier}}{R_{amplifier} + R_{brain}}.$$

From this equation, one can see that if the amplifier resistance is very low with respect to the resistance of the brain, little of the voltage generated by the brain will be seen by the amplifier. Unless the resistance of the amplifier is very large in proportion to the resistance of the brain, one will see or amplify only a portion of the voltage that the brain produces. For this reason, amplifiers used in recording have high input resistance.

The resistors in a circuit can also be combined in parallel as shown in Figure 6.5. When the switch is closed, current will flow through both resistors R_1 and R_2 as indicated by the arrows.

There are two important aspects of parallel circuits: (1) the voltage across parallel elements in any circuit is the same; thus, if (as in Figure 6.5) the source voltage E is 10 volts, the voltage

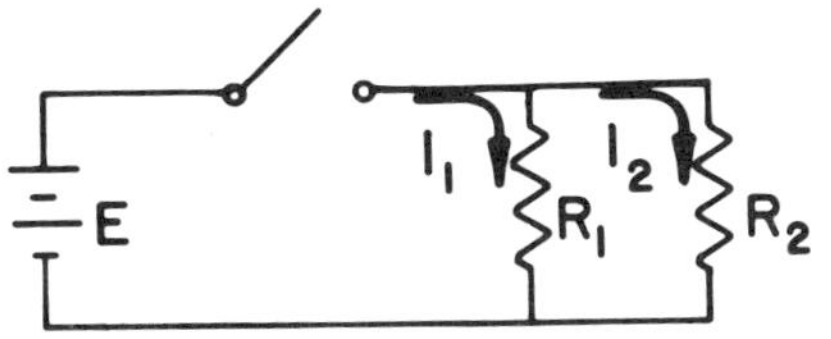

FIGURE 6.5. A Circuit of Parallel Resistors.

across R_1 and the voltage across R_2 is also 10 volts regardless of the size of R_1 and R_2, and (2) the parallel circuit acts as a current divider since the current through any parallel component is always less than the total current flowing from the voltage source.

In parallel networks the resistances do not add together as in a series network. The combined resistance or total resistance afforded by the parallel combination is always less than the smallest resistance in the combination. Mathematically, this can be stated as:

$$1/R_{total} = 1/R_1 + 1/R_2.$$

Rearranging, this equation gives:

$$R_{\text{total}} = \frac{1}{1/R_1 + 1/R_2}$$

and

$$R_{\text{total}} = \frac{R_1 \times R_2}{R_1 + R_2}.$$

Resistors can also be combined into series and parallel combinations as in Figure 6.6. R_1 is in series with the battery and also in series with the parallel combination of R_2 and R_3. The circuit is of theoretical importance in electrophysiological recording because of the voltage dividing properties of the series combinations of R_1 with the parallel combinations of R_2 and R_3. For example, let R_1 in Figure 6.6 be considered the resistance of the brain, R_2 a variable resistance, and R_3 the re-

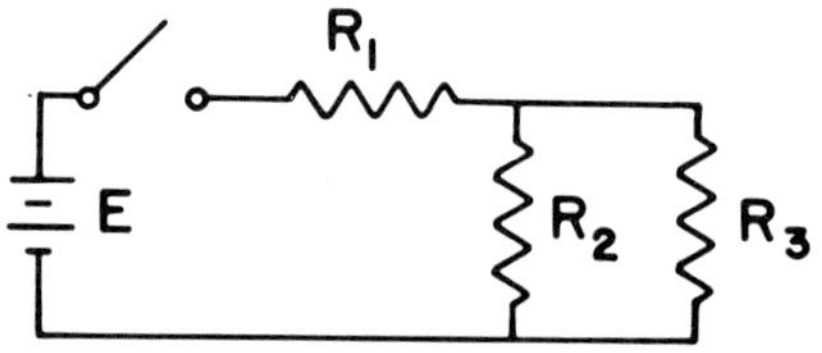

FIGURE 6.6. A Combination of Series and Parallel Resistors.

sistance of the amplifier. If R_2 changes during a recording session, the voltage across R_3 will change as a result of the voltage dividing properties of R_1 in series with the parallel combination. The result of such changes in the variable resistor would be that the magnitude of a recorded voltage from the brain would appear different at different times during an experiment even though the voltage actually generated by the brain was the same during the entire experimental session.

Normally, a variable resistor in parallel with the amplifier is not present in a recording situation; thus the circuit described above is mostly of academic interest. However, there may often be reactive elements that may cause capacitance to occur in parallel with the input to the amplifier. The capacitance is caused by electrodes, cables, and connectors. The opposition to current flow of an element with capacitance varies as a function of the rate of change of voltage generated by the brain; it may lead to unequal division of voltages by the resistance of the brain and the resistance of the amplifier. In other words, the recording circuit behaves as if there were a parallel variable resistor present; the magnitude of the resistance is different for voltages changing at different rates. Voltages changing at high rates would be seen as small by the amplifier and voltages changing at lower rates would be seen as large even though the magnitudes of these voltages were the same at the source in the brain.

Circuits Affecting AC Voltages or Currents

Most electrophysiological responses are voltages that change over time. An evoked potential, for example, is a voltage that rises to a peak and then falls. Since reactive properties such as capacitance and inductance are exhibited by various components of a recording system as well as by the brain, their behavior in various circuits is an important consideration.

As mentioned earlier, the rate of change of voltage or current is expressed in electronics by the frequency of a sine wave. A high-frequency sine wave represents a fast rate of change and a low-frequency sine wave represents a slow rate of change. The rate of change is represented by the term "omega" (ω) or angular velocity.

Voltages generated by the brain are rarely of the sine wave form; however, any complex wave form (although not a sine wave by definition) can be considered to be made up of combinations of sine waves of different frequencies and amplitudes. The analysis of a complex wave form into its constituent sine waves is called Fourier analysis.

An important concept in recording methodology is that of frequency response of various components of a recording system. The frequency response of a component can be expressed graphically to show that the ratio of output amplitude to input amplitude is a function of frequency. Suppose that a frequency-response graph were plotted for a pair of recording electrodes. Such a graph is presented in Figure 6.7 and shows that even though there is a low-frequency input, the voltage at

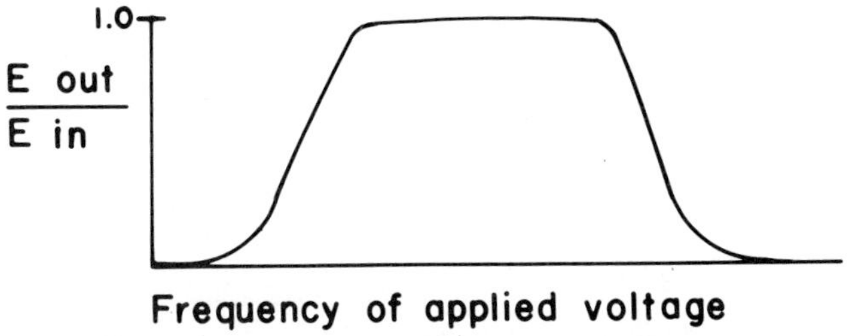

FIGURE 6.7. A Hypothetical Frequency-Response Curve for a Set of Recording Electrodes Showing that Some Frequencies of Voltages that Appear Under the Electrode Are Not Always Passed Through the Electrode.

the electrode does not equal the input voltage. The same can be said for the higher frequencies of input. In other words, the electrode is capable of passing only a restricted range of frequencies (frequency band) of voltage wave forms on to the cables and amplifiers. The electrode is said to filter out low and high frequencies or to act as a bandpass filter. The point on the graph at the low-frequency end where the output is one-half of the input voltage is called the low-frequency, one-half amplitude cutoff. At the higher frequencies it is called the high-frequency, one-half amplitude cutoff. One amplitude corresponds to −3 db; therefore, these cutoff points are sometimes called the −3 db points.

The form of a frequency-response curve can vary widely. Two common curves result from devices called, respectively, a high-pass filter and a low-pass filter. The frequency response of each of these devices is shown in Figure 6.8. Electrodes exhibiting the properties of a high-pass filter

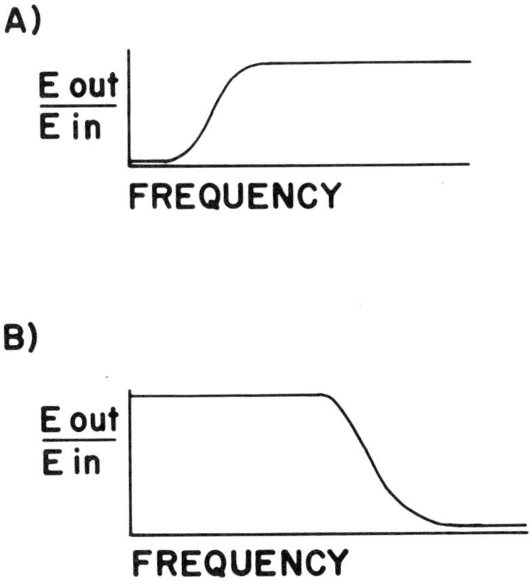

FIGURE 6.8. A. A Frequency-Response Curve of a High-Pass Filter, B. A Frequency-Response Curve of a Low-Pass Filter.

would not be usable for recording DC responses and slowly changing responses from the brain because there is no output from these electrodes at low frequencies of applied signal. The electrodes of choice for DC recording would be those that exhibit the properties of a low-pass filter. Each component of a recording system will show properties of one or the other type of filtering system.

Capacitive Circuits

One of the simplest combinations of capacitance and resistance is the RC series circuit shown in Figure 6.9. At the time that the switch is closed, current will flow through the circuit until

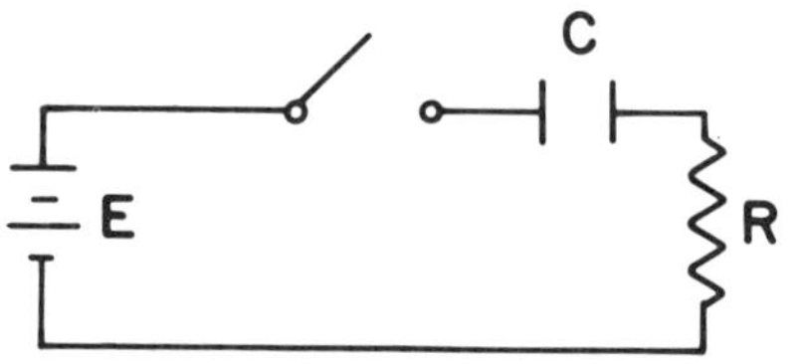

FIGURE 6.9. A Series Combination of a Capacitor and a Resistor.

the capacitor reaches its capacity of charge for the voltage applied. At that point, no further current will flow in the circuit. The voltage appearing across the capacitor is small at the time of switch closure and rises over time. As mentioned earlier, the opposition of a capacitor to current is an inverse function of the rate of change of voltage across the capacitor. Since the voltage across the capacitor changes more rapidly just after the switch is closed, the opposition to current, or reactance (X_C), is minimal initially and infinitely large after a long time period. These relationships are depicted graphically in Figure 6.10. The RC series circuit is a voltage divider circuit; thus, the proportion of voltage appearing across the resistor is directly proportional to the portion of opposition to current flow provided by the resistance. Since X_C varies from zero to infinity in an exponential manner from the time the switch is closed, the proportion of opposition to current flow by the resistor varies from one to zero exponentially. The voltage appearing across the resistor, then, is the inverse of the voltage across the capacitor.

The total opposition to current flow in a reactive circuit is called the impedance of the circuit and is represented by the symbol Z, which is measured in ohms. The total opposition, or impedance, is not the simple summation of R in ohms and X_C in ohms; rather the impedance is a complex addition. For an RC series circuit, the total impedance in ohms is:

$$Z = \sqrt{R^2 + X_C^2}.$$

One of the parameters of RC and other reactive circuits is the time constant of the circuit. The time constant (τ) of an RC circuit is the amount of time in seconds that the rise of voltage or fall of current takes to reach two-thirds of its eventual level. The τ in seconds of an RC circuit is equal to the product of resistance in ohms and capacitance in farads. Mathematically, τ can be stated as:

$$\tau = R \times C.$$

The behavior of the series RC circuit can be examined in a different way. Rather than applying a DC voltage source to the circuit, a sine wave voltage or AC source can be applied. For a given frequency of sine wave, the reactance X_C of the capacitor can be calculated by $X_C = 1/2fc$ and expressed in ohms. For a given frequency, the series RC circuit acts as a voltage divider where:

$$E_{\text{across the resistor}} = E_{\text{source}} \times \frac{R}{\sqrt{R^2 + X_C^2}}.$$

If the voltage across R is measured while the frequency of the voltage is being varied, the resulting graph of voltage across the resistor as a function of frequency shows the characteristics of a high-pass filter.

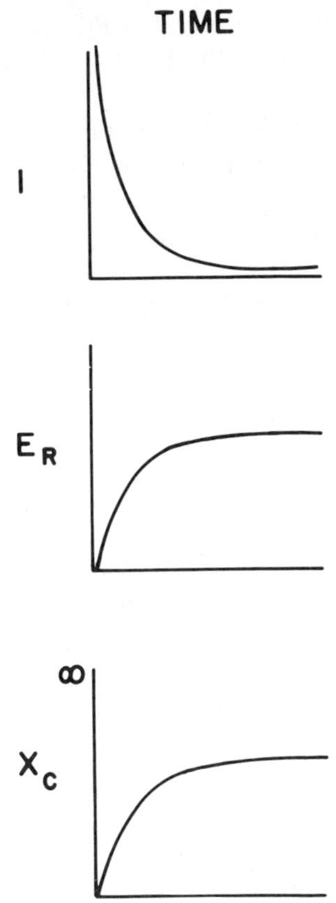

FIGURE 6.10. Graphic Representation of the Change Over Time of I, E, and X_C When a Voltage Is Applied to a RC Series Circuit.

The same principles that apply to a parallel resistance combination apply to the parallel combination of a resistance and a capacitance. The voltage across any member of the parallel RC circuit is equal to the source voltage, and the total impedance of the parallel combination is less than the reactance or resistance in ohms of the smallest member of the combination. Since the reactance of the capacitor (X_C) is an inverse function of frequency, the total impedance to current flow in the circuit is also an inverse function of frequency. Mathematically, the total impedance of a parallel RC combination is:

$$Z = \frac{1}{\sqrt{(1/X_C)^2 + (1/R)^2}}.$$

In electrophysiological recording, there is always some degree of capacitance in parallel with the input to the amplifier. Also, there is always some resistance in series with the voltage source in the brain and the parallel combination of the amplifier resistance and capacitance. The circuit shown in Figure 6.11 is a voltage divider circuit similar to those seen before. The voltage generated by the brain is divided by the brain's resistance and the parallel combination of C and the resistance

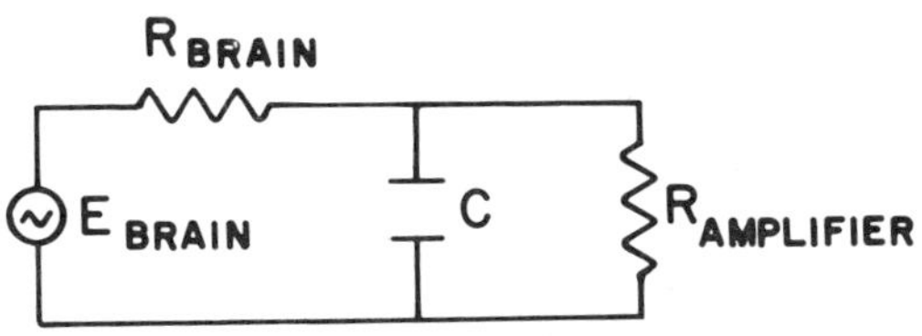

FIGURE 6.11. A Circuit that Includes a Capacitance in Parallel with a Recording Amplifier.

of the amplifier. Since the impedance of the parallel RC combination is an inverse function of frequency, one can see that relatively more of the brain's voltage will appear across the amplifier at low frequencies. As far as the voltage across the amplifier is concerned, the circuit is a low-pass filter. Its importance lies in the fact that data in the high-frequency range may be lost in one's recordings if this parallel capacitance is large. There are many sources of the parallel capacitance. The electrodes, cables, and amplifiers all have capacitive properties that contribute to the overall parallel capacitance. The total parallel capacitance is simply the sum of all the sources, since capacitances in parallel add together.

In many recording situations, another capacitance is added to the recording circuit. This capacitance is added in series with the brain and amplifier as shown in Figure 6.12. This series capaci-

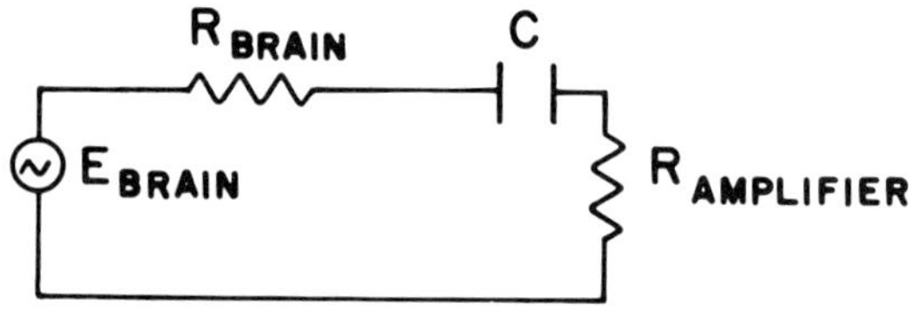

FIGURE 6.12. A Circuit that Includes a Capacitance in Series with the Brain and a Recording Amplifier.

tance will typically have its source at the amplifier or the electrodes or both. The result of adding such a capacitance is to stop DC signals from appearing across the resistance of the amplifier and to reduce low-frequency signals. The parallel and series capacitance properties in a recording system are important. Unknown capacitive elements cause distortion of data and should be understood. In general, it is desirable to reduce "stray" capacitance in a recording system. A method for such reduction is considered later.

GENERAL CONSIDERATIONS IN ELECTROPHYSIOLOGICAL RECORDING

The measurement of a voltage source in the brain always entails measurement of a voltage at one point compared with the voltage at another point or location. What is actually measured is the voltage or potential *difference* between two different points; thus, the measurement is always relative. One type of recording measures the differences between a location in the brain or elsewhere on an animal and "ground" (ground is the point that all voltages of the recording system are referred to). This is called "single-ended" recording. It is rarely used for recording from chronically prepared animals because of its susceptibility to noise and artifacts. The more commonly used recording system is called "differential recording," which is not as susceptible to noise and measures a difference in voltage from one location on an animal with respect to another location, neither of which is grounded. For example, one may wish to record the electrical activity of the lateral hypothalamus. This can be done by placing one electrode in that location and another electrode in another location, such as in a different brain area, the cerebrospinal fluid, the skull bone, the blood, or even the ear. This type of recording is called "referential" or "monopolar" recording. The voltage recorded from the hypothalamus is measured with reference to another spot. A second method is to place two electrodes so that their recording surfaces are relatively close together in the lateral hypothalamus. The voltage across the pair is again measured differentially as the difference between the two electrodes. This type of recording is called "bipolar" recording.

There are advantages and disadvantages to both the monopolar or referential and bipolar methods. In the case of referential recording, the voltage recorded, since it is the difference between the two electrodes, may be caused by changes occurring at the reference electrode and not at the "active" electrode in the lateral hypothalamus. The diagram in Figure 6.13 shows some possible

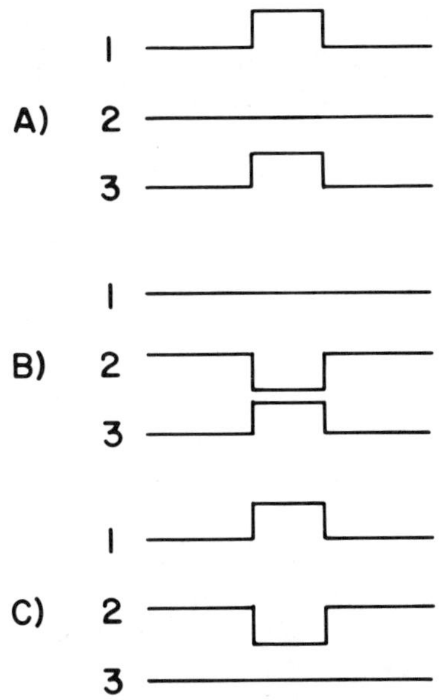

FIGURE 6.13. A Number of Possible Outcomes When Using Differential Recording Amplifiers. A: (1) change occurring at active electrode location, (2) change occurring at reference electrode location, (3) resulting recorded differences, 1–2; B: (1) change occurring at active electrode location, (2) change occurring at reference electrode location, (3) resulting recorded differences, 1–2; C: (1) change occurring at active electrode location, (2) change occurring at reference location, (3) resulting recorded differences, 1–2.

combinations that could occur in referential recording. In A of Figure 6.13, the recorded difference would accurately reflect the voltage occurring at the active electrode location, but in B, the recorded difference would not reflect activity occurring at the active electrode location. In C, there is an identical voltage change at both electrodes and the recorded difference is zero change. With a single pair of electrodes, there is no way of determining where the change is occurring.

Similar problems exist in bipolar recording with two electrodes in close proximity. If a large difference between the two electrodes is recorded, it is relatively certain that the source of the voltage is close to the electrode pair because voltages rapidly fall off or become smaller the farther the electrodes are from the source in the brain. This does not mean, however, that similar voltage sources are not acting in the same way at the same time in other brain locations. An identical voltage may be recorded at other places in the brain at the same time. Thus, even though a voltage source is close to the electrodes, many sources with similar behavior may exist. The only way one can accurately localize a given electrical response to a certain brain structure is to record from a large number of different locations at the same time.

Another problem exists in bipolar recording. A voltage change may be distributed widely throughout the volume of tissue; thus, the voltage change occurs identically at both electrodes. This will result in no difference between the two electrodes and no voltage change will be recorded.

THE NATURE OF VOLTAGE SOURCES IN THE BRAIN

Relatively brief and rapid voltage changes (less than 1.0 msec) are generated by the discharge of single neurons in the brain; these can easily be localized. These brief changes are called unit spikes or neuron spike discharges. They are difficult to record unless the electrode is very close to the neuron generating the voltage. The distribution of current around this voltage source falls off rapidly as the electrode is moved away from the nerve cell membrane so that even though the source may be around 100 mV, within 1 mm of the source one can typically record less than 1/10,000th of the source voltage. Since nerve cells are densely packed, it is difficult to distinguish the response of one nerve cell from the response of another one nearby unless the recording surface is closer to the membrane of one cell. The method of achieving this closeness is to use very small recording surfaces or microelectrodes. With a freely moving or even restrained but awake animal, it is difficult to achieve and maintain a close relation of the microelectrode with a single nerve cell membrane. The brain tissue constantly moves with respect to the electrode.

One way of recording the activity of single cells and populations of cells from a moving animal is to implant a relatively large electrode. With appropriate filtering of other voltages from the records, one can observe a large mass of unit spikes occurring. This is called the multiple unit technique. It picks up activity from a large number of nerve cells that are in the immediate vicinity (within 1 mm) of the electrodes. The active nerve cells that are closest to the electrode show larger spike discharges than those generated farther away. This technique works best in areas of the brain that have relatively large active cells. The large cells show spikes distributed over a larger volume; thus, their activity will be more easily discernible from that of other cells. In this situation, it is possible to use techniques that discriminate the activity of one cell from others. This technique of recording from single cells in unrestrained awake animals is currently being used with some success (Olds, 1965, and Hirano et al., 1970).

The etiology of other voltages recorded from the brain is less clear. Patterns of EEG activity, evoked potentials, slowly changing potentials, and steady potentials are complex and difficult to determine with certainty. The belief that these reflect the summation of many individual nerve cell discharges is a common misconception. These types of responses may occur as a result of one or a combination of many different voltage sources, many of which have little or nothing to do with neural activity. Such activity, however, can often be highly localized within specific areas of the brain. This does not mean that there is necessarily a neural origin for the response; at times, there is a clear neural relationship; at other times, the localized voltage appears only distantly related to neural activity.

The problem of specifying the electrical source of a voltage change is perhaps the most difficult experimental problem in electrophysiology. However, in spite of the uncertainty as to the exact source of certain voltage changes, their correlations with behavioral data have proved useful both in the clinic and in experimental work.

GENERAL PROPERTIES OF ELECTRODES

Different electrodes have different electrical properties that may eliminate or distort the voltages it is desired to record. One major factor that leads to differential electrode potentials is the size and shape of the surface area in contact with the solution. Other considerations such as toxicity of the electrode, ease of construction, and cost are also important. When an electrode is placed in the brain for either recording or stimulation purposes, electrical contact is made with the brain through a liquid medium or solution. The behavior of the electrode in such a solution is an important consideration since it can have a significant influence on the ability of the electrode to pick up signals occurring in the brain. The contact of an electrode with a solution is called the junction or electrode interface. All metals in contact with a solution tend to build up a potential across the interface. This is called the electrode potential. It results from the fact that charged particles or metallic ions initially leave the metallic surface and go into solution at a higher rate than the rate at which they are returned from solution to the metal. Eventually, the rate of ion transfer into and out of solution stabilizes to a point where no net movement occurs. Stabilization occurs when the metal, which has become negative because of its loss of positive ions, tends to retain other positive charges in accordance with the law of charged bodies. On the other hand, positive charges have built up in solution so that there is an electric charge difference between the metal and solution. This charge difference generates potential energy. If a current path is provided between the electrode and the solution by connecting a wire to an identical electrode in contact with the solution, no current will flow through the current path if the other electrode has an equal electrode potential across its junction. The two metals, which have an equal negative charge, will oppose each other equally. However, if one electrode has a junction potential greater than that of the other, current will flow until both electrodes restabilize. In the brain, the difference between the electrode potential on one electrode and that of the other will be completely confounded with sources of voltage from the brain. Obviously, it is desirable to minimize this effect by minimizing the difference in electrode potential between the pairs of recording electrodes. Another problem occurs when movement, heat, or other factors cause electrode junction resistances or potentials to change differentially. This situation generates an artifactual voltage change in the recording system that is not attributable to a change of the brain source.

Two classes of electrodes are used in electrophysiology: (1) a reversible electrode and (2) a nonreversible electrode. The former tends to minimize difficulties caused by unequal electrode potentials. Another characteristic of the reversible electrode is that it can pass low-level DC currents in direct proportion to the voltage generated by the brain, while the nonreversible electrode cannot.

In other words, the liquid junction of the nonreversible electrode acts like a capacitor in series with the metal of the electrode, the degree of capacitance being proportional to its surface area. If DC currents do not pass through the electrode, no current will travel through the amplifier inputs and thus no voltage can be amplified and recorded. The nonreversible electrode, however, can pass rapidly changing currents so that it is often used in applications of this sort. A stainless steel or steel alloy wire electrode is often used for recording EEGs, evoked potentials, and unit activity from the brain in spite of the nonreversible characteristics of the electrode.

The capacitive characteristics of the nonreversible electrode result from the existence of an effective dielectric between the liquid junction and the metal, which greatly opposes the physical movement of a charged body. The nature of the dielectric varies from metal to metal, but in stainless steel part of the dielectric effect is probably caused by an oxide film on the metal and partly by the fact that the electrode metal junction polarizes. The polarization of the junction refers to the fact that when a voltage from the brain is applied to the junction, the force of that voltage will overcome the opposing force of charge on the metal. Current will flow across the junction, causing either further depletion of positive charges from the metallic surface or addition of positive charges. A current will flow until the force of charge on the metal builds up to a point where it equalizes with the force from the voltage source in the brain. When the two forces equalize, no further current will flow. A steady DC current cannot flow through such a junction; thus, DC signals cannot be recorded.

To record slowly changing or DC sources, a reversible electrode is used. With a reversible electrode, the capacitive effect of the liquid junction is eliminated, at least at the low voltage levels generated by the brain. The elimination of the capacitive effect is achieved by breaking down the dielectric properties of the metal-liquid junction through imposing a film of metallic salt between the metal and the liquid.

The most commonly used reversible electrode in electrophysiology is the silver:silver chloride electrode. Voltage alterations in the solution of the brain cause negatively charged chloride ions to be combined with positive silver ions at the metallic surface of one electrode, forming silver chloride. At the opposite electrode, chloride is liberated from associated silver chloride at the electrode surface and the silver ion is combined with the metal. A charge is thus transferred across the junction without a buildup of an equal and opposite charge on the electrode. This reaction can occur as easily in one direction as the other. Thus current flows between the two electrodes, and DC voltage can be measured as long as silver chloride and chloride exist at each electrode surface.

Care must be taken with the silver:silver chloride electrode so that too large a current is not applied through it by any external source. The electrode will polarize slowly and show capacitive effects if too large a current density is passed through it. The polarization caused by amplifier currents is related to a phenomenon called "concentration polarization" in which large concentrations of certain ions are generated by the large currents flowing through the electrode and the high concentration of these ions causes an opposition to current flow across the junction. One way to ensure that large currents will not flow through the electrodes is to use amplifiers of high-input impedance. Another way to reduce the influence of external currents on the electrodes is to use large electrode surfaces whenever possible.

Another source of distortion of voltage wave forms by electrodes is the parallel capacitive properties of electrodes in contact with a solution. This property will tend to cut off the high-frequency end of voltages generated by the brain. This is generally not a serious problem with large electrodes, but it can be serious with microelectrodes. The insulation or glass wall of a microelectrode is a very thin dielectric. The bulk of the solution that the electrode is immersed in and the conductive core of the electrode can act as "plates" or charge-storing surfaces of a capacitor. The larger the capacitance, the lower the impedance to high frequencies; thus, high-frequency signals are in effect shorted out between the conductive core and the solution that the electrode is in.

The toxicity of various electrode materials to brain tissue also varies widely. Of the commonly used electrode materials, the silver:silver chloride electrode has some toxic effects when it is directly implanted in a brain. The toxic effects are not major and they can be minimized by implanting a glass pipette filled with agar-saline and using the glass pipette as a bridge or conductive core to a glass cell containing a silver:silver chloride electrode. The technique of construction of this electrode, which can be used for DC, slow potential, EEG, and evoked potential recording is described by Rowland (1961) and Rebert and Irwin (1973). The author has used a combination of this type of silver:silver chloride electrode with steel electrodes placed immediately below the tip of the silver:silver chloride electrode for recording multiple unit (MU) activity. No change in MU responses has been observed over a year with electrodes implanted by this technique, which indicates little toxic effect of the silver:silver chloride electrode.

GENERAL PROPERTIES OF CONNECTIONS AND CABLES

Perhaps the most tedious problem in recording from behaving animals is movement artifact. The major sources of movement artifact are at the connection of the electrodes with a cable and in the cable itself. High-frequency vibrations can also affect the liquid electrode junction in the brain and result in artifacts. Typically, the leads from the electrodes go to a small connector that is mounted on the implant plug of the animal. The cable connects directly to this plug with a mating connector. If the mating connector can move with respect to the connector on the implant plug, voltages will be generated at this junction. Voltages at this point can be generated directly by friction or by movement that causes the contact resistance to vary. This problem can be resolved simply by bolting the two connectors together to ensure that the cable and plug connections fit firmly.

Movement artifact generated by cables is more difficult to deal with. The source of this artifact is capacitance between each wire in the cable. Static charges can build up on the insulation on the wires of the cable. The charges on the insulation result in a charge field that can act through the dielectric material of the insulation and the air space between the wires. As each wire moves with respect to the other, the movement of the charge field with respect to the core conductor of the wire induces electron movement or currents to be generated in the wire. These currents are recorded as voltage changes.

Capacitance between each wire in a cable can also limit the high-frequency response of the recording system, since the capacitance is in parallel with the input impedance of the amplifiers. This is typically not a significant problem unless the cables from the animal to the amplifier are extremely long. In other applications, interwire capacitance of the cable can be a significant problem. For example, when using a radio-frequency lesion maker, one should separate each wire going from the lesion maker to the animal by some distance to reduce the capacity between the wires. If the wires lie close together, the capacity between them is sufficiently large that the energy of the lesion maker can be dissipated between the wires instead of in the animal.

Cable-induced movement artifact caused by interwire capacitance can be reduced by a number of methods. One method is to insert a second conductive material between the fixed charges and the core conductor. Movement of the charge field then sets up currents in the second conductive material but not in the conductive core. The currents are then led to ground. Another method is to prevent the buildup of the static charges by surrounding the insulation with a conductive medium that is led to ground. The methods of constructing cables of this type have been described by Straw et al. (1967) and Poschel and Ho (1972).

Another method of reducing movement artifact is to mount a small amplifying system directly on the implant plug. The amplifier then moves with the subject, and there is no differential movement of leads to the amplifier. Reducing the output impedance and partially amplifying the recorded signal before it is passed through another cable to other amplifiers and display devices increase the signal magnitude in comparison to movement artifact. A device of this sort that is capable of amplifying signals from three different electrode pairs but small enough for a rat to carry on its head has been described by Sia et al. (1971). (See also Rossetto and Vandercar, 1972.)

A final method of eliminating noise caused by movement of cables is simply to eliminate the cable and substitute a system that broadcasts the signal via a radio transmitter mounted on the implant plug to an antenna located elsewhere.

Connections of the cable with the recording amplifiers can be a problem. With freely moving animals, the cable will become twisted and impede the animal's movements, which can be solved by placing a swivel connector between the animal and the amplifiers. A commonly used swivel in recording situations has its cable contacts rotating in a mercury pool. The device is often constructed of materials with high dielectric properties that can store a charge, and the electrical contacts of the cable with the mercury can become polarized. These factors result in a system that is highly susceptible to movement artifact. A swivel system that tends to minimize movement artifact is described by Mundl (1967). (Also, see Chapter 5.)

OTHER SOURCES OF NOISE IN RECORDING SITUATIONS

Artifacts and spurious voltages generated by electrodes, cables, and connectors are discussed in terms of capacitive characteristics; however, noise can appear during recording as a result not only of capacitive properties but also of inductive and resistive properties of the recording system.

The "coupling" of the noise to the recording system is commonly thought of as capacitively, inductively, or resistively coupled. This means that currents are caused to flow in the input circuit of the amplifier by having the force of the noise source act on the input circuit via a charge field (electrostatic field), via a magnetic field, or via charges (currents) running directly to the input circuit through a resistance. The effect of the noise source on the input circuit of the recording amplifier is given by Coulomb's Law of charged bodies for capacitive noise coupling where the input circuit acts as one plate of the capacitor. The currents are induced by the charge field. Currents in the input circuit are similarly induced by a magnetic field, and the induction resulting from the force of the changing magnetic field causes electrons to move.

Most laboratories have many noise sources, and elimination of noise effects takes many forms. Generally, the animal should be directly grounded so that it is not capacitively or inductively coupled to ground. The animal and the remainder of the input circuit are shielded or surrounded with a material, such as bronze or copper screen or aluminum foil, which is grounded. This grounded material acts as a shield against electrostatic fields and, to a lesser extent, electromagnetic fields. The theory behind this type of shielding is to interpose another conducting plate of a capacitor between the noise source and the input circuit so that the force of the fields causes currents to flow in the shielding and not in the input circuit. Shielding against magnetic fields tends to be difficult, but it can be accomplished by interposing a material of high magnetic permeability between the magnetic noise source and the input circuit. Soft iron is generally the material of choice. Commercially available shielded rooms generally are constructed from either soft iron or other high permeability material.

Control of resistive noise coupling requires ensuring that there are no "ground loops" in the grounding system. This means that there should be no loop or circular path in which current can flow in the grounding system. The grounding system should branch from one physical point only, much like a tree branches from a central trunk. For example, several different items of equipment may be operating during a recording session, each with a different power cord. Each power cord has a chassis ground pin. The ground should be taken out of the power circuit on all but one piece of equipment by using a common three-pin to two-pin adapter on the power cord plug. The ground point on the chassis of all other pieces of equipment should be connected to the chassis of the one grounded item by separate wires. Finally, the shielding and animal ground should be wired separately to this chassis ground point.

Commercially installed shielded rooms are commonly connected to ground at some inaccessible spot. In this case, it is necessary to use the shielding as the common grounding point even though the recording equipment may be located some distance away. However it is desirable to be able to have control over the point where grounds lead. If a shielded room is to be installed, it should be designed so that the ground point is readily accessible.

Noise on power lines is often a source of difficulty, particularly high-frequency spikes and other high-frequency signals. The filtering networks of the power supplies in most equipment items are designed to convert 60-cycle AC power to DC. Other high-frequency signals on the power lines may partially pass through the power-supply filtering networks and invade the amplifiers, appearing in recordings as noise. This noise can be reduced by using a commercial power line filter that plugs directly into the power outlet.

Unplugging power cords from components of the experimental system and moving power cords to different outlets or to different orientations to the input circuit often are effective in identifying noise sources and eliminating or reducing noise effects. Moving the experimental apparatus to another location or room may also help.

GENERAL PROPERTIES OF AMPLIFIERS

The major point of control of the characteristics of a recorded signal is the amplifying system. The amplifying system in most biological experiments consists of a preamplifier, which is designed to match the particular characteristics of the signal source (including electrodes), and a driver amplifier, which is capable of supplying the power to drive a display device and accepting the output signal of the preamplifier. Each of the large variety of preamplifiers is designed for a particular application or set of applications. One way of classifying a preamplifier is whether it has single-ended input or differential input. The single-ended input preamplifier accepts voltage signals with reference to ground. One of the problems associated with this type of preamplifier is that extraneous noise sources may cause voltages to appear on the animal with respect to ground, and these will be amplified along with other biologically generated voltages. The differential input preamplifier tends to reduce this problem in that it amplifies signals from one point on the animal with respect to another point. The differential type of preamplifier is usually used in biological research. Extraneous noise signals appearing on the animal with respect to ground will most often be equal or "common" at the two points of contact that the differential preamplifier has with the animal. Since the differential preamplifier amplifies only the difference in voltages between the two points, it does not amplify the common signal at the two points with respect to ground. The degree to which a common signal at the two points (called the "common mode signal") is ignored or not amplified is called the "common mode rejection ratio" of the preamplifier.

A further classification of preamplifiers is based on the type of coupling that the preamplifier has with the biological preparation and electrodes. A preamplifier is usually capacitively coupled or directly coupled to the electrodes. A capacitively coupled preamplifier has a capacitance in series with the inputs. This blocks DC components generated by the preparation but passes higher-frequency input signals. In other words, the preamplifier acts as a high-pass filter. Usually the unit has controls that allow one to select the one-half amplitude low-frequency cutoff point over a wide range. Such controls are useful in eliminating low-frequency noise or other unwanted low-frequency signals but make it impossible to record DC signals or slowly changing signals.

An additional problem with this type of preamplifier occurs with a large signal or artifact. The large signal tends to charge the capacitor to a voltage level that is higher than the acceptable range of input signals. Although this will not normally damage the amplifier (most amplifiers can accept much larger currents and voltages than they can amplify before actual damage occurs), the amplifier will cease functioning for a period of time and is said to be "blocked." The length of time that it remains blocked is directly proportional to the size of charge on the input capacitor, its capacitance, and the input resistance. The stored charge on the capacitor must discharge through the resistance of the input circuit until its voltage again reaches the level where the preamplifier can function. The blocking time can be on the order of tens of seconds, during which time all data are lost. Large artifactual voltages that block amplifiers are usually associated with movement. If the resistance of the electrodes is high or if they are polarized to some DC level (which they normally are), large charges can occur.

A directly coupled preamplifier is capable of recording DC or slowly changing signals. The coupling does not include a series capacitance. Directly coupled preamplifiers can be used for relatively large DC signals; however, they are not useful at the low level of signals generated by the brain. The major problem of this type of amplifier is that it "drifts" over a wide range, which means that the amplifier generates slowly changing voltages that are confused with those of the brain. Rather than a directly coupled preamplifier, a "chopper" stabilized DC amplifier is normally used in biological recording. This preamplifier "chops up" or modulates the input signal into an AC signal before it goes to the amplifier portion. The amplifier portion then amplifies the AC signal using a capacitively coupled preamplifier to the input chopper. The amplified AC signal is then demodulated or pieced together at the output of the amplifier to reform the DC character of the original input. Although this preamplifier works well in recording low-level, slowly changing, and DC signals, it is not usable for recording higher-frequency signals. Its high-frequency, one-half amplitude cutoff is limited to frequencies below the frequency of the chopper. Since the chopper is a mechanical device that must be moved, the inertia of the mechanical system limits the chopping rate. Typical one-half amplitude cutoffs are on the order of 50 Hz. This amplifier is limited to brain slow potential, EEG, GSR, and skin potential recording types of applications. For recording faster-changing signals, a capacitively coupled amplifier is necessary.

CONTROLS IN AN IDEALIZED AMPLIFYING SYSTEM

Most amplifying systems have a variety of controls for modifying the output characteristics of the amplified signal. Most modern amplifiers will have such controls as:

1. Gain or sensitivity
2. One-half amplitude, low-frequency cutoff

3. One-half amplitude, high-frequency cutoff
4. Output DC balance
5. Input DC balance (in directly coupled or chopper amplifiers only)
6. Input capacity compensation.

Other amplifier parameters that are usually not subject to variation are input resistance and output resistance.

The gain or sensitivity of an amplifier is the degree to which the amplifier multiplies or magnifies the input signal. For example, if the input signal is 1 mV and the gain of the amplifier is 1000, the output voltage will be 1000 mV. Voltage gain by itself is not a sufficient indicator of the usefulness of an amplifying system. If it is desired to display or analyze the recorded signal, it is often necessary to have the output of the amplifying system provide voltages and currents sufficient to drive a display or analysis device such as an oscillograph, oscilloscope, computer, or tape deck. Some of these devices may require input voltages on the order of 1 volt or higher and currents in the ampere range for some applications. This can be achieved by having a preamplifier with a high voltage gain feed a power amplifier with a high power gain. The gain necessary for any application can be determined if one knows the voltage range required to drive the data display device and the range of voltage generated by the brain. For example, it is often necessary to have at least 1 volt of output to operate a display device. The signal in the brain can be 10 μV or less. The needed gain is 1 volt divided by 1/100,000 of a volt or a gain of 100,000. If a single preamplifier does not have sufficient gain, additional amplifiers can be placed in series with the preamplifier. The gains of amplifiers in series multiply each other so that sufficient gain can be achieved. However, care must be taken so that the filtering characteristics of the amplifiers placed in series do not distort the recording and so that succeeding amplifiers are not overloaded by the output characteristics of the previous ones. Specification of input and output characteristics and requirements of amplifiers will be given in user's manuals for commercially obtained amplifiers.

The one-half amplitude, low- and high-frequency cutoff controls vary that point in frequency where the amplification is one-half of peak. These controls vary the frequency response curves of the amplifier. The use of these controls is well illustrated by the single unit or multiple unit recording technique. The frequencies of voltages inherent in a nerve cell spike discharge are in a band from roughly 800 to 5000 Hz. The electrodes that are used also pick up voltages in the low frequencies (1 to 40 Hz) associated with EEG wave forms. If the relatively larger voltage EEG wave forms are not selectively eliminated from a recording, the relatively smaller unit discharges are swamped out or masked by the EEG. If one sets the one-half amplitude, low-frequency cutoff at around 500 Hz, the much slower EEG waves are so strongly attenuated that the faster nerve cell discharge wave forms appear much larger than the EEG and can be readily discriminated from it. Alternatively, if one wishes to record slow wave forms in the EEG range but not faster wave forms associated with noise, one would set the one-half amplitude, low-frequency cutoff at a low value and the one-half amplitude, high-frequency cutoff at a value higher than the EEG frequencies but lower than the frequencies of noise.

Most amplifiers are operated so that when no signal appears at the inputs (for example, if the inputs are shorted together), there is also no DC output from the amplifier. However, this condition can be changed so that a steady DC level will appear at the output even with no input signal. The output DC balance control balances this output DC level back to zero. In certain special applications, it may be desirable to have a certain DC output level associated with no signal at the input. This function is controlled by the baseline control or pen zero control on polygraph systems. Other applications of this feature include its use to DC bias a device at the output of an amplifier such as a diode bridge circuit or other device.

An input DC balance control is present on most DC amplifiers; its function is to balance out steady DC voltage levels that come from the animal or electrodes. In many situations, it is desirable to record small changes occurring on a large DC level. At the high gains needed to detect the small changes, the large steady DC level output from the animal may overload the amplifier or force it to operate in a nonlinear portion of its range. This large DC component can be balanced out by the input DC balance control through placing an equal and opposite voltage back on the animal. The amplifier will then be able to operate within its range to amplify the smaller changes occurring on the larger DC level. One must take care when recording DC phenomena from the brain to ensure that the DC input to the amplifier is balanced so that the amplifier is operating around its null-balanced input point. If the amplifier operates much beyond this point, currents could flow in the input circuit that would be sufficient to cause polarization of the DC recording electrodes.

Input-capacity compensation is usually found on amplifiers designed for recording higher-frequency signals in biological systems. This is a feature that tends to overcome the high-frequency distortion of signals caused by the capacitive properties parallel to the amplifier input of the electrodes and cables. By varying this control, one can improve the high-frequency response of the recording system. Such a device is useful in single-unit, microelectrode recording situations. This control is normally not useful in recording from electrodes larger than microelectrodes.

CALIBRATION

Calibration is essential for accurate quantification of data. The basic procedure is to introduce a known signal into the amplifier inputs and note resultant output on the display device. Comparisons between the magnitude of the change produced by the calibration signal with those produced by a subject allow for specification of the magnitude of the subject's change to be quantified in known units. In general, the calibration signal must have the same magnitude and frequency characteristics as the data to be recorded.

The two basic methods of calibration are off-line calibration and on-line calibration. With off-line calibration a calibration signal is placed in the amplifiers either before or after data have been collected. Usually, it is wise to calibrate each day with the amplifier settings at the values used to collect data. Most amplifiers designed for electrophysiological work have built-in calibration circuits, and their use is clearly explained in the user's manual for the equipment.

On-line calibration requires placing a calibration signal in the amplifiers at the same time data are being collected from a subject. This method has both advantages and disadvantages compared with off-line calibration. The major advantage is that the calibration signal is applied directly across the subject so that variations in the subject's impedance over time or variations in the equipment during data collection will be taken into account. Also, such systems are usually designed to be more convenient and flexible in use than off-line systems. The major disadvantage is the greater difficulty and cost in designing an on-line calibration system. Most commercial amplifiers do not include on-line calibration. It is therefore necessary to either purchase additional equipment or build an on-line system, which is beyond the scope of this chapter. However, descriptions have appeared in the literature (Emde, 1964, and Scobey, 1972).

DATA DISPLAY AND STORAGE SYSTEMS

Methods of displaying and storing data are numerous and varied, but, in general, a display system needs to be capable of satisfying three basic conditions:

1. The data should be displayed in a way that faithfully represents their characteristics.
2. The display should be readily amenable to quantification.
3. The process of quantification must be reliable.

The problem of display is essentially that of reproducing voltage (or any other electrical property) as a function of time. The two devices commonly used for this purpose are the oscilloscope and the oscillograph.

An oscilloscope has a screen similar to a television screen. Behind the screen is an electron gun that emits a focused beam of electrons directed toward the screen. The screen is made of phosphor; when the beam of electrons strike it, the phosphor emits light. If the electron beam is directed to a single spot on the screen, a single stationary dot of light appears. Since electrons are negatively charged particles, they are attracted by an opposite charge and repelled by a like charge. This principle allows for the movement of the dot of light on the screen. If one places a charged plate on either side of the beam of electrons and charges one more positively than the other, the electron beam will be attracted to the positively charged plate and thus the dot on the screen will be moved toward the positively charged plate. The dot can be caused to move from left to right on the screen at a constant rate, providing a time base. For example, if the screen is 10 cm wide and the dot moves from left to right in 1 sec, one can convert time to distance across the screen. Similarly, if the output of the amplifier is connected to two plates, one above and another below the electron beam, changes in voltage from the amplifier will be converted to changes in the vertical position of the dot on the screen. For example, if the screen is 10 cm high and a change of 1 volt on the plates above and below the electron beam causes the dot to move from the bottom of the screen to the top, the voltage can be expressed as a vertical distance on the screen. By this method, it is possible to plot voltage as a function of time with a visual display.

There are limitations to oscilloscope display. The voltage-time function is plotted as it occurs, and once the dot reaches the end of the screen the function is no longer visible. If the dot moves rapidly, it may not be possible to quantify reliably the function for storage. Other storage devices can be used with oscilloscopes so that even if the voltage change is too rapid, a memory device will memorize the voltage change and display it as a constant visual display on the oscilloscope.

The oscilloscope, in combination with a storage device that will remember the original display, is commonly used for displaying and analyzing voltages that occur at relatively high frequencies. Such storage devices include tape recorders, films of the oscilloscope screen, and computers.

One common solution to displaying and storing voltage-time functions, where the voltage changes occur in frequencies below 50 Hz, is the use of an oscillograph. In this device, the voltage change is converted to the vertical movement of an ink pen writing on a roll of paper. The paper is caused to move under the pen at a constant rate so that its movement results in time being expressed as horizontal distance on the paper. Unlike the oscilloscope, the oscillograph gives one a permanent and continuous record of voltage changes. However, the pens are mechanical devices with inertia; thus there is an upper frequency limit to the voltages that can be displayed by this method. Evoked potential, MU, and single unit data cannot be displayed by this method.

ELECTROPHYSIOLOGICAL RECORDING SYSTEMS USED WITH BEHAVING ANIMALS

Multiple Unit Recordings

Multiple unit (MU) recording is a method of recording the total of nerve spike discharges from small areas in the brain (Rebert, 1973). It has the advantage of providing data that are directly interpretable in terms of excitation and inhibition of neural activity. In contrast, EEG, evoked potential activity, slow potential activity, and so forth are not directly interpretable with respect to neural excitation and inhibition. The disadvantage with the MU technique lies in its relative difficulty compared with others. For this reason, the technique is not commonly used in behavioral research, although it is a valuable technique. With appropriate diligence and equipment, the technique can be mastered by the novice in a few months.

ELECTRODES

Stainless steel and platinum iridium wire are the best electrode materials for MU recording. The wire can range from 40 gauge to 30 gauge or even larger, since the larger the wire, the larger the number of units picked up. Either monopolar or bipolar pairs of electrodes can be used; however, bipolar recordings are preferable with behaving animals since they reduce movement artifact. For this purpose, the wires are straightened and insulated. The two wires are glued together with insulation material and cut so that one of the bipolar pair extends 0.5 mm below the other. The cut uninsulated ends serve as the recording surface.

The wires are implanted in specific brain locations using stereotaxic techniques. It is highly instructive to record from the electrodes while they are being implanted. Various brain locations have distinctive patterns of MU responses. During surgery, these can be displayed on an oscilloscope and also fed into an audioamplifier connected to speakers in the surgery room. The audio display of the MU activity is more readily analyzed by the human ear than is the visual display on an oscilloscope, and slight differences in activity between different brain areas can be readily identified with experience. One should be careful not to penetrate neural areas below the depth chosen for chronic implantation, since resulting damage tends to reduce subsequent MU responses. It is also necessary to shield the preparation with a grounded screen enclosure while recording during surgery, which usually results in procedures that slow the surgery substantially. However, the gain in precision of electrode localization is often worth the extra trouble.

CONNECTORS

The electrodes are led to a connector device and carefully soldered to the connector assembly that will be mounted on the skull. The connectors should fit tightly to preclude movement between the receptacle on the animal's head and its mating connector on the cable. It is also advisable to use a nonpolarizing connection such as that afforded by gold-plated connector pins. (See Chapter 5 for a discussion of several types of connectors.)

CABLES

Many cable materials can be used; however, it is necessary to reduce to a minimum the movement artifacts generated by cables. The author has obtained excellent results in free-moving rats and cats using a movement-free cable described by Straw et al. (1967).

PREAMPLIFIERS

Characteristics of preamplifiers that are important for successful recording of MU responses are as follows.

1. The noise amplitude generated by the amplifier must be less than the amplitude of the MU activity. Typically, MU activity recorded by means of 30-gauge stainless steel bipolar wires is on the order of 20–30 μV.
2. The input impedance of the amplifier should be relatively high (above 4–5 megohms).
3. It is essential that high-amplitude, low-frequency signals (EEG), as well as high-frequency noise, be filtered out of the records. A bandpass filter that results in good MU recording is one-half down at 800 Hz and 4000 Hz.
4. The preamplifier should have sufficient gain to drive another amplifier or display device.

Preamplifiers with the above characteristics are available from several manufacturers of biomedial amplifiers. It is highly advantageous to have the animal cables and preamplifier located within the electrically shielded space necessary for such recording. Preamplifiers with rechargable batteries for power are ideal for this purpose.

SHIELDING OF THE PREPARATION

An adequate preparation shielding can be constructed using copper or bronze screen material grounded at one point. Commercially shielded chambers may also be used.

FURTHER AMPLIFICATION AND TREATMENT

The output of the preamplifier can be displayed on the face of an oscilloscope. The resulting pattern shows a mass of activity and noise. The MU activity appears as a mass of voltage spikes. In this form, the data are nearly useless for quantification; thus, it is necessary to convert this activity into a form more amenable to reliable measurement and quantification. For this purpose, the output of the preamplifier is amplified further until it is capable of driving an integrator. The integrator converts the high-frequency spikes into a DC level; the amplitude of the DC level is proportional to the number of spikes, their amplitudes, and their durations. The integrated signal can then be displayed on an oscilloscope or on the paper of an oscillograph. Such amplification and integration devices are available from several polygraph manufacturers.

CALIBRATION

The integrated MU activity does not indicate how many neural spikes are occurring at any time. Neurons near the electrodes contribute more to integrated records than neurons farther away. Large neurons contribute more to integrated records than small neurons, and neurons firing at higher rates contribute more to integrated records than neurons firing at lower rates. Nevertheless, increases and decreases in the integrated records do provide information about the state of excitation and inhibition in small populations of nerve cells. To provide a reference for quantifying changes in the integrated record, a series of known signals is inserted into the inputs of the preamplifier and the total effect on the integrated record is determined. These known signals must approximate the characteristics of the unit activity. Square wave calibration signals are often used in this application; however, these wave forms contain frequencies that can fall outside the band of frequencies passed by the filtering system used during recording. It is more desirable to use sine wave calibration signals, since the frequency of a sine wave falls approximately in the middle of the bandpass filter system.

The unit of measurement of the integrated MU activity is microvolt seconds. If one applies a sine wave calibration signal that is 10 μV peak to peak for 1 second, the resulting integrated output of the recording system will represent the integral of the 10-μV signal over 1 second. The integral of any sine wave is .707 times the peak-to-peak value. The resulting integrated output of the calibration signal would then represent 7.07 μV sec. Although the wave forms of the unit spikes are not the same form as a sine wave, one can refer their output to that of the sine wave and express their activity level as a known number of microvolt seconds. Decreases in the number of microvolt seconds indicate less MU activity, while increases indicate more MU activity. Figure 6.14 shows two examples of MU data recorded in the manner described.

Single Unit Recording in the Behaving Animal

Modifying the MU technique, one can record the activity of single units. Difficulties are encountered with single unit recording, but useful data can be generated with care and patience. The goal is to discriminate the activity of one nerve cell from another. The first step is to reduce the

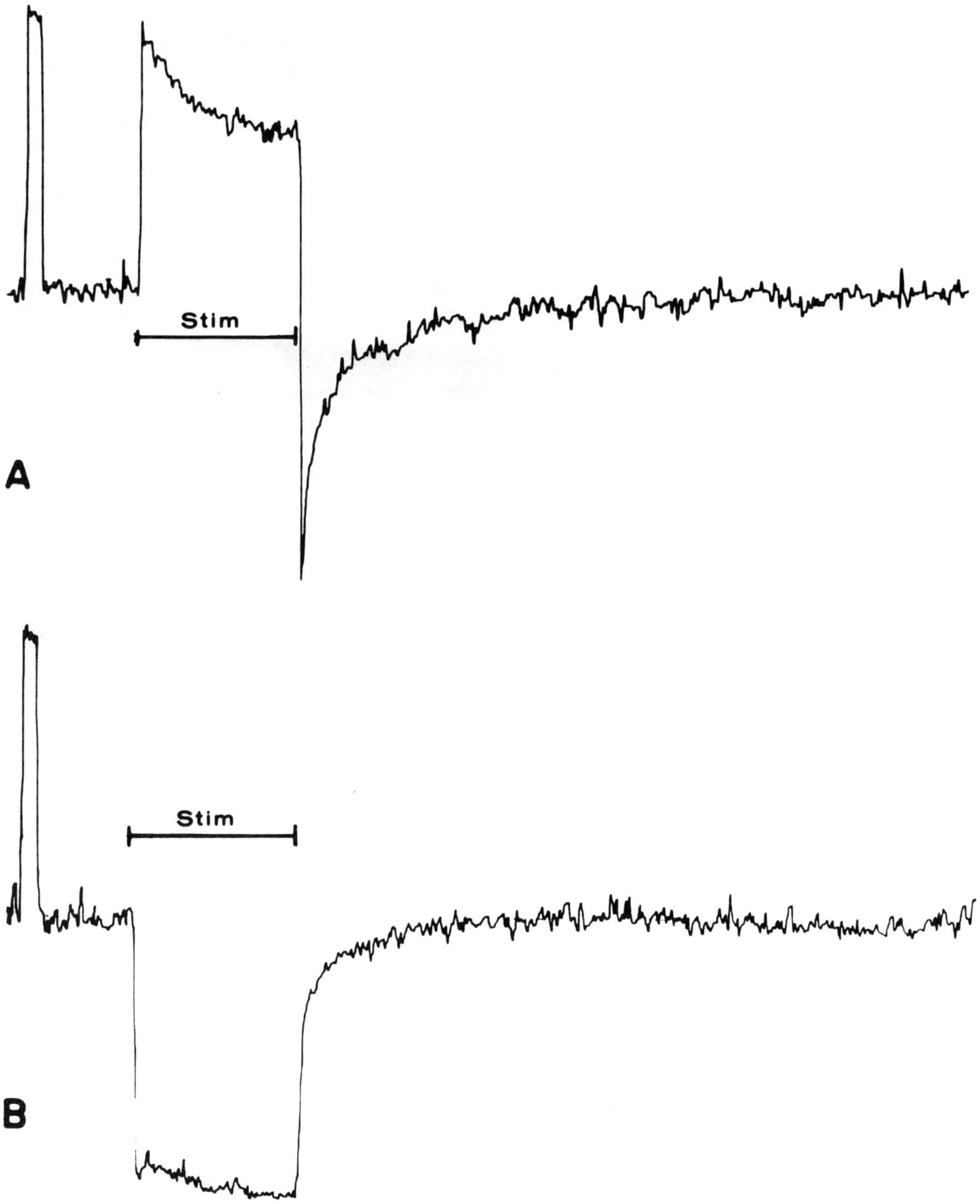

FIGURE 6.14. Integrated Multiple Unit Responses from the Inferior Colliculus of the Cat in Response to Sound Stimulation of 30 Sec Duration. Preceding each stimulation (Stim) is a 50 μV/sec calibration signal. In (A) the upward deflection of the record indicates a neural excitation, with adaptation, produced by a white noise stimulus. In (B) the downward deflection of the record indicates an inhibition of neural activity to a sine wave tone.

size of the electrode wires to 36 to 40 gauge. The same connectors, cables, and preamplifiers used for MU recording can be used for single unit recording. The smaller electrodes will pick up spikes from a smaller population of cells; however, the output of the preamplifier will still show a multiplicity of different spikes.

In oscilloscope displays of the preamplified activity, it can be noted that some spikes are larger than others, and a careful analysis will reveal wave form differences. Also, as a result of the refractory periods of neurons, there is an upper limit to the rate of discharge of a single nerve cell.

Discriminating the activity of one nerve cell from another requires taking into account the knowledge that the amplitude of discharge of a single nerve cell is constant within narrow limits, that the form of the spike discharge is relatively constant, and that there is an upper limit to the rate of discharge. Using a variety of instruments that can detect amplitude limits and noting the differences in spike discharges, one can identify neural spikes that are assumed to occur as the result of the activity of one cell. (See Olds, 1965 and Hirano et al., 1970.)

Evoked Potential Recording with Implanted Electrodes

Recording sensory evoked potentials (EPs) from the brain is similar to recording MU activity. The difference is in the frequencies of the signals one allows to pass through the recording apparatus and the magnitudes of those signals. Most of the frequencies contained by EPs are below 1000 Hz. Also, EPs are typically of larger magnitude when recorded through similar electrodes than are the unit spike discharges. This is probably because the EP source (or sources) is more widely distributed in the brain than is the source of a single spike discharge.

The major problem with recording EPs is to be able to distinguish their form and occurrence from the normal waxing and waning of the constantly present EEG activity. In other words, the problem is one of detecting a signal that is buried in noise. In the case of MU recording, EEG noise is eliminated by filtering it out, which is possible because most of the noise is in a different frequency band than the signal. However, when recording EPs, the frequency band of high noise overlaps the frequency band of the signal to be recorded.

The typical solution to the problem of extracting a signal from noise entails using averaging techniques with the data once they have been recorded. The signal or EP is assumed to be evoked identically with each occurrence of an identical stimulus and the EEG activity is assumed to be random noise with respect to the signal; thus, if one averages the records obtained from many stimuli, the resulting average record will show less noise and more signal. In practice, these assumptions of a constant stimulus and EP and a random EEG noise are rarely encountered. Accordingly, the resulting records are extremely difficult to interpret. For example, the EP that occurs on each trial of one block of trials may be of the same magnitude and form as the EP that occurs on each trial of a second block of trials. However, if the variability of the latencies of the EPs differs in different trial blocks, the average EP for the two trial blocks will be different in both magnitude and form.

Figure 6.15 shows an example of a sensory EP recorded from a human head using the technique described above.

Recording of EEG Activity

The recording of EEG activity from freely moving animals is similar to the two techniques described previously with the exception that the amount of gain in the amplifiers is not quite as high and the frequencies of signals recorded are different. EEG activity is considered to lie in the frequency band at approximately 1 Hz to 40 Hz. One usually implants a pair of bipolar Nichrome steel electrodes for depth recordings. Stainless steel screws placed through the skull and resting just above the dura mater will work for cortical recordings. Other electrode materials are also suitable for this

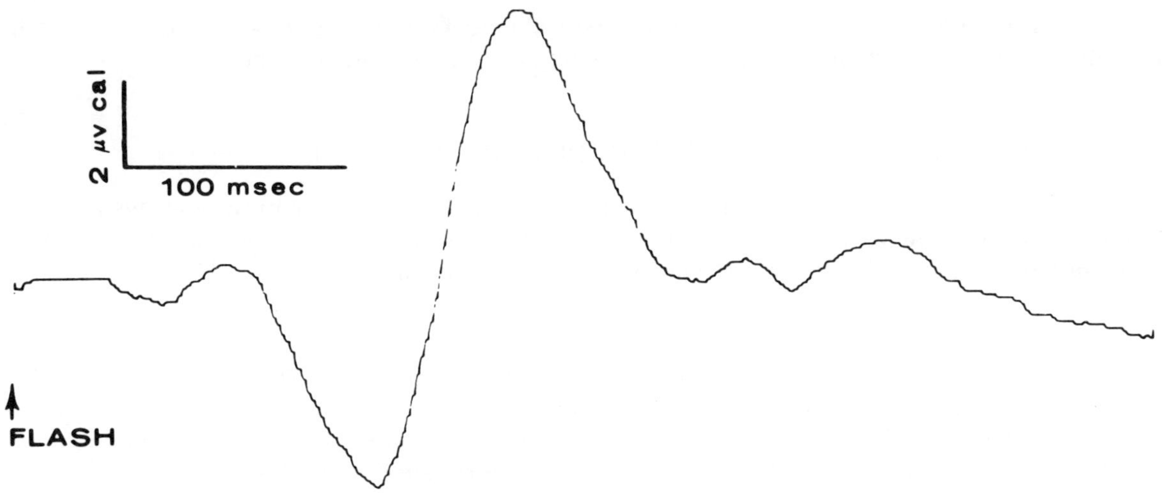

FIGURE 6.15. An Example of an Averaged Evoked Potential to a Brief Light Flash Presented to a Human Subject. The evoked potential was obtained from scalp electrodes located over the occipital cortex.

technique, since the frequencies of EEG signals place no special requirements on electrode material. The primary considerations are ease and cost of construction and toxicity.

Appropriate connectors and cables are described in the section on MU recording, and differential input amplifiers for EEG applications are readily available. The display of EEG is best achieved with an oscillograph.

The problem with EEG recording is not in the actual recording or display but in the analysis. Visual analysis of polygraph records can give a gross impression of the predominant type of activity—whether it is large, slow-wave activity, whether spikes are present, or whether the EEG displays a fast, low-amplitude character. With a ruler, one can often calculate the percentage of total time that the EEG displays one or the other types of activity.

More sophisticated analysis of the EEG activity can be performed with such equipment as tape decks and computers. Three common methods of analyzing EEG activity are power spectrum analysis, autocorrelation, and cross correlation. The consideration of the details of these analyses is beyond this chapter; only brief definitions of the methods are given here (see Brazier, 1961, for complete descriptions).

A power spectrum analysis plots the relative amplitudes of the sine wave components of the complex EEG wave forms recorded over some time period. In power spectrum analysis, one is typically concerned with comparing the spectral analysis obtained in one condition with another obtained in a different condition to determine the influence of those conditions on the EEG activity.

An autocorrelation is an analysis in which components of a period of EEG activity are compared with each other to determine periodicities of complex wave forms over time. The information obtained is that some degree of periodicity and reproducibility of a wave form exists (or does not exist) over time. Again, comparisons of autocorrelations under different conditions give one information as to how the EEG changes under various conditions.

A cross correlation is similar to autocorrelation. Rather than components of an EEG record being compared with each other, one EEG record is compared with another EEG record. The second EEG record can be obtained from the same electrode at a different time or from a different electrode location at the same time. In the latter case, the cross-correlation record would indicate similarities of EEG wave forms from different brain locations and also whether one condition shows the similar wave form earlier or later in time. Such analyses are often interpreted as reflecting the degree to which one area of the brain controls another brain area, although other logical interpretations are possible. Again, comparisons of such records under different conditions provide information as to the effect of those conditions on dependency relationships among brain structures.

Slow Potential and DC Recordings from Brain

A considerable body of literature has developed relating behavior to voltages from the brain that change slowly over time. The term "slow potential change" (SPC) encompasses potentials that can literally last the lifetime of an animal or those that last only a few seconds.

ELECTRODES

Reversible electrodes are required for the SPC application. The silver:silver chloride electrode is the most widely used one. Construction of implantable electrodes of this type is described by Rowland (1961) and Rebert and Irwin (1973). The recording of SPCs is generally monopolar. In this case, one electrode is placed in a brain area that is presumed to be the active site of voltage generation and referenced to a second point on an animal that is electrically inactive. Unfortunately, there is really no electrically neutral point on an animal; thus, a point of reference must be chosen to avoid voltage sources at the reference site to the maximum extent possible. For example, if one wishes to eliminate the possibility that SPCs are generated by sources other than those in the brain, such as the blood, the reference electrode should not be in contact with locations outside the brain. The reference site should be in other brain areas or in cerebral spinal fluid. In larger animals, such as cats, this can be achieved readily by placing the references in a cerebral spinal fluid cisterna such as the superior cisterna. One can also record transcortically—that is, place one electrode on the surface of the cortex and the other in the white matter of the cortex.

A common extraneural reference site is the skull bone, but one should be aware that use of this reference site means that one is recording across the blood-brain barrier and the obtained measures can be contaminated by a large variety of extraneural changes.

CONNECTORS AND CABLES

Tightly fitting connections between the head plug and cable are helpful in avoiding movement artifacts as are specially constructed cables to the amplifiers.

AMPLIFIERS

The only type of amplifier that is effective in this recording situation is the chopper-stabilized DC preamplifier. Some investigators have argued that specially designed, long time constant, capacity-coupled amplifiers are sufficient for recording SPCs that have durations measured in a few seconds or less. However, the possibility exists that changes of longer duration may be discovered during experimentation, and these would be severely distorted or eliminated by such amplifiers.

A second problem may be encountered in using a chopper-stabilized preamplifier. It is often necessary to balance the input DC level from the electrodes and animal, which is achieved with the input DC balance control. This balancing places an equal and opposite voltage back on the animal and electrodes. When the DC level from the animal is equally opposed by the amplifier, the amplifier is said to be in the balanced state. If the amplifier is not in a balanced state, a net current is being driven through the electrodes with some amplifiers of this type. Within the limits of recorded signals, the unbalanced state can cause sufficient current to flow through the electrodes so that they will react against the current or will polarize. Although this is usually not the case when recording at microvolt levels, it can be a significant problem when recording at millivolt levels with the type of implantable electrodes commonly used. The solution to this problem requires using chopper amplifiers that balance at a later stage of amplification. A second solution is to use a high-impedance input, unity gain, direct-coupled preamplifier placed in series ahead of the chopper amplifier. However, this usually introduces additional slow-wave noise into the recording.

DISPLAY

The raw record display of SPCs is readily achieved on the oscillograph of a polygraph system, which gives one a continuous permanent record. Additional data analysis such as that offered by signal averaging techniques is often needed to extract the SPC signal from noise. Slow potential change recorded simultaneously from three brain locations is shown in Figure 6.16.

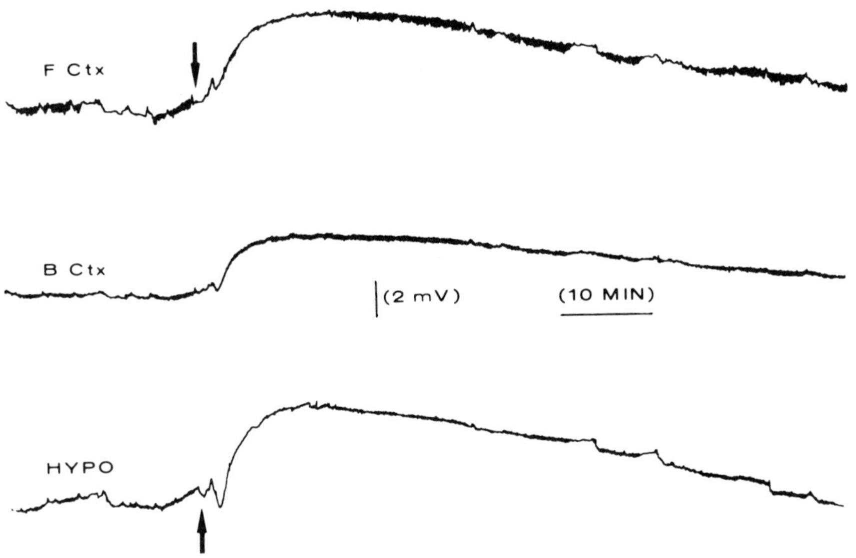

FIGURE 6.16. An Example of a Prolonged, Slow Potential Change Recorded Simultaneously from the Front Cortex, the Back Cortex, and the Hypothalamus of a Rat. The slow potential change was evoked by a penetration wound of the cortex by a stimulating electrode at the time indicated by the arrows.

Brain Impedance Recording

Electrical properties exhibited by the brain, other than voltage changes, are impedance and impedance changes. The measurement of brain impedance has seldom been used in behaving animals to study neuro-behavioral relations. One of the factors that may have inhibited investigators in using this technique is the problem of the physiological meaning of brain impedance data. In this respect, impedance recording is no less meaningful than the recording of voltages such as EEG, slow potentials, and sensory evoked potentials. The interested investigator may therefore expect to find some unknown and interesting data in using the impedance recording technique.

The specific impedance of cortical grey tissue has been calculated to average about 250 ohms per linear centimeter (Van Harreveld, 1966). The impedance of white matter is higher. In addition, changes in impedance have been shown to be evoked by sensory stimuli as well as by a variety of other physiological manipulations (Klivington and Galambos, 1968).

Brain impedance is primarily resistive in nature. Impedance to current can have either a resistive component or a reactive component. Most of the reactive component results from the capacitive property of neural tissue, but this is usually small, contributing little to the overall impedance level or to changes from that level.

In recording brain impedance from freely moving animals, electrodes that have low resistance interfaces with the extracellular fluids and that have reversible properties must be used. Large silver:silver chloride electrodes or platinum electrodes have been used. The normal way of measuring impedance is to use a bridge circuit in which the animal forms one end of the bridge. The bridge is activated by a sine wave voltage source at frequencies in the audio range (usually 1000 Hz). The output of the bridge is then measured using a preamplifier capable of passing the frequency of sine waves activating the bridge circuit. (An informative discussion of impedance measures can be found in Malmstadt et al., 1963.)

The circuit diagrammed in Figure 6.17 illustrates a typical method of impedance record-

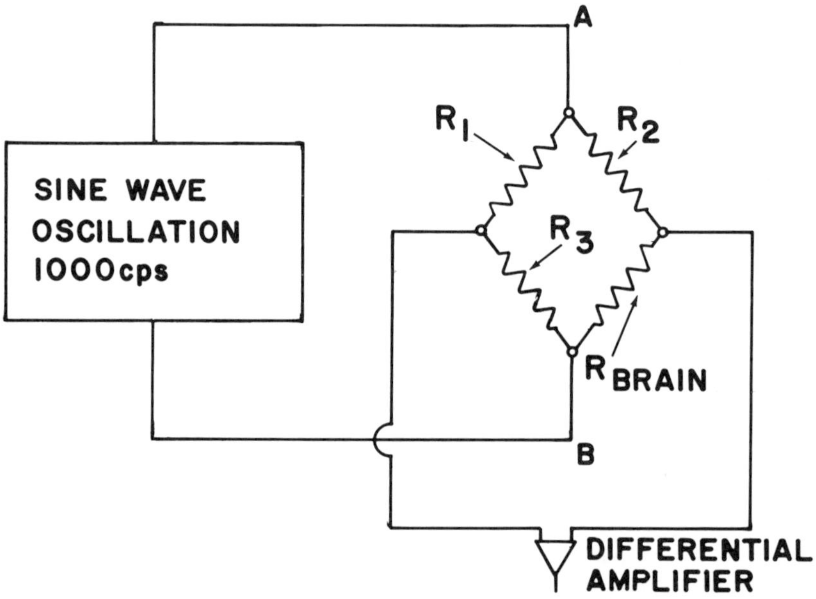

FIGURE 6.17. A Bridge Circuit Used in Recording Brain Impedance Changes.

ing. It is usually convenient for the resistors R_1 and R_2 to be equal; thus, they should be carefully matched. With effective electrodes, the overall impedance of the brain and electrodes is in the neighborhood of 1000 ohms; thus, the variable resistor, R_3, should be variable up to approximately 5000 ohms. The variable resistor is usually a precision decade resistance box. A small capacitor of around 0.02 microfarads is often placed in parallel with the variable resistor to compensate for the capacitive properties of the brain. The principle of operation of the bridge circuit is as follows: if $R_1 = R_2$ and $R_3 = R_{brain}$, there will be no voltage difference recorded between points A and B. When these conditions are met, the absolute impedance of the brain is known by knowledge of the value in ohms of R_3. Usually one wishes the value of R_3 during an experiment to be less than that of R_{brain} so that if the brain impedance decreases, the recorded voltage between A and B decreases, and if the impedance of the brain increases, the recorded voltage between points A and B increases. The system is easily calibrated by switching in various values of resistance in place of the animal, leaving R_3 fixed at the same level as used during the data collection.

The voltage changes that occur at points A and B as a result of brain impedance changes are amplified by a differential amplifier, and they can be displayed on an oscilloscope. If a permanent record of changes occurring over time is desired, the output of the differential amplifier can be integrated and displayed using an oscillograph or polygraph.

The selection of the values of the parameters of the bridge circuit will vary depending on the size of the electrodes used in recording. The parameters of applied voltage, R_1, R_2, and R_3, should be selected with the restriction that no more than 10^{-10} amperes per square micron of electrode surface area be passed through the animal. At the frequency of applied signal, this current density is considered to have no effect on neural functioning (Klivington and Galambos, 1968).

When using electrodes of readily implantable size, it is useful to reduce other voltage sources in the situation. Reduction of movement artifact in cables and connectors as discussed above is desirable, and the output of the differential amplifier can be filtered to attenuate signals at frequencies other than the frequency of signal that activates the bridge.

RECORDING EPs, SPCs, AND EEG FROM HUMANS

Slow potentials, evoked potentials, EEG, and other variables can be recorded from a human without implanting electrodes directly. In general, the recording techniques are the same as those used with animals with the exception of the placement and type of electrode.

Electrode Locations

In the slow potential, evoked potential, EEG, and eye movement recording techniques, the placement of the electrode on the head is important. A standard scheme for electrode placement is called the ten-twenty system, as presented in an article by Jasper (1958). This placement system, or variations of it, is commonly used for EEG recording. For sensory evoked potential recording, the placement is determined by the particular sense modality to be studied. Even so, many different electrode locations have been used, and the investigator should study the literature in this regard to guide his electrode placement.

In slow potential recording from the human scalp, a particular response (called the "contingent negative variation" or CNV) has been extensively studied (Walter et al., 1964). This response is commonly recorded from the vertex of the scalp with reference to one or both mastoid bones. The vertex is defined as a point in the midline of the head measured halfway between the inion (the bony protuberance on the back of the head) and the nasion (the place where the brow starts just above the nose). The mastoid bone is the large surface of bone just behind the ear. An example of a human CNV is shown in Figure 6.18.

Using slow potential recording techniques, one can also record the movement and position of the eyes by placing one electrode just above the eye on the forehead and another just below the eye. This placement will detect vertical eye movements. If one places one electrode laterally to the eye and another at the nasion, lateral movements of the eye can be detected. It is imperative that eye movement records be obtained when attempting CNV experiments since movement of the eyes can cause CNV-like activity at other head locations.

Preparation of Skin Surface for Electrode Placement

Careful cleaning and preparation of the skin where the electrode is placed serve two purposes: (1) they reduce the resistance of the electrode contact with the skin, thereby reducing noise and movement artifact, and (2) they eliminate slow voltage change from the skin itself.

The first step in preparation is to remove skin oils by lightly brushing the skin with a gauze pad soaked in acetone. If one is working around the eyes, one should use alcohol since acetone will damage the cornea. One must also exercise great care to avoid getting alcohol in the eyes, but it is not as dangerous as acetone. After cleaning the skin, a small amount of electrode paste such as

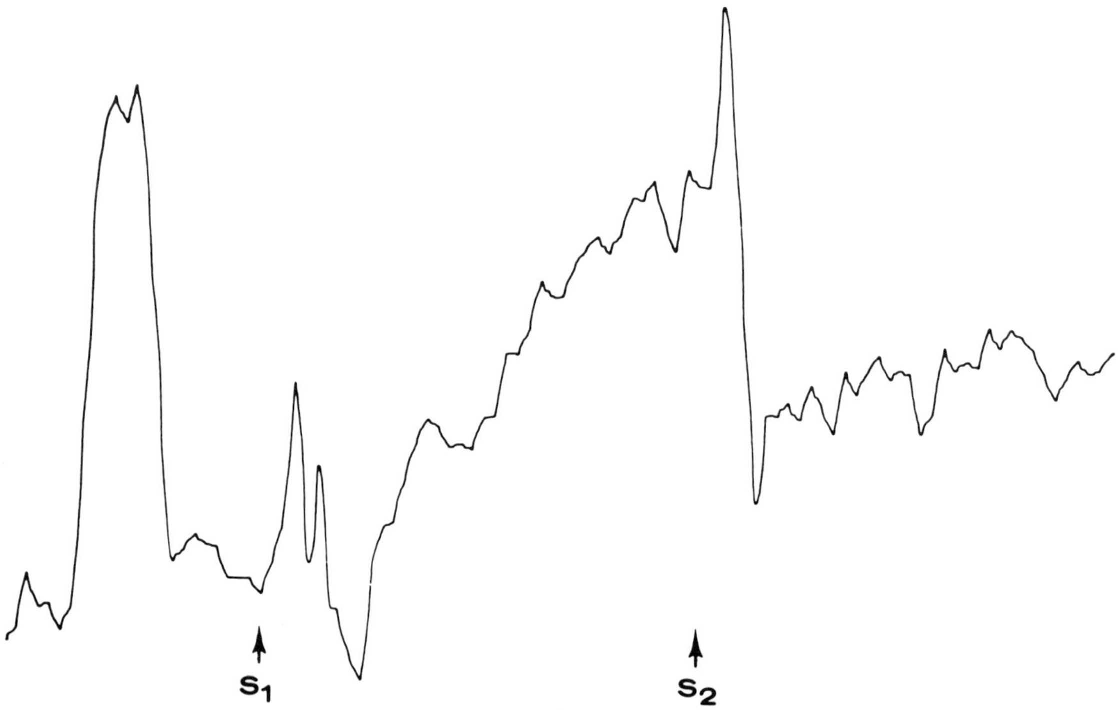

FIGURE 6.18. An Example of a CNV Recorded from the Human Scalp Between a Light Presentation (S_1) and a Loud Noise (S_2). The large wave preceding S_1 is an on-line calibration signal of negative 25 μV. The record is an average of ten trials.

Redux should be placed on the tip of a cotton swab and briskly rubbed into the skin until the skin takes on a pronounced blush. Then any excess electrode paste should be wiped off.

Fixing Electrodes to the Scalp

Many methods have been used to fix electrodes to the scalp; the primary goal of each is to fix the electrode so that it cannot move with respect to the skin. The method used depends on the size and shape of the electrode. A common and adequate technique entails placing the electrode with a conductive paste material directly in contact with the skin, covering the top of the electrode and the skin with a broad piece of cotton gauze soaked in a colloid glue, and drying the glue with an air stream. Carefully applied, the electrodes can be used continuously for many hours. In places where this technique will not work, the simple expedient of taping the electrode down often works well. The type of electrode used depends on the particular response one wishes to record. The most demanding technique in terms of electrode characteristics is the slow potential recording technique. This is usually done with the silver:silver chloride electrode. It is essential that an electrode's metal surface is not in direct contact with the skin. Usually the metallic electrode is contained within a plastic cylinder filled with a conductive electrode paste (NaCl solution), which is the conductive bridge with the skin. Electrodes of this type are commercially available. It is usually necessary to wash the electrode carefully with distilled water after its use (do not contaminate the electrode with other metallic ions) and repack the electrode with the conductive paste. Pairs of electrodes can be stored shorted together through the electrode paste for periods up to a few days to avoid polarization problems. For longer storage periods, the electrodes should be dried and stored after cleaning. It is usually necessary to match pairs of electrodes for minimum drift and minimum polarization difference.

For EEG and EP responses, the care and selection of electrodes are less critical. Silver:silver chloride disk or gold disk electrodes are commonly used. However, the silver:silver chloride disk electrode has a limited life, and it is often necessary to clean and rechloride the electrode after several uses. Hydrochloric acid is an effective cleaning medium. The electrode can be chlorided by connecting the electrode to the positive pole of a voltage source with a second silver plate connected to the negative pole. When both silver surfaces are immersed in a weak NaCl solution and 1 to 2 volts are applied to them, the silver electrode will slowly darken in color. The electrode is ready for use when it is evenly coated by the dark chloride material. Freshly prepared and matched for electrode drift, such electrodes are usable for slow potential recording. Gold disk electrodes for EEG work are less troublesome and longer lasting; however, they must be discarded after a time. The other techniques for recording responses from humans are the same as described previously for animals with implanted electrodes.

Recording Other Electrical Events from Humans

Other electrical responses that are commonly recorded from humans and other organisms are electroretinograms (ERG), electrocardiograms (EKG), skin potentials, and galvanic skin resistance responses (GSR). The methods for recording them are similar to those previously discussed although there are some minor differences.

The ERG uses an electrode configuration with an active lead in contact with the cornea of the eye and with the reference electrode clipped on the ear or pasted to the side of the head. Silver:silver chloride is generally used for the metallic part of the electrode. The metallic part is embedded in a contact lens so that its surface is slightly removed from the lens surface that makes contact with the cornea. Moisture from the eye forms the conductive bridge between the cornea and the metal electrode.

A silver:silver chloride disk electrode can be used as the reference electrode. The method is identical to that for EP recording with similar cables, differential amplifiers, and display devices. However, the ERG is usually several magnitudes larger than sensory EPs from the brain. This method is potentially damaging to the cornea, and the investigator is strongly advised to consult an ophthalmologist before attempting its use.

EKG recording is similar to sensory EP recording although the EKG activity usually has lower frequencies associated with it. Almost any electrode material will work, and large electrodes with steel surfaces strapped on the arms or legs are commonly used. The EKG can provide different information, depending on the placement of the electrodes; however, in the behavioral laboratory, the information generally needed is the time of occurrence of the Q-R-S complex associated with each heartbeat. Again, an electrode paste material should be used to provide good contact of the electrode with the skin, and each electrode can be held in place by rubber straps or tape.

One problem that arises in EKG work is the quantification of data. If the heart rate is the variable of concern (as it usually is), the EKG can be fed to a cardiotachometer amplifier. Each interbeat interval is then converted to a DC level output that is proportional to the heart rate associated with each interbeat interval. This can be displayed on an oscillograph for a permanent record.

The recording of slowly changing skin potentials is similar to the recording of slowly changing scalp potentials; however, skin potentials from the palms are usually much larger. The electrodes of choice are silver:silver chloride electrodes.

One must clean the skin carefully over the point from which the potential is to be recorded, but one *must not* abraid the skin since this will destroy the source of the potential. The skin under the reference electrode must be carefully and vigorously abraided so that it can serve as a nonactive reference point. The electrodes can easily be held in place with tape wrapped around the hand or arm when recording palmar skin potentials. (Skin potentials of lesser magnitude can be recorded from almost all areas of skin other than the palms.)

Similar data are obtained from recordings of palmar resistance changes or GSR. The same type of electrode and their placement are used as in skin potential recording. In this case, however, a special type of GSR amplifier passes a small constant current through the electrodes and skin. The output of the amplifier is proportional to the DC resistance of the skin and is typically displayed on an oscillograph. It is important that the current density passing through the electrodes be small. This will ensure that the electrodes do not polarize and that the GSR responses are not altered by the current. There are two ways that the current density can be controlled; (1) using an amplifier that passes low currents and (2) using electrode surfaces that are as large as possible.

REFERENCES

Brazier, M. A. B. (Ed.) Computer techniques in EEG analysis. *Electroenceph. Clin. Neurophysiol.*, 1961, **supl. 20,** 1–98.

Emde, J. W. A time locked, low level calibrator. *Electroenceph. Clin. Neurophysiol.*, 1964, **16,** 161–168.

Hirano, T., Best, P., and Olds, J. Units during habituation, discrimination learning, and extinction. *Electroenceph. Clin. Neurophysiol.*, 1970, **28,** 127–135.

Jasper, H. H. The ten-twenty electrode system of the international federation. *Electroenceph. Clin. Neurophysiol.*, 1958, **10,** 371–375.

Klivington, K. A., and Galambos, R. Rapid resistance shifts in cat cortex during click-evoked responses. *J. Neurophysiol.*, 1968, **31,** 565–573.

Malmstadt, H. V., Enke, C. G., and Toren, E. C. *Electronics for scientists.* New York: W. A. Benjamin, Inc., 1963.

Mundl, W. J. An improved swivel for recording from behaving subjects. *Electroenceph. Clin. Neurophysiol.*, 1967, **23,** 483–485.

Olds, J. Operant conditioning of single unit responses. *Proc. XXIII Congress Physiol. Sci.* Tokyo, 1965, 372–380.

Poschel, B. P. H., and Ho, P. M. Post reinforcement EEG synchronization depends on the operant response. *Electroenceph. Clin. Neurophysiol.*, 1972, **32,** 563–567.

Rebert, C. S. A technique for simultaneous measurement of DC and multiple unit responses. *Electroenceph. Clin. Neurophysiol.*, 1973, **34,** 326–328.

Rebert, C. S., and Irwin, D. A. Simple electrode configurations for chronic or acute recording of DC potentials from subcortical nuclei of the brain. *Electroenceph. Clin. Neurophysiol.*, 1973, **34,** 440–442.

Rossetto, M. A., and Vandercar, D. G. Lightweight FET circuit for differential or single-ended recording in free-moving animals. *Physiol. Behav.*, 1972, **9,** 105–106.

Rowland, V. Simple non-polarizable electrode for chronic implantation. *Electroenceph. Clin. Neurophysiol.*, 1961, **13,** 290–291.

Scobey, R. P. A time-locked photon isolated calibrator. *Electroenceph. Clin. Neurophysiol.*, 1972, **32,** 568–570.

Sia, J., MacNeil, D. A., and Sigg, E. G. A miniature three-channel preamplifier for unit recording in freely moving animals. *Physiol. Behav.*, 1971, **7,** 121–122.

Straw, R. N., McAdam, D., Berry, C. A., and Mitchell, C. L. A simple cable for reduction of movement artifact in electroencephalographic recordings. *Electroenceph. Clin. Neurophysiol.*, 1967, **22,** 90–92.

Van Harreveld, A. *Brain tissue electrolytes.* Washington: Butterworths, 1966.

Walter, W. Grey, Cooper, R., Aldridge, V. J., MacCallum, R. D., and Winter, A. L. Contingent negative variation: An electric sign of sensorimotor association and expectancy in the human brain. *Nature*, 1964, **203,** 380–384.

ADDITIONAL READINGS

Brown, C. C. *Methods in psychophysiology.* Baltimore: The Williams & Wilkins Company, 1967.

Bures, J., Petran, M., and Zachar, J. *Electrophysiological methods in biological research.* New York: Academic Press, 1967.

Burns, B. D. *The uncertain nervous system.* London: Edward Arnold Ltd., 1968.

Caceres, C. A. *Biomedical telemetry.* New York: Academic Press, 1965.

Cooper, R. Recording changes in electrical properties in the brain: EEG. In R. D. Myers (Ed.), *Methods in psychobiology.* Vol. 1. New York: Academic Press, 1971.

Geddes, L. A. *Electrodes and the measurement of bioelectric events.* New York: Wiley-Interscience, 1972.

Jenkner, F. J. *Rheoencephalography*. Springfield, Ill.: Charles C Thomas, 1962.
Nastuk, W. L. *Physical techniques in biological research*. Vol. 5. New York: Academic Press, 1964.
Regan, D. *Evoked potentials in psychology, sensory physiology and clinical medicine*. London: Chapman and Hall Ltd., 1972.

CHAPTER 7

Histological and Related Procedures

Barbara L. Case*

FELS RESEARCH INSTITUTE

INTRODUCTION

A frequent objective in histological preparation of the brains of experimental animals in behavioral research is to locate centers of electrode tracks and the areas of lesions. For this kind of work, relatively thick sections are desirable since they are easier to handle and can be analyzed more efficiently. At the same time, special requirements of the work demand complete sections that are nearly bilaterally symmetrical and that can be cut in any desired plane. Often a given plane is repeated almost exactly from brain to brain. The descriptions given below are intended to aid in preparing such sections and to suggest ways of assessing them for correlation with behavioral data. The author has used these methods on rats, hamsters, guinea pigs, rabbits, and cats.

PREPARATION OF THE TISSUE FOR SECTIONING

The brain is prepared for sectioning by bringing it into contact with 10 percent formalin, which causes it to become firm and somewhat bleached. Histologists call this process "fixation." Under some experimental conditions, it is desirable to kill the animal rapidly by decapitating it with a guillotine, dissecting out the brain as quickly as possible, and dropping the brain into a jar of formalin. Such brains should be blocked—that is, cut into smaller pieces in the approximate plane of future sectioning—as soon as they are firm enough, so that fixation can take place as rapidly and evenly as possible. Most of the blood either drains out or is decolorized; in either case, it is not an obscuring complication in stained sections. Using a freezing technique, a brain treated in this way can be sectioned 52 hours after the animal was sacrificed. It is possible that it could be done even sooner.

Another technique for accomplishing even fixation of the brain is called "perfusion." It is necessary to use this technique when there are electrodes or cannulas implanted in the brain since the brain must be hardened before dissection. Otherwise the position of the electrode/cannula tip will be obscured when the soft brain tissue moves with respect to the hard implanted object. The following procedures have been devised to harden the brain before dissection.

The animal is first anesthetized with either Equithesin or sodium pentabarbitol injected into the abdominal cavity. It is then laid on its back on a dissecting tray with its legs extended and fastened down so that the chest cavity can be opened without cutting major blood vessels and so that the heart will be revealed, since the perfusion is accomplished by means of the circulatory system. Physiological saline solution (0.8 percent NaCl in distilled H_2O) is used for washing out the blood. As mentioned earlier, 10 percent formalin is used for fixation (that is, 10 percent of a standard commercial formalin, which is usually about 37 percent formaldehyde in H_2O). The solutions are introduced into the left ventricle of the heart with a hypodermic needle. After coursing through the blood vessels, they flow out from the right auricle, which is cut open for this purpose just prior to or immediately after injection of the needle. It is desirable, although not absolutely necessary, for the heart to still be beating when washing out begins. Some investigators prefer to clamp the dorsal aorta with a hemostat, especially for larger animals, thus restricting the flow to the upper body and head, but the author has found that this procedure makes little difference in the quality of fixation or in the time required for fixation. At times with this procedure, the solutions back up into the left auricle and then to the lungs, reversing the pulmonary circulation. Droplets of fluid come out through the nose; however, this does not necessarily interfere with perfusion of the brain.

The hypodermic needle is attached to a rubber tube, which in turn connects with tubes running from large plastic jars containing the two solutions. These jars are set on a shelf several feet

* This article discusses techniques developed in connection with Fels Research Institute during research supported by National Institute of Mental Health Research Grant M-4529 and National Aeronautics and Space Administration Grant NGL 36–005 to Elliot S. Valenstein.

above the dissecting tray so that gravity helps the formalin perfusion, since the heart usually stops beating before the saline washing is complete. Individual preference varies somewhat as to the actual method; some investigators leave the needle and attached tubing in the heart while switching to formalin, while others carefully place another needle and tube into the hole made by the first. The first method requires some kind of connecting valve between the tubes leading from the formalin and saline jars and the tube connected to the hypodermic needle. Several sizes and kinds of plastic valves are commercially available for this purpose. A third method, which the author has used on infant rats, is to fasten the hypodermic needle and tubing to a tube leading from a double stopcock connected at both ends to the jars of saline and formalin. In this way, it is possible to switch from one solution to the other without disturbing the preparation. A fourth method that has been described is simply to force the solutions in by pushing them out of a large hypodermic syringe. This presumably takes considerable physical strength but will work in smaller animals.

In any event, the procedure should be done carefully to try to prevent bubbles of air from entering the circulatory system and to keep the system full of fluid so that the blood vessels cannot collapse. The saline washing usually requires from 5 to 15 min; it is considered to be complete when little or no blood flows out with the saline from the right auricle. The formalin perfusion usually also takes only a short time. It is considered to be complete when there is general stiffening of the animal's body, especially the front legs, neck, and shoulder girdle. However, there is no absolutely reliable means for predicting the efficacy of the perfusion; accordingly, the initial dissecting or opening of the skull should be approached with caution and some estimate should be made of the hardness and whiteness of the brain before continuing. If the brain is pink and soft, it is best to dissect away only enough bone to allow formalin to enter. Removing as much extraneous muscle as possible, since it hardens in formalin also and becomes difficult to cut away, one should put the brain and attached electrodes into formalin for 12 to 24 hours to allow the brain to harden before the electrodes are pulled out and the dissection completed. Where perfusion appears to have accomplished whitening and hardening of the brain, the initial dissection can be carried further if desired before implants are removed. Here too, however, caution should be exercised and an adequate amount of dura and skull left to prevent the brain's being pushed or pulled against the implants. In general, turning the preparation upside down after dissection has proceeded to the point of removing lateral skull bones should be avoided. All brains with implants should be left in formalin for several hours to overnight before proceeding with implant removal. It is quite possible, and even desirable where implants have penetrated deeply, to leave the ventral bones in place during electrode/cannula removal. If the brain is small or does not contain electrodes and if the perfusion was successful, it is possible to freeze and section it 24 hours after the animal is sacrificed. The brains of squirrel monkeys have been processed in a similar manner. The method of freezing probably has general applicability to nerve tissue.

Electrodes can be removed easily by placing the hardened brain and the remainder of its supporting skull upside down on hardware cloth in chloroform or acetone or some other fluid that will dissolve acrylic cement. Methyl methacrylate monomer works very well. Soaking the brain overnight is usually sufficient. If the ventral surface is exposed, drying can be prevented by covering it with a piece of cotton soaked in formalin. The electrodes can then be pulled out easily, the dissection completed, the brain blocked in whatever way is best for future cutting, and the pieces preserved in a jar of 10 percent formalin. They can be sectioned immediately or sectioning can be postponed to a more convenient time.

Rapidity or evenness of fixation need not be of special concern in preparing sections for electrode localization or lesion assessment since the fine structure of cells is not a consideration in this case. Nevertheless, a technician should work toward rapidity and evenness since there is a limit beyond which an unfixed brain is no longer useful for any purpose. Brains that show blotchy pink areas after perfusion, however, can yield excellent sections after staining; in fact, on rare occasions when animals were found dead in their cages, good stained sections have been obtained from their brains. The author's experience is that the step that is the most important in producing an effective, anatomically revealing stain is soaking the mounted sections in chloroform before they are stained.

In addition to dissolving some lipids, particularly from the myelin sheaths, the $CHCl_3$ extracts traces of H_2O. As a result, the sections adhere more evenly to the slide, and this evenness or lack of it has a profound effect on the quality of the stain of these thick sections.

REMOVAL OF THE BRAIN

The essential tools for extracting the brain are rongeurs, straight scissors, and forceps. The beginner should decapitate the animal and cut away the lower jaw. All of the skin and underlying muscle should be removed until the skull is bare. Once a good impression of the skull structure is acquired, it is not necessary to peel the underlying muscle before starting to chip the skull. Figure 7.1 shows a five-step procedure for removing the brain of a rat after any implants have been removed according to the previously described procedure. The skull can be peeled either ventrally or dorsally, although it is easier to work dorsally since the skull plate is smooth and uniform. In any case, the lip of the rongeurs should be slid gently between the dura and skull. The rongeurs should then be firmly clasped, and a piece of skull bone should be cut by forcing the rongeurs in opposite directions to the

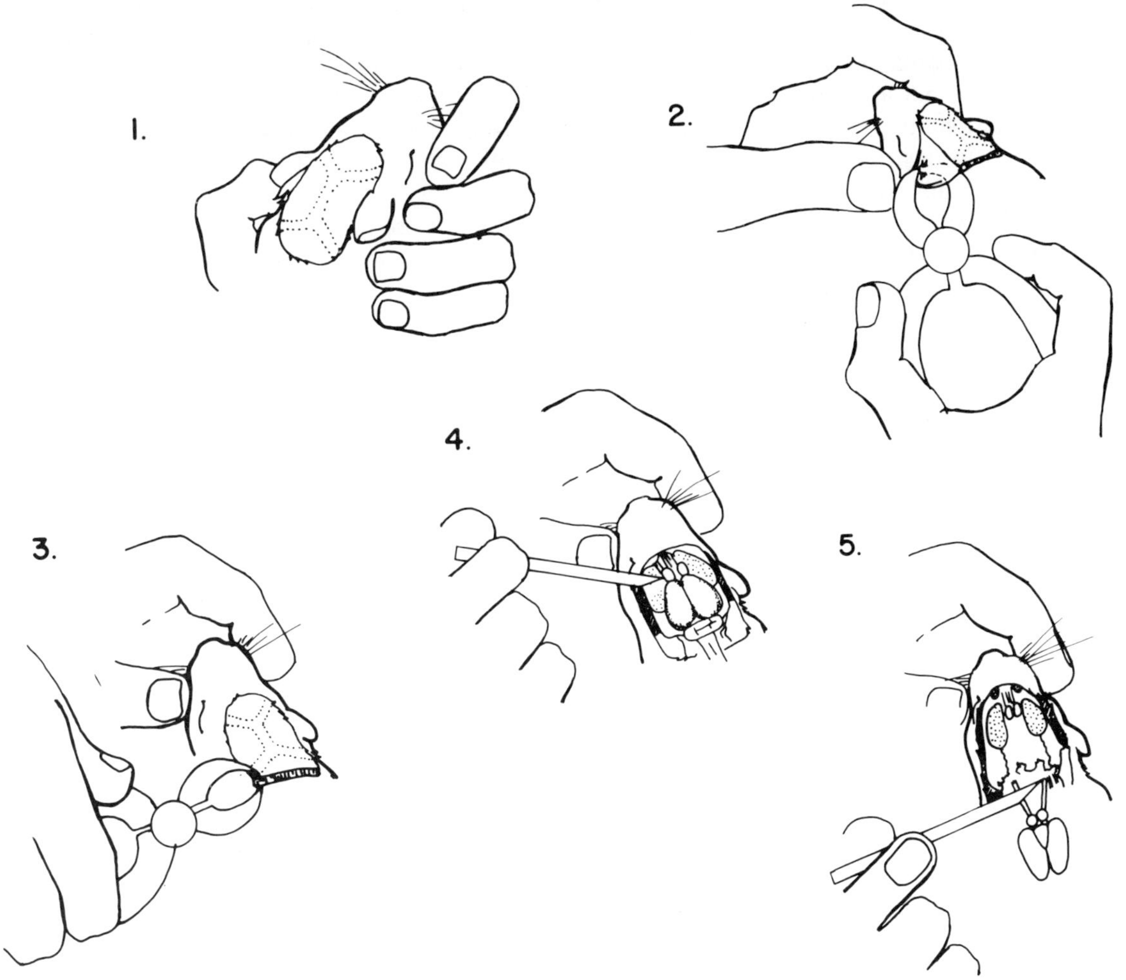

FIGURE 7.1. Technique for Removing the Brain from the Rat. The head is severed from the body (1), and skin is pulled away anteriorally to expose muscles. The lateral muscles and underlying bone are cut with rongeurs (2). The skull is chipped away (3). When all the skull bone is removed, the head is raised vertically and the optic tract is cut (4). The brain is gently pushed away from the remaining skull cavity, and gravity causes it to hang down, exposing the remaining fiber tract and cranial nerves (5). This technique works satisfactorily with both perfused and nonperfused brains.

brain. The rongeurs should be used carefully, and only a small piece of bone should be picked off. Special care is required in those areas where holes in the skull were drilled for lesions or electrode implant since the dura mater under the drilled area invariably fuses with the new bone growth; a jerky movement may pull a piece of the cortex along with the cut piece of the bone. Care should also be taken to avoid breaking the dura mater when chipping the skull bone. When the dorsal plate is peeled, the brain should be lifted from the anterior portion by cutting through the olfactory bulbs. If the lateral portions of the skull are peeled sufficiently, when the skull is lifted, the brain will hang from the optic tract and cranial nerves, which can easily be cut with small scissors. Once the brain is removed, the dura mater can be cut and peeled away with forceps. Brains can be stored in 10 percent formalin in tightly sealed bottles for several months without significant morphological changes.

SECTIONING

A sliding microtome is better than a rotary microtome for obtaining complete, bilaterally symmetrical sections because it is easier to adjust the plane of cutting with a sliding microtome. Accordingly, in the following general discussion, use of sliding microtomes is assumed.

A microtome is a precisely machined piece of equipment that should be kept oiled. The knife should be handled carefully and it should occasionally be examined under a dissecting microscope to ensure that it is free of nicks, which would rip sections as they are cut. Many laboratories have automatic honing devices. The author routinely sends blades out for sharpening at the factory and does not use a strop. Although stropping is relatively easy, it must be done with great care and there is considerable disagreement as to its usefulness.

The brain must be supported while it is being cut or sectioned. Earlier methods called for embedding the tissue in paraffin or celloidin. For larger brains such as those of cats and monkeys many psychology laboratories prefer celloidin embedding; however, celloidin embedding is a time-consuming procedure and, since sections generally do not need to be thinner than 80 microns, a freezing method is both adequate and quick.

One method of freezing is to place the tissue in a stream of expanding CO_2. Most microtomes come fitted with special platforms and tubing so that they can be attached to compressed CO_2 tanks and so that the gas can be released through pores in the platform. The tissue is frozen to the platform with a few drops of water and is itself frozen by the expanding CO_2. It is then hard enough to be sliced in reasonably uniform sections. There are also thermoelectric freezing devices that can be attached to sliding microtomes; however, such equipment is not available in the author's laboratory, and several thousand brains have been processed successfully with simple equipment. The tissue is frozen on a specially designed brass platform that has a trough at one end to hold absolute alcohol and powdered or very small pieces of dry ice. As the dry ice sublimes, the platform is chilled. A piece of filter paper, 1-in. square and wetted with distilled water, is frozen to the gridlike surface of the platform. Then a little mound of ice with a flat top is built up on this frozen paper to a height convenient for slicing and the brain is frozen to the ice. Once the brain is attached to the platform, it is itself frozen by being packed with powdered dry ice held in place by a narrow circle of soft metal. This process takes about 10 min for a rat brain.

Whichever technique is used, it is desirable to practice on an expendable brain to learn how high above the platform the tissue should be raised so that as much of it as needed can be cut. Experience in cutting frozen brains will also be useful in judging the optimum degree of freezing for the particular tissue to be sectioned. In general, the brain must be hard enough to be sliced evenly without holes or tears from spots that have begun to thaw but not so hard that the tissue shatters when the knife is drawn through it. A rule to keep in mind is to pull the knife through at a slower rate for tissue that is frozen very hard than for tissue that is softer in consistency. Occasionally, a brain will thaw rapidly and it will have to be repacked with powdered dry ice before it is sectioned. Fortunately, it is possible to refreeze the brain without damage. Dry ice can be powdered by hitting it with a hammer while it is wrapped in kitchen towels. If conventional apparatus is being used, one can simply refreeze the specimen with compressed CO_2.

As the sections are cut, they are lifted off the knife with a small brush and placed in serial order into a compartmented plastic box containing 40 percent ethyl alcohol. They can either be mounted and stained immediately or left in the alcohol a convenient length of time. If they are to be left for more than two weeks, they should be checked to be sure that the alcohol does not evaporate or that sections do not become moldy. If it is known that they must be left for a long period before being mounted, a few drops of chloroform added to the alcohol will prevent mold from growing. The sections can also be stored in formalin, but alcohol is less unpleasant to work with during mounting. They will shrink slightly, but this does them no harm since the brain swells somewhat in formalin. Even staining is enhanced by leaving the sections in the 40 percent ethyl alcohol for about 24 hours before mounting.

MOUNTING

Since the sections are arranged in serial order, they can be mounted in any desired pattern such as every second or third section. Every other section through the useful parts of the brain is mounted, stained, and examined. The intermediate sections are thereby left available for future staining in case the first set of slides was inadequate or for a complementary stain. Staining consecutive sections through electrode tracks is often necessary for reconstructing the position of the electrode tip. Alternate sections are sufficient for analyzing large lesions. The actual mounting is done by lifting the sections with a small brush one at a time out of the compartments into a Petri dish of highly dilute (0.01 percent) gelatin solution (Case, 1969). Then it is lifted with the brush from the gelatin solution and oriented on a glass slide that has been appropriately labeled with a diamond marking pencil. This orientation is aided by making a hole in the left or right side of the cortex or another area that is not to be examined at the time that the brain is being frozen and cut. A dissecting scope is used to check the section to avoid excessive manipulation of the section during the orientation procedure because it apparently results in stretching, which distorts some structures, notably the ventricles, during the subsequent drying time. It is also desirable to avoid a hot, dry laboratory environment since the sections may become shriveled. It is theoretically possible to dry the sections on a standard histology warming plate, but such a procedure is not recommended for these thick sections of complex tissue. It is convenient to set the sections on a dark background on the laboratory counter so that the change in appearance from opaque, white myelin fiber tracts to transparent myelin is readily observable. This indicates that the section is dry enough to stain. The time varies but about 30 min are usual in the author's laboratory. If the sections are not thoroughly dried, they will tend to loosen in watery solutions. Any number of sections can be mounted in this way and kept indefinitely as long as they do not become moist again.

STAINING

Recipes for staining nervous tissue are given in many books on histology technique. There are some combination stains that color myelin, cell bodies, and nuclei differently; however, unless one is studying fiber degeneration or cytological details, a simple nuclear stain is sufficient for locating both fiber tracks and nuclear areas. Cresyl violet (Cresylecht Violett, Chroma-Gesellschaft, Schmid & Co.) has been extensively used by neuranatomists and is highly acceptable because it is easy to control. One procedure (Jones, 1966) that has been used successfully is to pass the dried sections through chloroform for 1 min, then through a graded series of ethyl alcohols (95 percent and 70 percent are sufficient) for 1 min each, and then through distilled H_2O for 1 min. They are then stained in two jars of cresyl violet buffered to pH 4.0 and pH 3.0 in succession for 1 min each. The depth of staining seems to be highly sensitive to differences in the pH of the sections themselves. Because the author literally does thousands of sections, it is convenient to use the two pHs to achieve a more uniform stain. A technician doing only a few sections could probably use either one. The stain baths are followed by baths of 1 min each in distilled H_2O, 70 percent ethyl alcohol, 95 percent ethyl alcohol (usually with a small percentage of glacial acetic acid added to hasten differentiation), chloroform, 95 percent ethyl alcohol, and 100 percent ethyl alcohol. The sections are then placed in xylene for 5 minutes followed by a second xylene bath from which the sections are cover slipped using a synthetic resin.

The schedule just described has proven convenient, but it can be altered considerably without reducing the quality of the stained sections. There are, however, a few critical points. The initial chloroform bath is necessary to achieve even staining. The length of time in watery solutions should be kept to a minimum. The graded series of alcohols is designed to avoid convection currents that can literally tear the sections away from the glass slides. The reason for two successive xylene baths is to avoid carrying solutions of low pH on the sections to the point of cover slipping since they may cause gradual fading of the stain. If this happens, the cover slips can be removed by soaking the slides in xylene. The sections can be rinsed free of xylene in absolute alcohol, carried back down to H_2O through a graded series of alcohols, and restained. In general, avoid a heavy or dark stain since it will obscure details needed for interpretation of the sections.

METHODS OF RECONSTRUCTION AND REPORTING

The reconstruction of the position of an embedded object after its removal from the brain is based on the scar of glial cells that forms around the surface of such objects in the living tissue. When the object is removed, the scar is usually left relatively intact. The nuclei of these glial cells stain deep purple with the cresyl violet method described, and the scar thus becomes visible. If the object was a twisted-wire electrode, for example, the impression of the twists is often visible in the sections. By looking at the slides in consecutive order from anterior to posterior positions of the channel that is left after removing the implant, a technician can easily visualize the shape and former location of the object. The desirability of thick compared with thin sections, in addition to their ease of handling during mounting, lies in the fact that one can see more of a channel in a single section.

Before reconstruction is begun, the formerly embedded object should be examined under a dissecting scope, since small variations in the size or shape of such objects can often be correlated with otherwise inexplicable details of the glial scar. It is convenient to do this as the electrodes are removed, writing a brief description of each one to avoid confusion when there is more than one electrode in a brain.

The slides can be examined effectively with a binocular dissecting microscope designed to be used with transmitted light (older dissecting scopes sometimes provided for reflected light only). Two or three slides can easily be moved back and forth on the stage and thereby compared. Also, only low magnifications are required. (Low magnifications are actually helpful to the beginning technician since more of the section is seen at once than with higher-power microscopes.) Binocular dissecting scopes also have the advantage of providing a three-dimensional image. The kind of microscope that splits the image so that one can see parts of two slides simultaneously might also prove useful, especially for describing and comparing lesions.

At times, it is difficult to interpret slides, and a higher-power magnification is needed to decide, for example, whether a piece of tissue is the edge of a rip or part of the glial scar. Even with extremely careful handling of brains, there are often artifacts of this kind that must be assessed. Because of the abundance of artifacts, a set of criteria is needed to assist in making decisions as to the usefulness of the slides. When examining electrode or cannula channels, the technician should rate separately his ability to reconstruct the position of each of the usual three relevant dimensions—that is, the anterior-posterior extent, the lateral extent or width, and the depth. One can set up a range of estimated measurements and require that a series of slides conform to these measurements. If it is assumed, for example, that a twisted electrode is about 500 μ in diameter and that the sections are about 80 μ thick, and if swelling, shrinking, and variations in the thickness of the sections and the size of the electrodes are also assumed, seven to twelve slides should encompass the anterior-posterior dimension of the channel. If they do not, something is wrong with the interpretation or there was too much tearing to determine the dimension unequivocally. If there are thirteen to seventeen slides, reconstruction is less certain; and, if more than seventeen slides are required, one could say that, at least for the anterior-posterior dimension, the position of the electrode could not be reconstructed. Each variable should be rated independently, and the final reconstruction should be rated equal to the lowest one used.

The interpretation of electrolytic lesions is more difficult, but the center of the lesion can usually be reconstructed by following the channel left by the electrode that made it. Also, the centers of lesions have a characteristic appearance. A beginner should have a set of slides made from a control brain for comparative purposes. By comparing normal, undamaged brains with damaged ones, even a beginner can perceive the differences and make an approximate outline of the relevant area. However, assessments of damage or functional loss should be made only by those with considerable experience in interpreting changes in cellular morphology. The determination of the size of electrolyte lesions is further complicated by the fact that lesion morphology changes as a function of elapsed time between the production of a lesion and the sacrifice of the animal. For example, Rowland (1966) points out that lesions shrink approximately 50 percent in size in the animal sacrificed 28 days after surgery compared with those in an animal sacrificed 3 days after surgery. Since most behavioral studies are long-term studies, it would be useful to sacrifice a few lesioned animals 3 days after surgery and conduct a histological examination to obtain an estimate of the maximum lesion size.

Many atlases of brains of experimental animals are available; it is necessary to find an appropriate one and to compare one's sections with it to determine what part of the brain was affected. Most atlases are made from frontal sections (that is, cross sections) of brains. This is convenient since it assists in the process of cutting bilaterally symmetrical sections. With such sections, one has only to compare the altered side with the intact side to report the relevant structures. As one's knowledge of anatomy increases, this becomes less important, but it is always helpful. Reconstruction and reporting are also made easier by cutting one's sections not only in the dorsal-ventral plane of the atlas but also in the same plane as the insertion of the electrode, cannula, or lesion probe if it is possible. Diagrams of the brain made in other planes, such as sagittal and horizontal planes, are useful in elucidating anatomical relationships in the brain. Sagittal diagrams can also be used for reporting after one has gained experience.

REFERENCES

Case, B. Simplified mounting of frozen sections of brain; drying and $CHCl_3$ extraction prior to nissl staining. *Stain Technology*, 1969, **44,** 207–208.

Case, B., and Valenstein, E. S. Methyl methacrylate monomer; a solvent for removal of implanted electrodes. *Stain Technology*, 1963, **38,** 201–202.

Jones, R. M. *Basic microscopic technics*. Chicago: The University of Chicago Press, 1966.

Rowland, V. Stereotaxic techniques and the production of lesions. In L. Martini & W. F. Ganong (Eds.), *Neuroendocrinology*, Vol. 1. New York: Academic Press, 1966.

SUGGESTED READINGS

Akert, K., and Welker, W. I. Problems and methods of anatomical localization. In D. E. Sheer (Ed.), *Electrical stimulation of the brain*. Austin: University of Texas Press, 1961.

Drury, R. A. B., and Wallington, E. A. *Carleton's histological technique*. New York: Oxford University Press, 1967.

Skinner, J. E. *Neuroscience: A laboratory manual*. Philadelphia: W. B. Saunders, 1971.

Wolf, G. W. Elementary histology for neuropsychologists. In R. D. Myers (Ed.), *Methods in psychobiology*. New York: Academic Press, 1971.

CHAPTER 8

Gastrointestinal Manipulation in the Rat

Charles T. Snowden*
THE UNIVERSITY OF WISCONSIN

INTRODUCTION

For more than a hundred years, investigators have been fascinated by the operations of the peripheral digestive organs. The first notable contribution was William Beaumont's series of observations on the stomach of Alexis St. Martin, which was permanently exposed through a fistula made by a gunshot wound (Beaumont, 1833).

Early experimental work on the gastrointestinal system was done by Claude Bernard at the University of Paris in the mid-1800s and by Ivan Pavlov in Leningrad at the turn of the century. Pavlov eventually won a Nobel Prize for his studies on the physiology of digestion. Early in the 1900s, Walter Cannon found that peripheral sensations such as throat dryness and stomach contractions were important cues of thirst and hunger.

Since Cannon's findings, little attention has been given to peripheral digestive organs and the role that they might play in behavior, relative to central neurological mechanisms. In the past ten years, interest has revived in examining peripheral digestive organs as they relate to behavior. Rats have been trained to inject all of their daily food through a chronically implanted intragastric tube (Epstein & Teitelbaum, 1962b), and chronic injections have been made into the stomach (Thomas & Mayer, 1968), the bloodstream (Corbit, 1965; Adair, Miller, & Booth, 1968), and the upper intestines (Ehman, Albert, & Jamieson, 1971; Snowdon, 1974). Chronic fistulas have been devised to allow removal of foods from the stomach or upper intestines (Snowdon, 1970; Davis & Campbell, 1973); and feeding has been studied in rats whose stomachs have been partially denervated by vagotomy (Snowdon & Epstein, 1970).

Although the techniques described below have been useful primarily for studies of feeding and drinking behavior, most have other applications. For example, the chronic oropharyngeal bypass (intragastric tube) can be used for chronic intragastric injections of drugs, chemicals, or other solutions that animals would not ordinarily ingest voluntarily. The tube can also be used to administer solutions in precisely determined quantities. Intravenous catheterization can serve a similar purpose for more rapid delivery of materials.

Four techniques are described in this chapter. They are: (1) gavage, a nonsurgical technique for stomach intubation; (2) a nasopharyngeal intragastric tube, which is chronically implanted to the skull and allows injections of solutions directly into the stomach without abdominal surgery and without disturbance to the animal once it has recovered from surgery; (3) two gastrointestinal

*The author is grateful to Alan N. Epstein who first introduced him to gastrointestinal research techniques, to Harry R. Kissileff for countless discussions about each of the techniques described here, and to Richard S. Wampler for a meticulous critique of an earlier version of this chapter. Development of the duodenal fistulation technique and preparation of this chapter were supported by funds from National Institute of Mental Health Grant MH 17, 933, and from the Graduate School Research Council of the University of Wisconsin.

fistulation techniques, one that can be used for chronic injections into the intestines and one that can be used for the removal of gastric contents; and (4) vagotomy, a technique for eliminating a major source of gastrointestinal sensory and motor innervation, although it does not provide complete denervation.

Any person planning to investigate abdominal neural or organ functioning should first consult a good anatomic reference. For the rat, Eunice Greene's *Anatomy of the Rat* (1935) is the best source. One should also become familiar with abdominal anatomy first-hand by careful dissection of dead animals before attempting surgery on living ones. The dimensions given below for tubes and fistulas relate to the rat; however, the techniques and measurements can easily be adapted for use in other species.

GAVAGE

The word "gavage" derives from the French word "gaver," meaning "to gorge." In English, the term applies equally to the poultry farmer's common practice of using funnels to stuff grain down the throats of fowl and to feeding by means of a stomach tube. The latter technique is of concern here. It is frequently used clinically to intubate human patients and to sample gastric contents, as an example, for excessive acidity when an ulcer is suspected. The technique is most useful in situations where fluids must be intubated infrequently and when the stress that accompanies gavage is not likely to interfere with experimentation.

Materials

Materials needed are:

1. A Number 8 French catheter (Davol Rubber)
2. A 5, 10, or 15 cc syringe
3. A 15-gauge stainless steel hypodermic needle with the tip cut off
4. Mineral oil
5. A ring stand with clamp to hold syringe (optional).

Procedure

First, tie the catheter onto the 15-gauge needle by sliding the large open end over the needle tip. Surgical thread will provide a suitable tie. Mark the catheter with a dark Magic Marker between $5\frac{1}{2}$ and 6 in. from the tip of the catheter (at 6 in. for a 350-g rat, shorter distances for smaller rats). Fill the syringe with the solution to be intubated (liquid food, water, saline solution, drugs) and hold it under a running hot water faucet to heat the contents approximately to body temperature. Add the catheter needle assembly, and place the syringe in the ring stand clamp. Hold the animal gently with one hand pressing the hind legs firmly against your rib cage. With the other hand pass the catheter, the tip of which has been dipped in light mineral oil, into the rat's mouth. Pass from the side of the mouth, avoiding the incisors. As the tip reaches the back of the oral cavity, the rat will gag slightly, and the tube will begin to slide easily down the esophagus. Gentle handling of the animal will minimize its struggling. Slide the tube down until the black mark on the catheter is reached and then inject the fluid slowly from the syringe. By using preheated solutions and injecting at approximately 0.5 cc per sec, discomfort to the animal will be minimized.

If the tube does not slide easily all the way up to the mark on the catheter, if the animal appears to be in great respiratory distress, or if its tongue, ears, or paws turn bluish, remove the catheter immediately. Do not inject anything unless the rat is breathing relatively normally and is showing normal color.

The volume to be injected is important. Balagura and Coscina (1969) reported that intragastric loads of more than 5 cc pass immediately from the stomach to the intestines. In the case of saline or a drug, this may not be important, but if one is injecting foods that must be broken down by the stomach enzymes, a small intragastric load is advised. The laboratories of Epstein and Kissileff have claimed that animals can be adapted to accept larger loads by working up gradually from 5 cc to as high as 15 cc, but the intestinal fate of a large load in an adapted stomach has not been demonstrated. For long-term testing requiring intubation, the author's perference is the nasopharyngeal intragastric tube described below. For applications in which only hydration is necessary, the investigator may find it easier to inject 10 cc per day of isotonic saline intraperitoneally and not bother with stomach intubation.

NASOPHARYNGEAL INTRAGASTRIC TUBE

The nasopharyngeal intragastric tube was designed by Epstein and Teitelbaum (1962b) and has subsequently been used for studies of voluntary food and water intake regulation in the absence of oropharyngeal sensations in both normal and brain lesioned rats (Epstein & Teitelbaum, 1962b; Rodgers, Epstein, & Teitelbaum, 1965; and McGinty, Epstein, & Teitelbaum, 1964). The advantages of the method are that the tube is chronically implanted and fixed to the skull, and repeated injections can be made without the trauma of acute stomach intubation or surgical manipulation of the stomach. The tube is passed into the stomach through the esophagus, which eliminates gastric surgery. The tube lasts much longer than any other method of fistulation. If the operation is done properly and the animal is kept free of infection, an intragastric tube will remain functional for up to six months. However, when the animal is trained to self-inject its nutrient intake, the mean useful life of the intragastric tube is approximately 10 weeks. This shorter life results from the chronic stress placed on the skull rig by the tubing needed to carry food for injection and the counterweights needed to prevent the animal from destroying the tubing. Recovery from surgery is relatively slow (seven to ten days), but, after that period, there is no observable change in the animal's oral feeding behavior as a result of the presence of the tube (the lumen of the tube is considerably smaller than that of the esophagus).

The intragastric tube can be combined with the watertight swivel joint devised by Epstein and Teitelbaum (1962a) to provide for long-term injections. The tube described below is based on modifications of the original design and was presented first by Epstein (1967).

Construction of the Tube

MATERIALS

Materials needed are:

1. 17-gauge stainless steel needle tubing (Superior Tubing)
2. Polyethylene chloride tubing (PE 50), .023-in. i.d., .038-in. o.d. (Clay-Adams)
3. Polyvinyl chloride tubing, 1/16-in. i.d., 1/16-in. wall (Tygon, from A. H. Thomas, Fischer, Scientific Products)
4. A 1-ft length of tinned copper wire .017–.020 in.
5. Eastman 910 cement (Armstrong Cork)
6. A Bunsen burner, two pairs of blunt-nosed pliers, matches, small rattail file, hemostat, and a syringe with a 15-gauge needle
7. A cutting wheel (Dremel).

PROCEDURE

To construct the tube, cut off a 1-in. piece of 17-gauge stainless steel needle tubing with the cutting wheel. The ends must then be polished and slightly rounded, which can be accomplished by burnishing each end on the flat side of the cutting wheel. Then ream the inside of each end with a small rattail file to remove interior burrs. Hold each end of the tube with a pair of pliers and heat it over the Bunsen burner flame until the tube is red hot. Then bend the hot tubing to form a 100° to 110° angle. (Heating the tube before bending minimizes the crimping that occurs if the tube is bent while it is cold. The angle allows the tube to rest perpendicular to the surface of the skull of the animal.) After the metal tube has cooled, pass a 1-ft length of polyethylene tubing (PE 50) through the inside of the stainless steel tube. (If the inside edges of the metal tube have not been reamed, there may be some difficulty in passing the PE 50 tube through.) The short end of the PE 50 tube should protrude about 1 in. beyond the metal tube.

The next step requires considerable practice. Because PE tubing is inert, it is an ideal substance for contact with the internal tissues of an animal; however, its inertness makes it impossible to glue it or seal it other than by force-fitting. PE tubing expands when it is heated; rotate the short tip of the PE 50 tubing approximately 1 to $1\frac{1}{2}$ in. from a heat source such as a match or soldering iron. The end of the tube will expand, and if rotation is regular and exposure to the heat is even on all sides, a symmetrical collar will form as shown in Figure 8.1a. Gently pull the PE 50 collar back over the edge of the stainless steel tubing (see Figure 8.1b). If the collar is uneven and misshapen, cut off the end of the PE 50 tube and try again. The PE tube must be handled gently as it is pulled back over the metal tubing and should be checked carefully for cracks. (Cracks are the most common cause of faulty tubes.) The collar formed will prevent fluid from seeping between the PE 50 and stainless steel tubings during injections.

Next, cut a 1-in. piece of the polyvinyl chloride tubing (PVC) ($\frac{1}{16}$-in. bore, $\frac{1}{16}$-in. wall), place a few drops of Eastman 910 cement on the half of the stainless steel tube with the collar on it, and gently force the PVC tubing over the collar and onto the metal tubing to the bend. If the PVC tubing is twisted as it is forced on, it is likely to shear off the PE collar, making the tube inoperable. With practice, one can easily force on the PVC tubing without damaging the PE collar (see Figure 8.1c).

The collar now functions as a leakproof seal between the metal tube and the PVC tube. After 5 to 10 min, the Eastman cement will have dried enough to allow the tube to be tested. Fill a 10 cc syringe with water, attach a blunted 15-gauge needle, and insert the blunted end into the PVC tubing. Gently try to push some water through the tube; the water should flow through easily. If there is resistance, the tube has been obstructed, probably because some of the cement has blocked the opening of the PE tubing. An obstructed tube should be discarded. After the patency of the tube has been checked, clamp the long end of the PE 50 tube with a hemostat and again attempt to force water through the tube from the syringe. Leaks are most likely to appear between the PE tubing and the metal piece or between the PVC tubing and the metal piece. If leaks appear, discard the tube. If no leaks appear, the tube is suitable for insertion.

Cut the long end of the PE tube to 8 in. from the bend in the metal piece and insert the piece of copper wire up to the entrance to the metal tube. It is necessary to produce a permanent bend in the PE tube where it will double back on itself at the animal's nose. Depending on the application, the metal tube may be placed at different locations on the skull. The bend of the metal tube will be located at the anterior edge of the parietal bone of a 350-g male rat if the nose bend is made in the PE 50 tubing at $1\frac{1}{2}$ in. from the metal bend. If one is implanting electrodes or performing lesions, it may be desirable to have the metal tube situated farther to the anterior by shortening the distance from the metal bend to the nose bend. Shape the PE tube with the wire inside around the closed tips of a small hemostat so that the tube doubles back on itself with both sides of the angle parallel to each other. Hold the tube in hot water (60°C) for 1 to 2 min. The wire prevents the tube from collapsing and forming a permanent kink, and the hot water makes the bend permanent (see Figure 8.1d). After heating the tube, remove the wire. Measure the length of the PE tube from the nose bend. A distance of $5\frac{1}{4}$ in. will locate the tip of the tube just inside the stomach of a 350- to 400-g male rat. (Shorten

FIGURE 8.1. Steps in the Construction of an Intragastric Tube: (a) the PE 50 tube inside the bent 17-gauge steel tube with collar formed; (b) collar folded back over edge of steel tube; (c) PVC tubing force-fit over the collar and steel tube; (d) completed tube with nose bend.

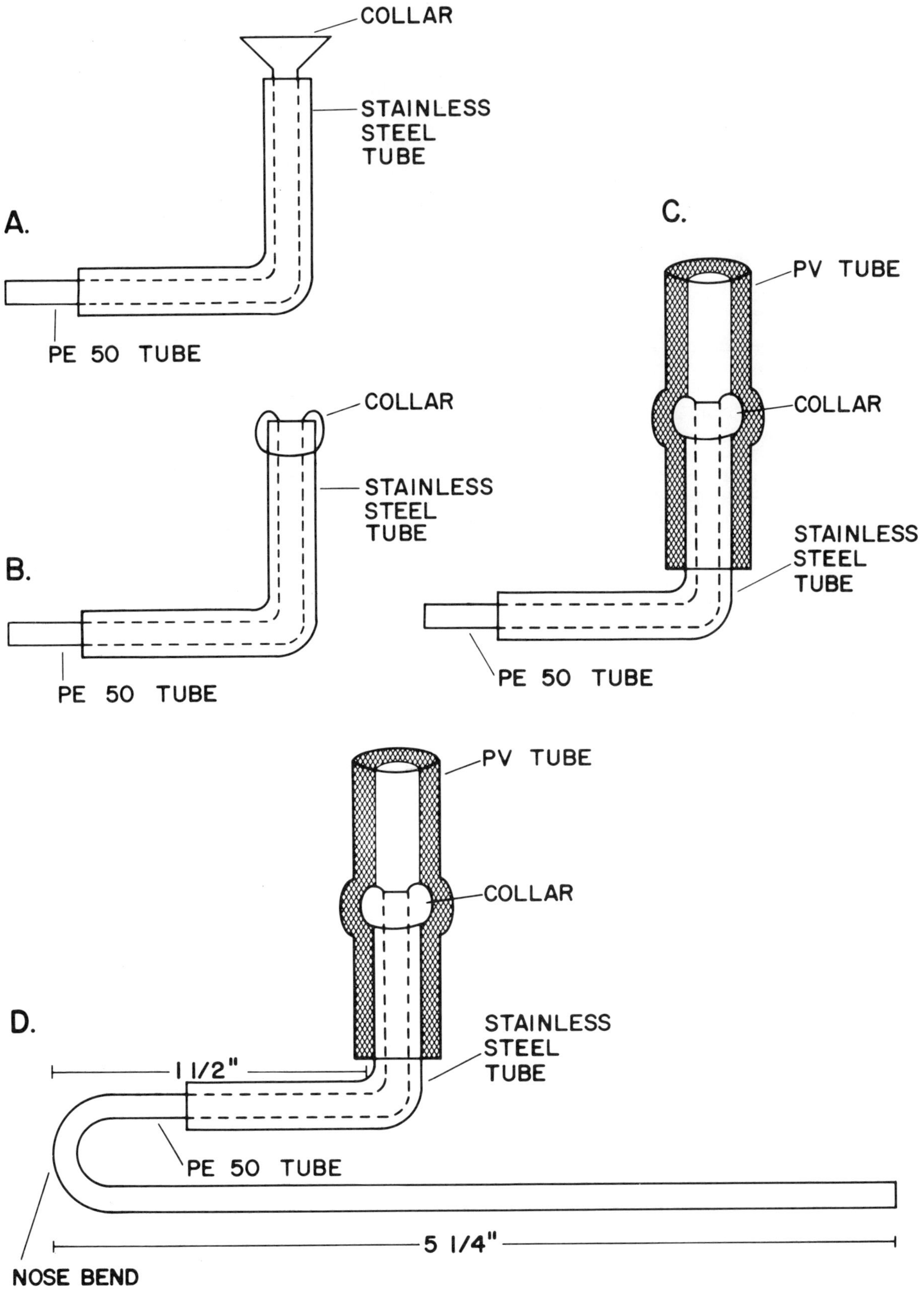
A.
COLLAR
STAINLESS STEEL TUBE
PE 50 TUBE
B.
COLLAR
STAINLESS STEEL TUBE
PE 50 TUBE
C.
PV TUBE
COLLAR
STAINLESS STEEL TUBE
PE 50 TUBE
D.
PV TUBE
COLLAR
STAINLESS STEEL TUBE
1 1/2"
PE 50 TUBE
5 1/4"
NOSE BEND

the tube by 1/4 in. per 100 g lower body weight.) If the tube is too long, it will irritate the stomach walls, causing hyperperistalsis and eventually rotation of the cecum (cecal volvulus), which occludes the intestinal tract and kills the animal. This symptom is prevented to some degree by using the tube length mentioned above. However, it appears fairly frequently when animals are forced to self-inject their food intragastrically (Snowdon, 1969).

It is generally more efficient to construct several tubes simultaneously, performing each step on all tubes before moving on to the next step. Thirty tubes can be made and tested in about two hours, and about 70 percent will test adequately.

Installation of the Tube

MATERIALS

Materials needed are:

1. A scalpel handle with a No. 10 blade (Bard-Parker)
2. Small sharp-pointed scissors (4 1/2 in. long iris scissors)
3. Small curved forceps (4 in. long eye forceps with serrated edges, not mouse-toothed)
4. Large curved forceps (7 to 8 in. long with blunt ends)
5. A stereotaxic instrument or headholder (Kopf, Scientific Prototypes)
6. A drill (power dental drill or jeweler's hand drill)
7. A No. 6 drill (dental)
8. 2 × 56 stainless steel machine screws
9. Surgical needle (half-curved, cutting tip, 18 or 20 gauge)
10. Surgical silk (3–0 or 4–0)
11. Nasopharyngeal tube (see above)
12. Dental cement (Special Justi Medical acrylic, type 1 superfine H. D. Justi)
13. Jeweler's screwdriver.

PROCEDURE

The nasopharyngeal tube implantation will work best if the animal has been deprived of food and water for several hours before surgery. It is also helpful to administer an injection of atropine sulfate (0.5 cc, 40 mg per cc) to prevent salivation about 30 minutes before anesthetizing the animal.

First anesthetize the animal and shave the hair from its skull with electric clippers. With the scalpel, make an incision just behind the ears to just in front of the eyes along the midline of the scalp. Carefully scrape away all the tissue beneath the skin so that a clear field of skull bone is available. The facial muscles insert at the edge of the skull, and one should clear the skull to the point where these muscle insertions are clearly visible. If bleeding occurs, it should be stopped by using cotton swabs, bone wax, or gentle buffing with a dental burr. The skull must be perfectly dry for the dental cement to hold. Fix the animal in the headholding section of the stereotaxic instrument. It is not necessary to level the head or to be sure the ear bars are inserted properly since the head need only be held firmly enough to allow installation of screws.

When the animal's head is secured, drill the screw holes, making sure that the drill just goes through the bone and does not penetrate brain tissue. For implantation of an intragastric tube, the best locations for screws are: one each on the lateral portion of each frontal bone just in front of the orbit, one on the postero-lateral portion of one parietal bone, and one on the postero-medial portion of the infraparietal bone. These are the thickest parts of the skull and will support screw placements for a longer time than other locations. Using the large curved forceps to hold a machine screw, drive each screw with a jeweler's screwdriver about three turns, so that the screw and attached bone move together when the screw is wiggled.

Once the screws are installed, remove the animal from the headholder, lift up the skin from the anterior portion of the scalp incision with one hand, and tunnel under the skin with the sharp-pointed scissors to the nostril. Tunneling is best done by inserting the scissors with the tips together, then spreading them apart to separate the tissue, closing them and pushing forward. Continue this process until the scissors' points emerge just above the nostrils. Little or no bleeding should result from this if it is done properly. Once the tunnel is open, push the PE end of the tube through the tunnel until the nose bend of the tube is right at the nostril.

The animal should be turned over on its back with its head hanging over the edge of the table. Before the tube is inserted through to the stomach, it should be remembered that the nasopharynx is heavily vascularized. Any roughness during tube insertion can cause bleeding that will complicate surgery. Because the animal will be manipulated in unusual positions, excess fluids and blood can block the trachea and cause respiratory difficulties. It is wise to have an aspiration system available to evacuate fluids from the pharyngeal area if necessary. An additional problem is caused by the anatomy of the nasopharynx. There are two diverticula (dead ends) as well as one passage that goes through to the esophagus. One is more likely to get the tube into one of the diverticula than into the correct path. Thus one must proceed gently and with minimal force to avoid bleeding.

Insert the tube into the nostril by holding the tube close to its tip and bringing it toward the nostril from a lateral position. Insert the first $^1/_4$ in. and then bring your hand closer to the medial part of the animal. The through passage runs along the roof of the mouth more or less parallel to the angle of the rat's lower jaw. The diverticula, on the other hand, run more or less parallel to the rat's forehead. Thus after the tube has been inserted from a lateral position for the first $^1/_4$ in. and the tube has been moved medially, attempt to direct it toward the roof of the animal's mouth (that is, in a ventral direction) as the tube is gently pushed in. Rotate the tube between the fingertips while pushing.

There will be some resistance when about 1 to $1^1/_4$ in. of the tube is inserted. Twist the tube and push it forward gently. If there is still resistance, the tube is probably in a diverticulum and should be withdrawn. If resistance is not met, continue to push until the tube is inserted up to the nose bend. If the tube meets with considerable resistance an inch or so from the nose bend (that is, with about 4 in. of tube already inserted), it is probably in the trachea and should be removed. Tracheal intubation is also indicated if the animal shows signs of respiratory distress such as gasping, cessation of breathing, or loss of coloration. Tracheal intubation is an extremely uncommon occurrence (less than 1 percent) if the animal's head is hanging over the edge of the table.

When the tube is fully inserted, make a small incision with the scissors through the outer cartilage of the nose between the nostril that contains the tube and the opening of the skin above the nose where the tube comes through from the skull. Push the nose bend of the tube into this slit, and apply tension to it by pulling the metal tube back on the skull. Carefully stitch the incision together so that no portion of the tube is visible at the nose. Be careful not to cut or puncture the tube with the scissors or needle. This step prevents the animal from pulling or scratching at an exposed tube.

Position the metal tube on the skull in the center of the screws and cement it to the screws with dental cement. Use a thin mixture of the cement at first to seal around the screws. As the cement gets thicker, add it around the base of the metal tubing. Cement the lower $^1/_8$-in. of the PVC tubing as well. Make sure that the end of the PVC tubing points in a vertical direction and that the outer edges of the cement are smooth. Also be certain that none of the cement is in contact with soft tissues such as skin and muscle. Once the cement has dried, stitch together the separated skin across the cemented area. Two or three stitches will suffice. It might be of value to sprinkle a topical antibiotic such as sulfathiozole or Furacin on the skin around the incision to prevent infection. Following completion of surgery, inject 0.4 cc of penicillin (300,000 U/cc) in two separate doses of 0.2 cc each into the muscles of each hind leg. Figure 8.2 indicates a cross-sectional view of the completed tube implantation.

The animal's food and water intake will be diminished for seven to ten days but will then return to preoperative levels. To prevent the tube from clogging, especially if the animal is feeding on a solid diet, the tube should be flushed with 1 cc of warm water or saline every two to three days.

The animals can be used for intragastric self-injection or for programmed injections on a 24-hour basis. The animals are housed in modified operant chambers at least 18-in. high, which pre-

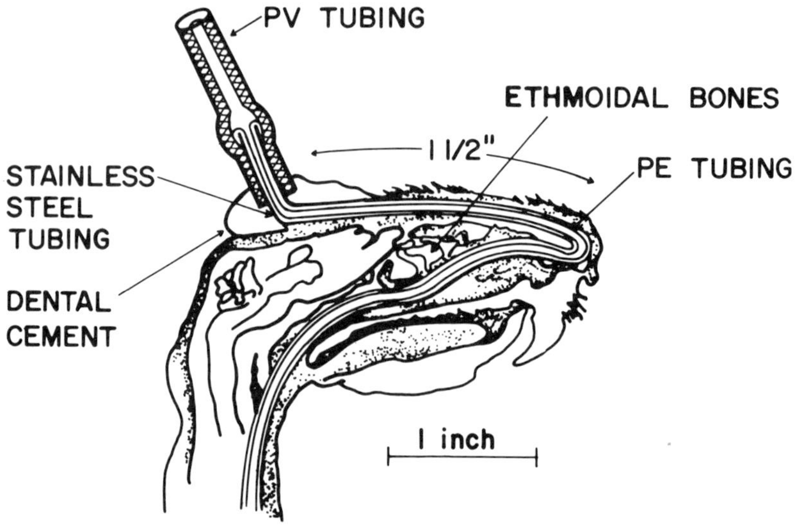

FIGURE 8.2. Cross-Sectional View of Rat Skull with Intragastric Tube Mounted in Place.

vents the animal from chewing the tubing connected to it. The swivel joint described by Epstein and Teitelbaum (1962a) allows the animal to move freely through the cage without twisting the plastic tubing that conveys the solutions to be injected (the swivel joint can be made by a machinist from published specifications). A length of PE 260 tubing is connected to the top of the swivel joint by force fitting and is interrupted at 18 in. so that the animal can be easily removed from the situation for weighing and other maintenance without detaching the swivel joint. The cut ends of the PE 260 tube are force-fit over a $^{3}/_{4}$-in. length of 15-gauge needle tubing. A pulley is suspended from a bar several inches above the top of the cage. A second pulley with a No. 5 one-hole stopper attached to it serves as a counterweight. The PE 260 tube is threaded through the fixed pulley, then through the counterweight pulley, and taped to the bar above the cage. From there, it goes through the pumping system to the dietary reservoir. The counterweight places tension on the tubing so that as the animal moves vertically, the tubing remains taut, preventing the animal from chewing at it.

The most satisfactory pump is the Sigmamotor, Model T-8, with Model E-1 Reveo vernier adjustment and with the pump head reamed to accommodate four $^{3}/_{16}$-in. tubes (Sigmamotor). These peristaltic pumps have been in operation for ten years without failure. The peristaltic pump requires a more flexible tubing than the PE 260, however, so PVC tubing ($^{1}/_{16}$-in. i.d., by $^{1}/_{16}$-in. wall) is used through the pump and joined to the PE 260 by another piece of 15-gauge stainless steel needle tubing.

It is easiest to program the injection of nutrients automatically, but such programming should closely approximate the animal's normal meal patterns (Quartermain et al., 1971). If an animal is to self-inject intragastrically, it should have been shaped to bar press for oral food. Then the pump speed is increased to its maximum of 19.2 ml per min where any brief bar press will deliver a fairly large amount of food. Over time, this rate can be reduced by successive halvings of the pump rate to the rate of .6 ml per min—the rate of delivery used by Snowdon (1969) to approximate normal ingestive rates. Two to three days will be needed for the animal to adjust to each level.

The choice of substances to be injected is important. Because of the small lumen of the intragastric tube, only completely soluble fluids should be used. For a nutritionally adequate diet, only that of Greenstein et al. (1960) has proved successful. An economical version with casein hydrolysate rather than individual amino acids and sucrose rather than glucose, which is adequate for stomach injections, is available (Diet 116 EC, General Biochemicals). Diets that contain raw eggs or that are suspensions will not work well in intragastric feeding.

GASTROINTESTINAL CANNULATION

Another means of manipulating the gastrointestinal system is through cannulae placed directly in the organs to be studied. The nasopharyngeal tube is suitable only for injections into the stomach. It cannot be inserted through the stomach to the intestines since it will cause irritation. Also, substances cannot readily be removed through such a tube. Direct cannulation is needed in these cases.

Two types of cannulas are described. One is mounted on the skull and can be used for direct injections into the intestines; the other has a much larger opening and can be used for removal of substances from the stomach.

Cannula for Injections into the Duodenum

MATERIALS

Materials needed are:

1. Polyethylene tubing (PE 50) (.023 in. i.d., .038 in. o.d.); (PE 260) (.070 in. i.d., .110 in. o.d.) (Clay-Adams)
2. Polyvinyl chloride tubing (PVC) ($^1/_{16}$-in. i.d., $^1/_{16}$-in. wall) (Tygon, from A. H. Thomas, Fischer, Scientific Products)
3. 17-gauge stainless steel needle tubing (Superior Tubing)
4. Usher's Marlex mesh (Davol 1265)
5. 5–0 silk with tapered BB needle (Ethicon K880H)
6. Scalpel with No. 10 blade, sharp-pointed small scissors, small curved forceps with blunt tips, and small (mosquito) hemostat
7. Dental cement (H. D. Justi)
8. Matches, headholder or stereotaxic, drill, screws, and isotonic saline.

PROCEDURE

Prepare a 1-in. piece of metal tubing, a 9-in. piece of PE 50 tubing, and the PVC tubing as follows. Cut and carefully file the metal tube, bend it while hot over a Bunsen burner flame, insert the PE 50 tubing through the cooled metal piece, form a collar by heating the PE near a match flame or soldering iron tip, bend it back over the metal tubing, add Eastman cement and the 1-in. piece of PVC tubing, and test for leaks. Next, cut a $^3/_4$-in. piece of the PE 260 tubing. Hold one edge above a match or soldering iron to expand the tubing. While the plastic is still hot, press the end against a table top to form a flat flange. Do the same at the other end. Cut a 1-in. square of Marlex mesh, round off the corners, and place a small slit in the center. Pass the flanged PE 260 piece through the slit and use dental cement to fix the mesh to the center of the flanged tube (see Figure 8.3a). Trim the piece of PE 50 tubing to 6 in. from the bend of the metal tubing and insert the piece of .017–.020-in. wire as with the nasopharyngeal tube and make a 90° bend $4^5/_8$ in. from the bend of the metal tubing. Then hold the tube with the wire in place for 1 to 2 min in hot water and remove the wire. This will allow the tube to be situated on the skull and reach just to the duodenum of a 350-g male rat. The remainder of the fistula construction will be done during surgery.

Anesthetize the animal, shave its skull and abdomen, prepare the skull, and insert the machine screws as described above for the nasopharyngeal tube. Then make a vertical incision of 1 to $1^1/_4$ in. on the abdomen about $^1/_2$ in. to the surgeon's left of the midline with the top of the incision beginning just below the rib cage. In making the incision, place a finger on the skin on each side of the scalpel blade and push the skin apart, keeping tension directly under the blade.

Using the small hemostats, tunnel under the skin from the abdominal incision to the posterior edge of the scalp incision. Grasp the end of the PE 50 part of the tube assembly at the skull between the jaws of the hemostats and withdraw the hemostats from the abdominal incision, bringing the PE tubing through the subcutaneous tunnel. Note that the position of the metal tubing will be opposite of that for the nasopharyngeal tube—the PE tubing faces backward on the skull.

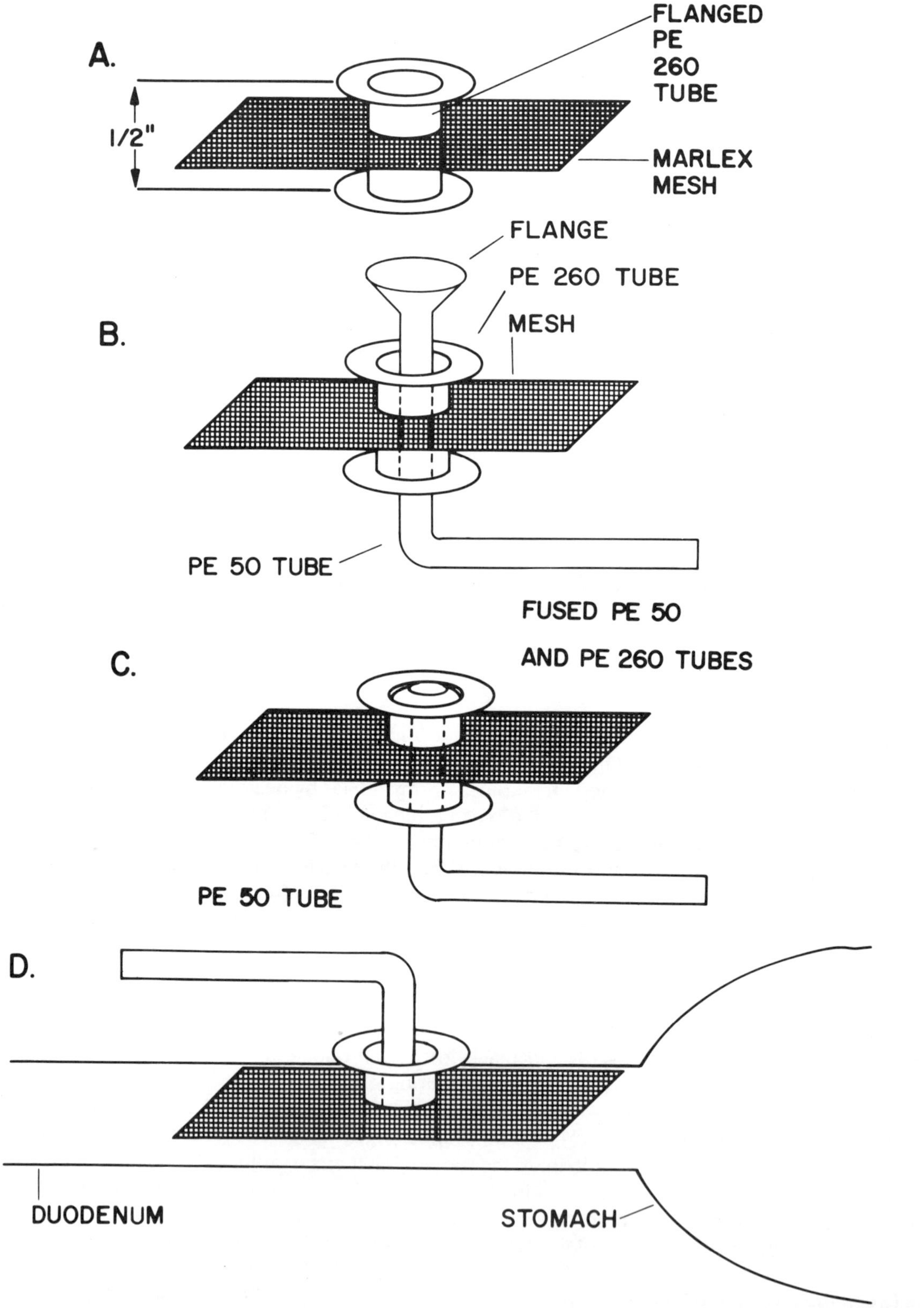

FIGURE 8.3. Steps in the Construction of the Intraduodenal Cannula: (a) flanged PE 260 tube with Marlex mesh cemented at center; (b) PE 50 tube passed through PE 260 collar and collar formed on PE 50 tube; (c) PE 50 and PE 260 tubes fused; (d) cannula in place in the duodenum.

Cut off the crimped end of the PE 50 tube so that about 1 in. extends from the 90° bend in the tube. Slide the flanged PE 260 tube over the end of the PE 50 and form a flange in the PE 50 tube by holding it near a match or soldering iron (see Figure 8.3b). Slide the flanged PE 50 tube back until it is flush against the PE 260 tube. (The flange on the PE 50 tube should now be large enough to prevent it slipping through the lumen of the PE 260.) Then heat both flanges so that they melt and fuse. (Be careful not to get the flanges too hot or they will collapse.) The tip of the PE 50 tubing should now be fused completely with the flange of the PE 260 (see Figure 8.3c).

With a pair of forceps, lift up the body wall and cut with a pair of scissors. One must never cut through the body wall with a scalpel. Always be certain to lift up the body wall with the forceps while cutting to prevent cutting into the abdominal organs beneath. Locate the duodenum (see Figure 8.3d) by deflecting the lobes of the liver to the side. (Locate the stomach below the liver; then follow the duodenum as it leaves from the left side [surgeon's left] of the stomach.) Lift the duodenum out of the abdominal cavity with the forceps. Any abdominal organ that is exposed must be kept moist. Frequently bathe the exposed duodenum with isotonic saline during the subsequent procedures.

With the atraumatic needle (Ethicon K 880 H), make four to six continuous stitches on the most ventral surface of the duodenum so that a circle about 3/8 in. in diameter is formed (see Figure 8.4). It is important to use an atraumatic or noncutting needle to minimize damage to the intestinal

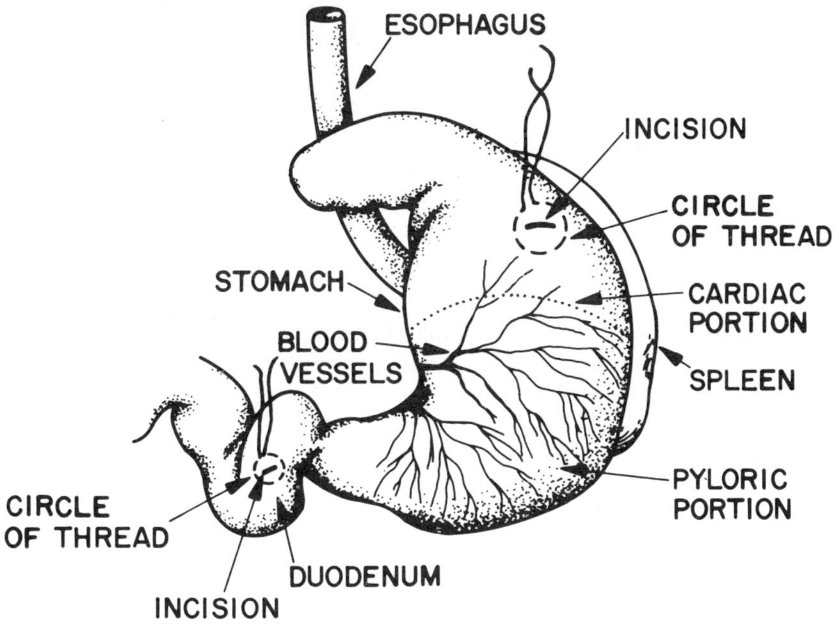

FIGURE 8.4. Stomach and Duodenum with Location of Purse-String Sutures for Duodenal and Gastric Cannulas.

walls. Then make an incision in the center of the circle of stitches with a pair of sharp-pointed scissors. Be careful not to cut any of the threads. Insert the free end of the cannula where the PE 260 and PE 50 were fused into the duodenum and pull on the ends of the thread. The continuous stitches act like a purse-string to draw the duodenal tissues tightly around the cannula. Tie the threads and then sew at least one more purse-string suture around the cannula. Spread out the mesh on the upper surface of the duodenum—it will help anchor the cannula since scar tissue will grow through the holes of the mesh (Figure 8.3d). Stitch the body wall together with discrete stitches and with just enough pressure to have the two cut edges meet each other without overlapping. Using a needle with a cutting edge, stitch the skin together in the same fashion. The body wall and skin must be stitched separately to eliminate the danger of intestinal herniation. Adjust the tension of the tube on the skull and cement it to the skull with dental cement as with the nasopharyngeal tube. Also give the same dosage of penicillin (0.2 cc intramuscularly in each hind leg) as with the nasopharyngeal tube.

This preparation requires care; first, a cap should be made for the skull end of the fistula. This is done by cutting a $^3/_4$-in. length of 15-gauge needle tubing and crimping one end closed with pliers. The open end is inserted into the PVC tube mounted on the animal's skull. To maintain the patency of the tube, it should be flushed out with 1 to 2 cc of warm water or saline every other day. This is especially important if the animal is on a solid diet. Failure to flush the tube routinely may cause permanent clogging and render the preparation useless. The animal recovers normal food and water intake in seven to ten days. Because of the incision in the intestine, the animal should not be given food until the day following surgery. If carefully flushed, the tube can remain useful for injections up to three months.

The duodenal fistula can allow examination of the role of the duodenum in controlling feeding. As an example, animals fitted with both intragastric and intraduodenal tubes were trained to press a bar for oral delivery of food. On some days, solutions such as glucose, sodium chloride, urea, liquid diet, or isotonic saline were injected into either the duodenum or stomach whenever the animal ingested by mouth. With intraduodenal injections of osmotically active substances—glucose, sodium chloride, diet—a satiety effect was produced. That is, the rat ceased eating sooner than he would if the same solutions were injected intragastrically. The animal's meals became small, and, to compensate for the reduced nutrient intake, meals were taken more frequently. Thus the duodenum may be more important than the stomach in producing satiety (Snowdon, 1974).

Cannula for Removing Substances from the Stomach

A larger opening must be used for removal of substances from the stomach or intestines, since gastric contents will obstruct the opening of a smaller tube. The precise details of the cannula described here can be modified for larger or smaller openings and can be made of different materials.

One type of cannula that has been used successfully by Settler and Smith (1969) and Snowdon (1970) is a piece of stainless steel tubing machined to have a $^7/_{16}$-in. flange at each end with a $^9/_{32}$-in. o.d. and $^7/_{32}$-in. i.d. along the shaft. The length from flange to flange is .420 in. The inside of the cannula is threaded, and a small knurled cap is machined to fit the threads of the cannula to screw it closed when not in use. To remove the contents, a hollow connecting tube is similarly threaded at one end and force-fit into .154-in. i.d. PVC tubing at the other end with a $^7/_{16}$-in. flange in the center. See Figure 8.5.

MATERIALS

Materials needed are:

1. A cannula with cap as described above
2. Usher's Marlex mesh (Davol 1265)
3. 5–0 silk with tapered, noncutting BB needle (Ethicon K880H)
4. A scalpel, with No. 10 blade, small sharp-pointed scissors, small curved forceps without teeth, hemostat, and dental cement.

PROCEDURE

First cut a square of Marlex mesh, round the edges, and cut a slit in the center through which the cannula can be placed. Cement the mesh to the center of the cannula with dental cement. The mesh provides an anchoring for the cannula since scar tissue formed at the point of incision will penetrate the holes of the mesh and secure it firmly.

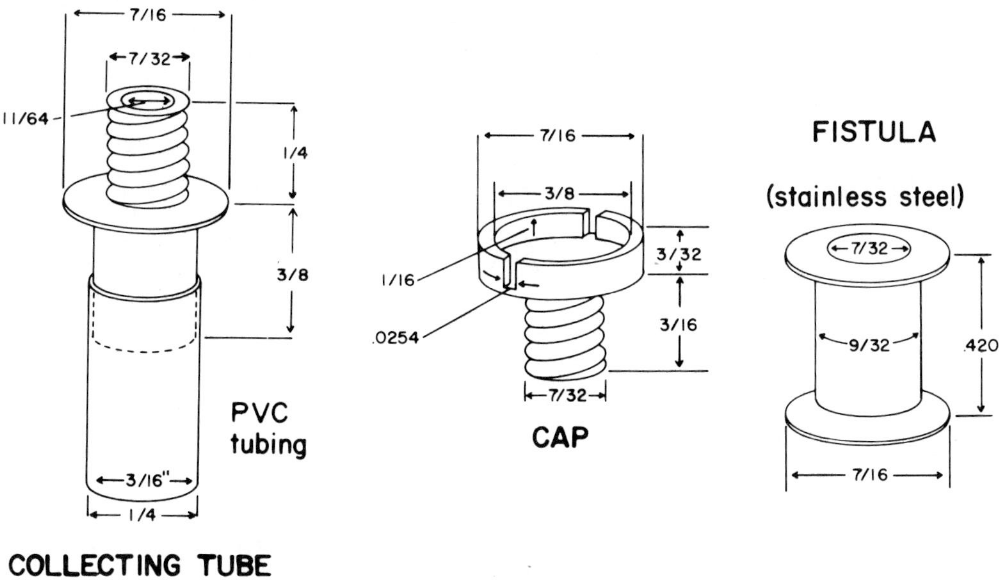

FIGURE 8.5. Dimensions for Cap, Fistula, and Collecting Tube of the Gastric Cannula. (All measurements in inches.)

Anesthetize the animal and shave the abdomen. Make a midline incision beginning approximately ¾-in. below the xiphosternum—the tip of cartilage in the center of the rib cage. Use fingers to spread apart the skin while cutting and take care not to cut the body wall beneath. Lift up on the body wall with forceps and make an incision with the sharp-pointed scissors, being careful not to cut any of the abdominal organs below. Gently deflect the lobes of the liver to locate the stomach deep within the abdominal cavity. Lift the stomach out of the abdominal cavity, being careful to keep it moist with isotonic saline throughout the remainder of the surgery. The stomach is anatomically divided into two distinct regions: (1) the cardiac region to the surgeon's right (the rat's left), which has a bluish cast and which distends to accommodate large volumes of food, and (2) the pyloric region to the surgeon's left (the rat's right), which has a yellowish cast and contains the secretory cells of the stomach and the muscles responsible for ejecting food to the duodenum through the pylorus. It is advisable to place the fistula in the cardiac portion so that the secretory and muscular apparatus are not impaired.

Locate the most ventral portion of the cardiac portion of the stomach. Find an area with relatively few blood vessels and construct a continuous circle (purse-string) of sutures (using the non-cutting needle) as with the duodenal fistula. Using the sharp-pointed scissors, make an incision in the center of the circle of stitches, being careful not to cut the thread (see Figure 8.4). Insert the fistula with the open end facing inward, pull the threads to form a tight fit around the fistula, and tie a knot. Make at least two more purse-string sutures around the fistula.

Place the stomach back in its normal position in the abdomen. (Notice where the fistula is located.) Grasp the body wall and skin with forceps, and, using a scalpel with a No. 10 blade, make an incision from *inside out* through the body wall and skin directly above the location of the fistula. Make one stab through these layers and withdraw the scalpel. With a pair of hemostats, reach from the outside in and clamp the top of the fistula. While holding the hemostat with the fistula in one hand, use a pair of forceps to thread the upper flange of the fistula through the hole. This is most easily done with movements similar to those for threading a tire on a wheel rim. No further closure of this opening is necessary. Spread out the netting smoothly over the surface of the stomach and return the lobes of the liver to their normal position. Close the original incision, first stitching the body wall and then the skin. Figure 8.6 illustrates the completed surgery. Give 0.2 cc of penicillin intramuscularly in each hind leg for postoperative prophylaxsis.

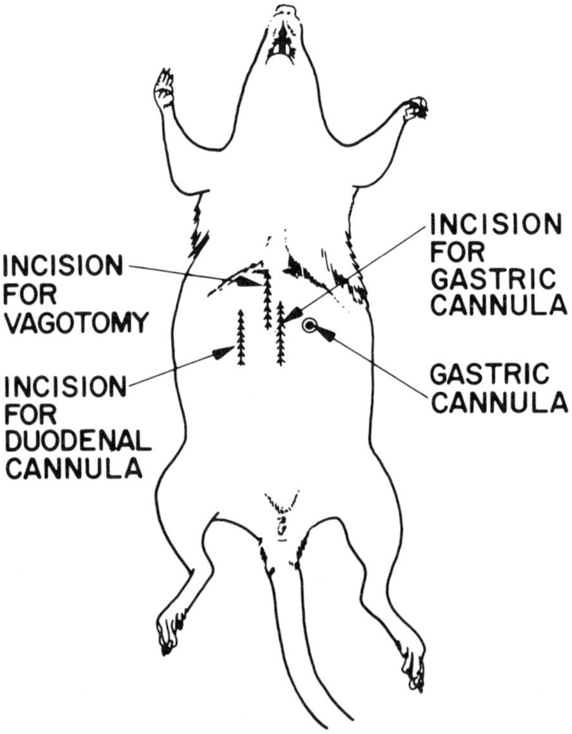

FIGURE 8.6. Position of the Body Wall Incision for Gastric Cannula and Final Position of the Cannula.

The animal should not be offered food or water until the day after surgery to allow time for the stomach incision to heal. The animal will be ready for experimental use four to five days later. The fistula will remain usable for up to six months if the animal is maintained on a solid diet. If liquid diets are used, leakage will develop in four to six weeks, rendering the preparation useless. Once leakage develops, the animal should be placed on a solid diet immediately, since the rapid loss of fluid from around the fistula may quickly lead to fatal dehydration.

Several uses have been made of the gastric fistula as described above. Settler and Smith (1969) and Snowdon (1970) used the fistula to measure gastric emptying time in chronic preparations. Snowdon equipped rats with gastric fistulas and intragastric tubes and injected a meal of fixed volume (5 cc) of various solutions into the stomach with the gastric fistula shut. After varying intervals of time, the fistula was opened and the stomach contents collected and the volume measured. Since dilution of the meal occurs with gastric secretions, it is also necessary to measure how much secretion has occurred. This is accomplished by adding a 0.04 percent solution of phenol red mixed in a 1:10 ratio with the test meal. When the test meal is removed from the stomach, it is centrifuged to spin down food particles and 1 cc of the supernatant is mixed with 9 cc of 1 M NaOH. This titrates the phenol red to the deep red it displays with a high pH. This solution is then placed in a colorimeter, and a reading of the optical density through a 540-nm filter is made. By comparing it with the standard curve and the optical density of the test meal before injection, one can evaluate the amount of gastric secretion that has occurred and the amount of the test meal that has emptied into the stomach by the following formulas:

1. [Dye concentration injected × volume injected] = [dye concentration recovered × volume recovered] + [dye concentration emptied × volume emptied] where dye concentration emptied = (dye concentration injected + dye concentration recovered)/2.
2. Volume injected + volume secreted = volume recovered + volume emptied.

For collecting accurate data on gastric emptying, the animals are deprived of food for 24 hours, the fistula is opened, and the stomach is washed thoroughly with distilled water. A connecting tube (see Figure 8.5) is force-fit with a piece of PVC tubing over it, and the PVC in turn is wrapped with a spiral of tinned copper wire for the first 4 in. to prevent the rat from chewing the tube attached to the fistula. Approximately 30 cc of distilled water is passed through the intragastric tube and collected from the fistula to ensure a clean stomach. After the stomach drains for two hours or more, it is ready for the test meal.

The animal is housed in a narrow chamber placed on a platform 10 to 12 in. above the table to allow the collecting tube to hang down. The dimensions of 12 × 3 × 15 in. are satisfactory. The floor should have a slot cut in it through which the collecting tube can hang.

Another use of the fistula is for meal removal. Snowdon (1970) waited until an animal had finished eating a meal, removed him from the cage, emptied out the stomach contents, and replaced the animal in the feeding situation. Normal rats quickly initiate a new meal in response to meal removal, but vagotomized rats (see below) do not. Davis and Campbell (1973) recently devised another type of fistula through which meal contents can be withdrawn during a meal without disrupting the animal. They found basically the same results as Snowdon (1970)—that is, meals are replaced rapidly.

Still another use of a cannula inserted in the stomach is to collect gastric secretions and determine their acidity. This has been used to show a correlation between the central neurological controls of feeding behavior and the mechanism that controls gastric secretion (Misher & Brooks, 1966). Another use of gastric secretion measurements is to verify the completeness of vagotomy, as described in the section on vagotomy.

VAGOTOMY

Although this section deals with a particular technique, some of the problems associated with it are common to all abdomenal denervation attempts. The vagus is one of three nerve sources for the stomach. The others are the sympathetic nerves, which pass through the coeliac plexus (ganglion) after coursing from the spinal cord and which branch from this plexus to cover all parts of the abdomenal viscera (McSwiney, 1931), and the visceral afferents, which appear to be direct afferent connections to the spinal cord (Hazarika, Coote, & Downman, 1964). Removing the vagus nerve thus denervates only part of the gastrointestinal tract. The vagus contains both sensory and motor nerves; thus its sectioning is likely to produce compound deficits that the experimenter must evaluate. Finally, the vagus does not always appear as a distinct collection of fibers. Lambert (1964) noted that the vagus often has branches running within the esophageal musculature and advises the surgeon to cut this musculature to be certain to eliminate the vagus. Unfortunately, this is advisable only for acute preparations. Rats appear to have impaired swallowing following damage to esophageal muscles and do not survive long.

The removal of all but 5 percent of the vagal fibers still permits the stomach to function normally (Burge & Vane, 1958); thus, an independent assessment of the completeness of the surgery is essential. Fortunately, one reliable technique exists. When small doses of insulin are injected, the chemical acts on the central nervous system, which then increases the rate of gastric secretion by means of impulses along the vagus nerve. This response is eliminated by a complete vagotomy (Hollander, 1946). With the gastric fistulation technique described above, one can test each putatively vagotomized rat for the gastric secretory response to insulin and confirm the success of the surgery. About 25 percent of the rats vagotomized by the procedure described below failed to show the abolition of the gastric secretory response. These rats were subsequently shown to have traces of the vagus nerve intact (Snowdon & Epstein, 1970).

One of the symptoms that develops as a result of the vagotomy is that the vagotomized animal eats small and frequent meals, although normal daily food intake is the same. This symptom appears only when rats are placed on a liquid diet. This may be a convenient "behavioral bioassay" of the completeness of vagotomy, but it cannot substitute for the use of the gastric secretory test in confirming the completeness of vagotomy.

Materials

Materials needed are:

1. A low-power binocular dissecting microscope (optional) or large magnifying glass that can be clamped to the table
2. Three pairs of curved, blunt-tipped, 4-in. forceps
3. One pair of sharp-pointed, 4-in. scissors
4. A scalpel, needle, thread, and hemostat
5. Angled microdissection scissors (Aloe Instruments).

Procedure

First, shave the abdomen; then with the scalpel blade make a 1 to 1½-in. incision on the midline of the abdomen, beginning at the posterior edge of the xiphosternum. With the forceps carefully lift up the abdominal wall, and use scissors to make an incision through the body wall, being careful not to damage any of the organs beneath. The liver will be exposed, and when the lobes are deflected to the side, the stomach will be exposed. Note the dividing line between the pyloric and cardiac portions of the stomach. When this line is followed toward the top of the stomach, it leads directly to the entrance of the esophagus buried below the liver (see Figure 8.4).

Carefully slide one pair of curved forceps under the esophagus and lift it out of the body cavity. Use this pair of forceps as a brace to hold the esophagus up out of the body cavity by placing the tips on one side and the handle on the other side of the incision. Be certain to keep the esophagus moist with isotonic saline throughout the operation.

The gastric artery and vein are located in a sheath on the underside of the esophagus; they can readily be discriminated by observing the pulsatile action of the artery. With a second pair of curved forceps, separate the sheath from the esophagus by carefully inserting the closed tips of the forceps through the connective tissue between the esophagus and the sheath and then slowly spreading the tips of the forceps. Continue this until the artery and vein are separated from the esophagus for a distance of 1 in. or more. Place the forceps that are being used to hold the esophagus in place between the esophagus and the sheath. The sheath should drop back into the abdominal cavity and only the esophagus should remain elevated as shown in Figure 8.7.

The vagi should be visible now as two thin whitish trunks running along the esophagus. One trunk runs along the left side (surgeon's left) and top of the esophagus, and the other on the right side and somewhat underneath the esophagus. The vagi are the only continuous white sheaths that run along the esophagus at this point. Other white threads in the area are strands of connective

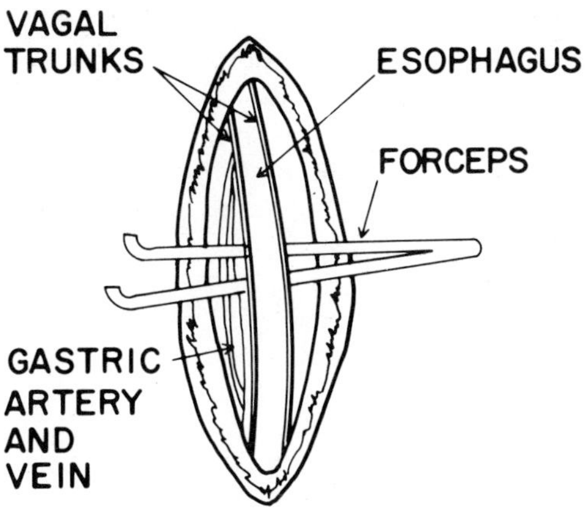

FIGURE 8.7. The Esophagus with Forceps as a Prop for the Esophagus, the Sheath Containing Gastric Artery and Vein, and Vagal Trunks.

tissue. Although the vagus fits this description, generally one should be prepared for a wide degree of variability between animals.

With a pair of curved forceps, nudge the closed ends between the left vagus and esophagus. Gently spread the forceps open. Separate approximately ½ in. of the vagus this way; then lift up the nerve with the forceps and cut off a piece of vagus ¼-in. long with the microdissecting scissors. Do the same with the right vagus; then gently strip away any other whitish sheaths along the esophageal surface, since the vagus may have divided into several small trunks in a particular animal. Be extremely careful not to damage the esophageal musculature in any way. Damage will impair swallowing and lead to eventual death of the animal.

With two pairs of curved forceps, gently roll the esophagus back and forth along the edge of the forceps on which the esophagus rests. This will allow one to examine all sides of the esophagus for traces of nerve. When the esophagus appears to be cleared of nerve, check again with a dissection microscope or magnifying lens. Then remove the forceps supporting the esophagus and let the esophagus fall back in place in the abdominal cavity. Replace the liver lobes, being careful not to damage them with the forceps. Sew the body wall closed, and then sew the skin closed.

The animal will recover best if it is placed on a liquid diet for a few days but will then eat normally on a solid diet, provided that the esophageal musculature has not been damaged. When experimentation is completed, install a gastric fistula as described above. When the animal has recovered from fistula surgery, deprive it of food for 24 hours. Wash the stomach thoroughly with warm distilled water and attach a collecting tube to the fistula.

Place the animal in a cage (12 × 3 × 15 in. with a slotted floor on a pedestal 10 to 12 in. above table height is sufficient). After the stomach has drained for 1 to 2 hours, inject the animal subcutaneously at the base of the tail with 1 U/kg of regular insulin (Iletin). Do not use the slower acting protamine zinc suspension. A microliter syringe will be needed since 8 to 12 μl will be injected. Alternatively, one can dilute the insulin with sterile isotonic saline on a 1:100 ratio and inject a larger volume with a 1-cc syringe. Collect the gastric secretions over the next 4 hours, recording the volume secreted. Either add 3 to 4 drops of phenol red solution or use a pH meter and titrate with a solution of 0.05 M NaOH until the phenol red changes color or the pH meter reads 7.0. One can compute the number of milliequivalents of H^+ ions present by knowing the number of OH^- ions needed to titrate the solution to neutrality. One milliequivalent of H^+ would be equal to 1 ml of 1 M NaOH. Since 0.05 M NaOH is used, 20 ml of NaOH are required to equal a milliequivalent. However, since fewer than 20 ml will titrate the solution to acidity, microequivalents are a better unit. One microequivalent is 0.001 of 20 ml of 0.05 M NaOH or 0.02 ml. The most accurate measurement possible would be to 0.2 ml or 10 microequivalents. An animal with an intact vagus always produces more than 250 microequivalents per 4 hours in response to insulin and usually less than this in response to a similar volume of isotonic saline. Vagotomized rats should give values below 250 microequivalents per 4 hours in response to both insulin and saline. After one day's testing, allow two to three days before depriving the animal for the saline test. If the animal does not respond to insulin with increased gastric secretion, it is likely to be successfully vagotomized (Snowdon & Epstein, 1970).

REFERENCES

Adair, E. R., Miller, N. E., and Booth, D. A. Effects of continuous intravenous infusion of nutritive substances in consummatory behavior in rats. *Communications in Behavioral Biology,* 1968, **2,** 25–37.

Balagura, S., and Coscina, D. V. Influence of gastrointestinal loads on meal eating patterns. *Journal of Comparative and Physiological Psychology,* 1969, **69,** 101–106.

Beaumont, W. *Experiments and observations on the gastric juice and the physiology of digestion.* New York: Dover Publications, 1833.

Burge, H., and Vane, J. R. Method of testing for complete nerve section during vagotomy. *British Medical Journal,* 1958, Part 1, 615–618.

Corbit, J. D. Effects of intravenous sodium chloride on drinking in the rat. *Journal of Comparative and Physiological Psychology,* 1965, **60,** 397–406.

Davis, J. D., and Campbell, C. S. Peripheral control of meal size in the rat: Effect of sham feeding on meal size and drinking rates. *Journal of Comparative and Physiological Psychology,* 1973, **83,** 379–387.

Ehman, G. K., Albert, D. J., and Jamieson, J. L. Injections into the duodenum and the induction of satiety in the rat. *Canadian Journal of Psychology,* 1971, **25,** 147–166.

Epstein, A. N. Water intake without the act of drinking. *Science,* 1960, **131,** 497–498.

Epstein, A. N. Feeding without oropharyngeal sensations. In M. R. Kare and O. Maller (Eds.), *The chemical senses and nutrition.* Baltimore: The Johns Hopkins Press, 1967.

Epstein, A. N., and Teitelbaum, P. A watertight swivel joint permitting chronic injection into moving animals. *Journal of Applied Physiology,* 1962, **17,** 171–172. (a)

Epstein, A. N., and Teitelbaum, P. Regulation of food intake in the absence of taste, smell, and other oropharyngeal sensations. *Journal of Comparative and Physiological Psychology,* 1962, **55,** 753–759. (b)

Greene, E. C., *Anatomy of the rat.* New York: Hafner, 1935.

Greenstein, J. P., Otey, M. C., Birnbaum, S. M., and Winitz, W. Quantitative nutritional studies with water-soluble chemically defined diets. *Journal of the National Cancer Institute,* 1960, **24,** 211–219.

Hazarika, N. H., Coote, J., and Downman, C. B. B. Gastrointestinal dorsal root viscerotomes in the cat. *Journal of Neurophysiology,* 1964, **28,** 107–116.

Hollander, F. The insulin test for the presence of intact nerve fibers after vagal operations for peptic ulcers *Gastroenterology,* 1946, **7,** 607–614.

Lambert, R. *Surgery of the digestive system of the rat.* Springfield, Ill.: Charles C Thomas, 1964.

McGinty, D., Epstein, A. N., and Teitelbaum, P. The contribution of oropharyngeal sensations to hypothalamic hyperphagia. *Animal Behaviour,* 1964, **13,** 413–418.

McSwiney, B. A. Innervation of the stomach, *Physiological Reviews,* 1931, **11,** 478–514.

Misher, A., and Brooks, F. P. Electrical stimulation of hypothalamus and gastric secretion in the albino rat. *American Journal of Physiology,* 1966, **211,** 403–406.

Quartermain, D., Kissileff, H., Shapiro, R., and Miller, N. E. Suppression of food intake with intragastric loading: Relation to natural feeding cycle. *Science,* 1971, **173,** 941–943.

Rodgers, W. L., Epstein, A. N., and Teitelbaum, P. Lateral hypothalamic aphagia: Motor failure or motivational deficit? *American Journal of Physiology,* 1965, **208,** 334–342.

Settler, P. E., and Smith, G. P. Gastric emptying in rats with chronic gastric fistulas. *American Journal of Digestive Diseases,* 1969, **14** (new series), 137–142.

Snowdon, C. T. Motivation, regulation and the control of meal parameters with oral and intragastric feeding. *Journal of Comparative and Physiological Psychology,* 1969, **69,** 91–100.

Snowdon, C. T. Gastrointestinal sensory and motor control of food intake. *Journal of Comparative and Physiological Psychology,* 1970, **71,** 68–76.

Snowdon, C. T. Production of satiety with small intraduodenal injections in the rat. *Journal of Comparative and Physiological Psychology,* 1974, in press.

Snowdon, C. T., and Epstein, A. N. Oral and intragastric feeding in vagotomized rats. *Journal of Comparative and Physiological Psychology,* 1970, **71,** 59–67.

Thomas, D. W., and Mayer, J. Meal taking and the regulation of food intake by normal and hypothalamic hyperphagic rats. *Journal of Comparative and Physiological Psychology,* 1968, **66,** 642–653.

CHAPTER 9

Chronic Intrajugular, Intraportal, Gastric, and Duodenal Cannulae for the Rat

John D. Davis and Constance S. Campbell
UNIVERSITY OF ILLINOIS AT CHICAGO CIRCLE

INTRODUCTION

The chronic cannulation of veins has proven to be a valuable technique for studying physiological processes that underlie behavior and for studying problems of drug dependence. Venous cannulae have been used in the study of the role that humoral factors play in the control of feeding (Davis et al., 1969) and maternal behavior (Terkel & Rosenblatt, 1972); for obtaining relatively large blood samples without disturbing the animal (Steffans, 1969); for obtaining serial blood samples (Beattie et al., 1973); for infusing chemicals (Smith, 1966) and chemically defined diets (Adair et al., 1968) in the study of feeding behavior; and in the study of drug dependence through self-administration of morphine (Weeks, 1962), barbiturates (Davis et al., 1968), and other drugs. Since the construction and surgical implantation of such cannulae require a minimum of experience and skill, it is likely that their use will continue to grow and be adapted to the study of an even greater variety of problems.

The construction and surgical implantation of jugular and portal vein cannulae present different problems; therefore, they are described separately in the material that follows.

INTRAJUGULAR CANNULAE

Construction

In principle, cannulae can be constructed from polyethylene, Teflon,® silicone rubber, or any other nontoxic tubing, but in practice the authors have found that a length of polyethylene tube joined to a shorter length of silicone rubber tubing offers some particular advantages. The silicone rubber portion, which is threaded into the vein, is flexible and can therefore be passed around bends in the vascular system without causing damage to the inner walls of the veins. It has been described by the manufacturers as having a particularly low tendency to promote blood clotting, but, in the authors' experience, silicone rubber and polyethylene tubing seem to be equal in this respect. The major advantage of this kind of construction is when the cannula is to be used for infusion only. With silicone rubber (but not with polyethylene), the intravascular portion of the cannula can easily be made into a one-way valve that eliminates the major source of cannula failure—blood clots in the end of the cannula. The polyethylene portion, which is threaded under the skin to its point of exit from the body, is more rigid than silicone. This is particularly important if the cannula is to be used for withdrawal, since if there are any bends in silicone tubing, it tends to collapse at that point and prevent further withdrawal. This feature of polyethylene and the fact that it is less easily punctured than silicone make it more resistant to damage and leakage. It is also easier to connect polyethylene tubing firmly to a hypodermic needle than silicone rubber tubing, especially when small-diameter tubing is used.

The first step in construction is to join a 30-mm length of silicone rubber tubing to a 20-cm length of polyethylene tubing. The tubing diameters should be selected so that the inside diameter of the silicone rubber tubing is equal to or slightly smaller than the outside diameter of the polyethylene tubing. For infusion cannulae, the appropriate sizes are Dow Corning's Silastic 602–101 (0.012-in. i.d., 0.025-in. o.d.) and Clay-Adam's Intramedic PE 10 (0.011-in. i.d., 0.024-in. o.d.). For withdrawal, where slightly larger cannulae are required to provide greater flow rates, Silastic 602–151 (0.025-in. i.d., 0.047-in. o.d., Dow Corning) should be joined to Intramedic PE 60 (0.030-in. i.d., 0.048-in. o.d., Clay-Adam). A firm and simple junction between these two can be achieved by first soaking one end of the silicone rubber tubing for 1 to 2 min in chloroform or trichlorethylene. This soaking softens and expands the tube so that it can easily be slipped over the polyethylene tube. In order to make a firm slip-proof junction, one end of the polyethylene tube is flaired slightly by holding the end near the flame of a match or a hot soldering iron. When cool, the flaired end is inserted into the softened and expanded silicone rubber tube. The tube should then be thoroughly flushed with water. When dry, the firm junction between the two tubes will resist any forces that are likely to be encountered in the normal use of the cannula.

Next a "U" curve is made in the polyethylene portion as illustrated in Figure 9.1. This is done by gently holding the polyethylene tube in the desired shape with forceps and lowering the curve briefly into water that is almost at the boiling point. The tube is then quickly immersed in a beaker of cold water. The hot water softens the plastic, permitting it to assume the shape in which it is held, while the cold water sets the bend. When this step is completed, two silk threads are tied firmly around the cannula at the places illustrated in Figure 9.1. A slight indentation on the silicone rubber and polyethylene shows that the threads are tied firmly enough to prevent slipping.

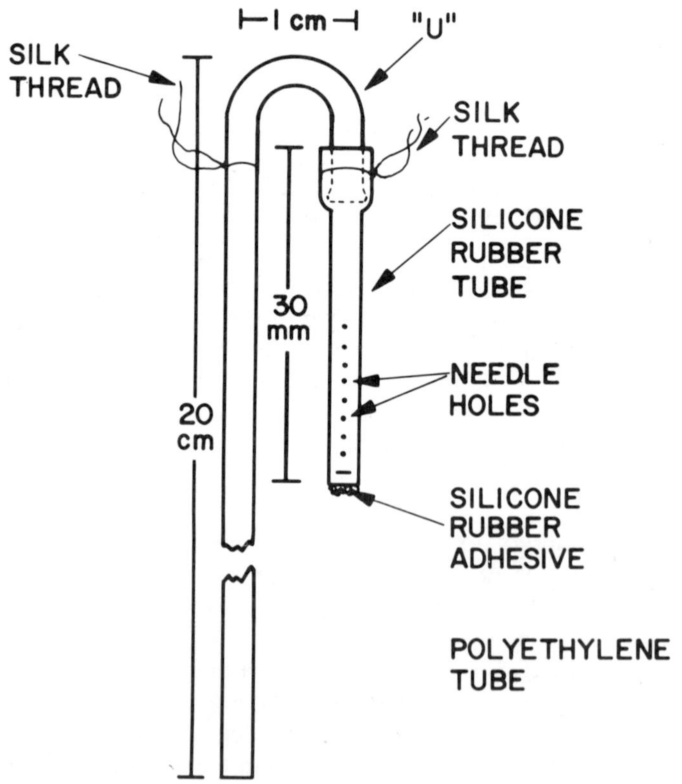

FIGURE 9.1. Diagram of the Completed Jugular Vein Cannula. (Details of construction are described in the text.)

At this stage, the cannulae should be thoroughly cleaned by soaking them in warm soapy water (Ivory Flakes is recommended by Dow Corning, the manufacturer of Silastic). They should then be thoroughly rinsed in distilled water. Since these cannulae cannot be autoclaved (the polyethylene will expand and become deformed), they should be stored in a dilute Zepharin solution (1:1000) to keep them sterile until they are used. Before they are implanted in the animal, the cannula should be thoroughly cleaned and flushed with sterile normal saline. If any Zepharin is left on the cannula, it can cause tissue reactions and infection sites.

If the cannula is to be used for infusion only, the construction of a one-way valve at the tip will prevent blood from entering the cannula and greatly prolong its useful life. This is done by filling the silicone rubber tip to the cannula a distance of about 1 mm with Silastic medical grade adhesive (Dow Corning). The adhesive should then be permitted to cure for 24 hours. The cannula is then placed on a soft surface, and a straight noncutting-edge needle is used to make a series of five or six holes along the length of the tube. The needle should penetrate both walls of the tube but should not be allowed to tear the tube. When the needle is removed, the holes should not be visible. The effect of this is to make pores in the end of the cannula that will open and allow fluid to pass out of the cannula when pressure is applied during infusion but will close when the pressure is reduced. The effectiveness of this valve should be tested before implantation by injecting normal saline through the cannula. If the holes have been properly made, small bubbles of fluid will appear where the tube has been punctured as pressure is applied to the injection syringe. If excessive pressure is required to force fluid through the cannula, more holes should be made.

The authors have encountered only one problem in the use of this one-way valve. The cannula becomes unusable if a solution crystalizes, becomes highly viscous in the tip of the cannula,

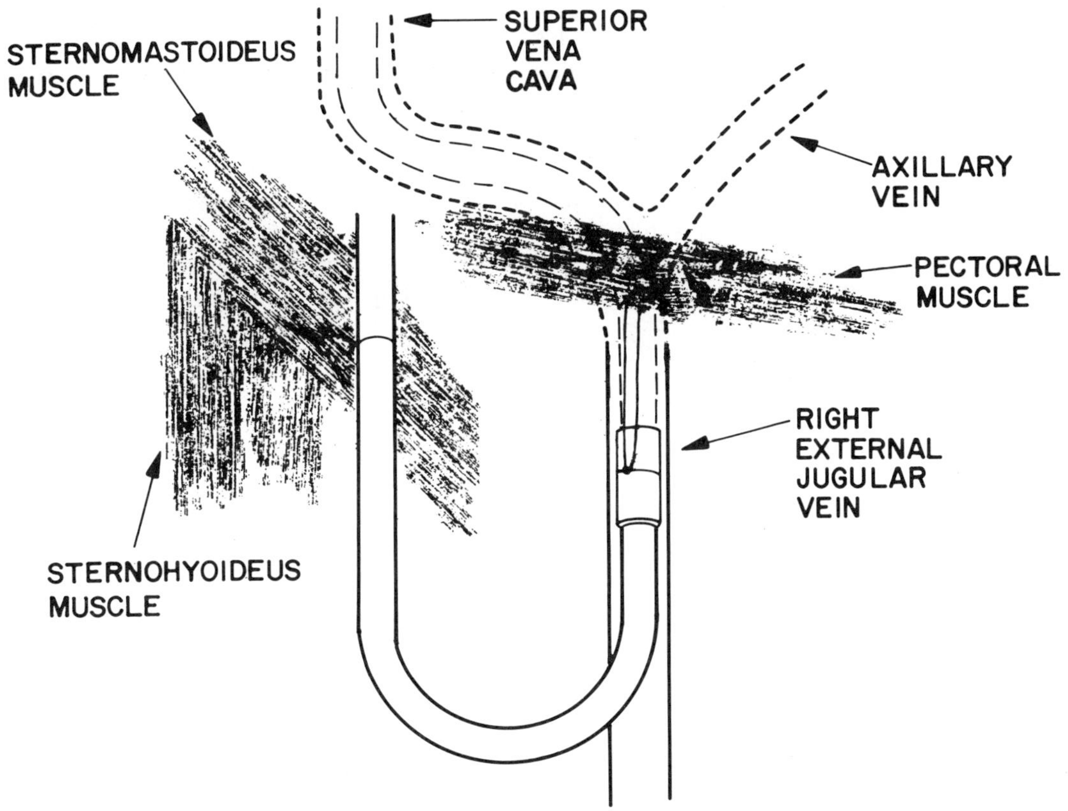

FIGURE 9.2. Schematic of the Position of the Cannula in the Jugular Vein. The muscles used for anchoring the cannula in place are shown as shaded areas.

or if foreign matter accumulates there. These situations effectively prevent the injected solution from passing through the pores. This can be prevented by thoroughly flushing the cannula after use with normal saline or some other nontoxic fluid that does not react with the experimental solution to produce a viscous solution or crystalization. All solutions injected intravenously should naturally be sterile and free of foreign matter, which can easily be achieved by passing solutions through a Millipore filter before they are used.

Surgery

The animal is anesthetized with pentobarbital, and the hair on the ventral neck region to the right of the midline and over the scapulae on the back of the animal is shaved. The shaved areas are then thoroughly cleaned with a disinfectant. A paramidline incision is made beginning just behind the anteriolateral margin of the pectoral muscle and extending about 1.5 cm rostrally. (This incision should barely penetrate the skin.) From this point on, only blunt dissection should be used. The subcutaneous tissue is separated until the right external jugular vein and the sternohyoid muscle are exposed. The subcutaneous tissue should then be separated as completely as possible from the muscle layer—on the animals' left side to just past the midline, on the right about 1 cm beyond the jugular vein, and from the pectoral muscle about 3 cm in an anterior direction. This will provide an open area in which the "U" portion of the cannula will later lie.

The vein must then be dissected free of all surrounding tissue for a distance of about 8 mm. It is essential at this stage to remove all tissue surrounding the vein. Otherwise, great difficulty will be encountered later in trying to insert the cannula. The animal is then turned over, and a 1-cm long incision is made on the back over the scapulae. The cannula is next attached to a trocar that is threaded under the skin beginning on the midline just over the clavicle. It should pass straight back in a posterior direction, following the line of the sternebra a distance of about 3 to 4 cm. Then it should be turned at a right angle and passed along the side of the animal to emerge through the incision over the scapulae. The trocar is then drawn out, bringing the end of the cannula with it.

The cannula is filled with normal saline, the animal is placed on its back, and the cannula is adjusted to approximately its terminal position. A small hole is then made in the vein with the point of a noncutting-edge needle. This step is greatly facilitated by placing a small diameter stainless steel rod under the vein and raising it in such a way as to stop the flow of blood. One should make certain at this point that the needle has completely penetrated all muscle layers of the vein. Closed needlepoint forceps are then inserted into the hole in the vein, and the cannula is held in the tips of another forceps. As the forceps in the vein are allowed to open slightly, the cannula is passed between their blades into the lumen of the vein.

This step is the most difficult part of the operation and requires considerable practice. In learning this step, one should practice with a small diameter polyethylene tube with a beveled end (for example, PE 10).

If the tube is inserted into the lumen of the vein, it can easily be pushed down to the heart. If any resistance is encountered, either the cannula has been inserted between two muscle layers of the vein, which is surprisingly easy, or it has entered the axillary vein rather than the superior vena cava. If the former has occurred, it is necessary to remove the cannula entirely from the vein, make a new hole, and reinsert it. If it has entered the axillary vein, it should be withdrawn until the tip is anterior to the anterior margin of the pectoral muscle but still inside the vein. Then it should be moved with the vein as far laterally as possible so that when it is pushed toward the heart, the tip is angled toward the midline of the body.

When the cannula has been inserted properly, it is pushed down the vein to the silicone rubber/polyethylene junction and the "U" portion of the polyethylene is laid under the skin. At this point with withdrawal cannulae, blood should be withdrawn into the cannula to be sure that it flows easily. The blood should then be flushed out with saline. One end of the thread tied at the junction is attached to a needle that is passed through the anterior margin of the pectoral muscle. The free end of the thread is then tied in a loose loop to the pectoral muscle. The function of this anchor is to prevent the cannula from backing out of the vein. There should be some slack in the threads when tied, but not enough to allow the cannula to move out of the vein more than 1 to 2 mm. The threads opposite these should then be tied to the sternohyoid muscle on the midline to form a second anchor point. The final position is illustrated in Figure 9.2. The incision is then closed by the conventional suturing procedures.

Postoperative Care and Maintenance of the Cannula

With cannulae designed for blood withdrawal and any other cannulae that do not have a one-way valve, it is necessary to keep blood from clotting in the lumen of the cannula when it is not in use. One technique is to fill the cannula with Heparin (1000 units per ml). The cannula is then sealed by holding the tip near a match flame until the plastic begins to melt and clamping it briefly with forceps or by inserting a small stainless steel wire plug in the end. The major difficulty with these precautions is that if the plug comes out or the heat seal is not perfect the Heparin will drain into the vein. A more satisfactory solution devised by Steffans (1969) is to fill the cannula with a mixture of polyvinylpyrrolidone (PVP) and Heparin (8 g PVP to 10 ml Heparin, 1000 units per ml). This is a viscous solution that will not be pumped into the vein by heart action but one that can easily be withdrawn before use. It should be made up at least 24 hours before use to permit the air bubbles that develop during mixing to dissipate from the solution.

With cannulae that have a one-way valve, these precautions are not necessary since blood cannot enter the venous end of the cannula. However, it is important to keep foreign matter out of the cannula. If unfiltered solutions are used, foreign matter can collect at the end of the cannula and will eventually occlude the pores, preventing further use. A small stainless steel plug inserted in the end of the cannula will keep dust and dirt out of it.

INTRAPORTAL CANNULAE

In cases where it is desirable to inject a substance to produce a known concentration in a specific target organ, intrajugular injection may not be suitable. By the time that the injected substance has reached the target organ, it may have been diluted or have been subjected to homeostatic adjustments that make concentration at the target organ difficult or impossible to estimate. In these cases, cannulae must be placed in the vessels that lead directly to the organ of interest. In many cases, the intrajugular cannula described in the preceding section can be adapted to vessels other than the jugular vein. In some cases, however, because of differing morphological features among the blood vessels of the body, a different approach must be used. The portal system of the rat is a good example.

The portal vein contains only longitudinal muscle fibers and a limited number of circular fibers (Bradley, 1963). It is therefore much more delicate than the jugular vein and is more likely to be damaged and to leak at the point where the cannula enters the vein. Furthermore, no suitable muscles surround this vein to which the cannula can be attached for support. Therefore, a cannula specifically designed for the portal system was developed for an investigation of the role that the liver plays in the control of feeding behavior (Campbell & Davis, 1974).

Portal cannulae have been developed for larger animals (Bessman, Magnes, Schwerin, & Waelsch, 1948; Jungblut, Lohmann, Schober, & Turba, 1955), but the authors are aware of only one preparation for the rat (it came to their attention after development of the cannula described below). The rat portal cannula described by Aziz et al. (1964) is a complex, but easily implanted cannula made of steel, polyethylene, and PVC tubing. They report that their cannula remains patent for as long as five weeks. The preparation described here has remained operative for up to three months, is easily constructed and implanted, and can be used for long-term infusion in freely moving animals.

Cannula Construction

The cannula consists of lengths of silicone rubber and polyethylene joined together. The intravascular portion is silicone rubber. This part is joined to a short length of polyethylene tubing permanently formed into a "U," which in turn is connected to flexible silicone rubber tubing that ends in another short length of polyethylene.

The first step is to cut two lengths of silicone rubber tubing (Silastic 602–101, 0.012-in. i.d., 0.025-in. o.d., Dow Corning), one 2 cm long, the other 15 cm long, and two lengths of polyethylene tubing (Becton-Dickinson PX-014, 0.014-in. i.d., 0.034-in. o.d.), one 3.5 cm long, the other 1 cm long. The longer polyethylene tubing is beveled on both ends, the shorter one on only one end. The longer polyethylene tubing is formed into a "U" by holding it with forceps in the desired form and immersing it briefly in nearly boiling water, then dipping it quickly in cold water to set the bend. The shape of the bend is illustrated in Figure 9.3. One end of both the longer and the shorter silicone rubber tubing is then soaked for 1 to 2 min in chloroform or trichloroethylene to soften and expand it and is then fitted onto the polyethylene tubing as illustrated in Figure 9.3.

When the junctions are made, silk threads are tied securely around them both to reinforce the junctions and to anchor the cannula in the body. A fourth silk thread is tied loosely around

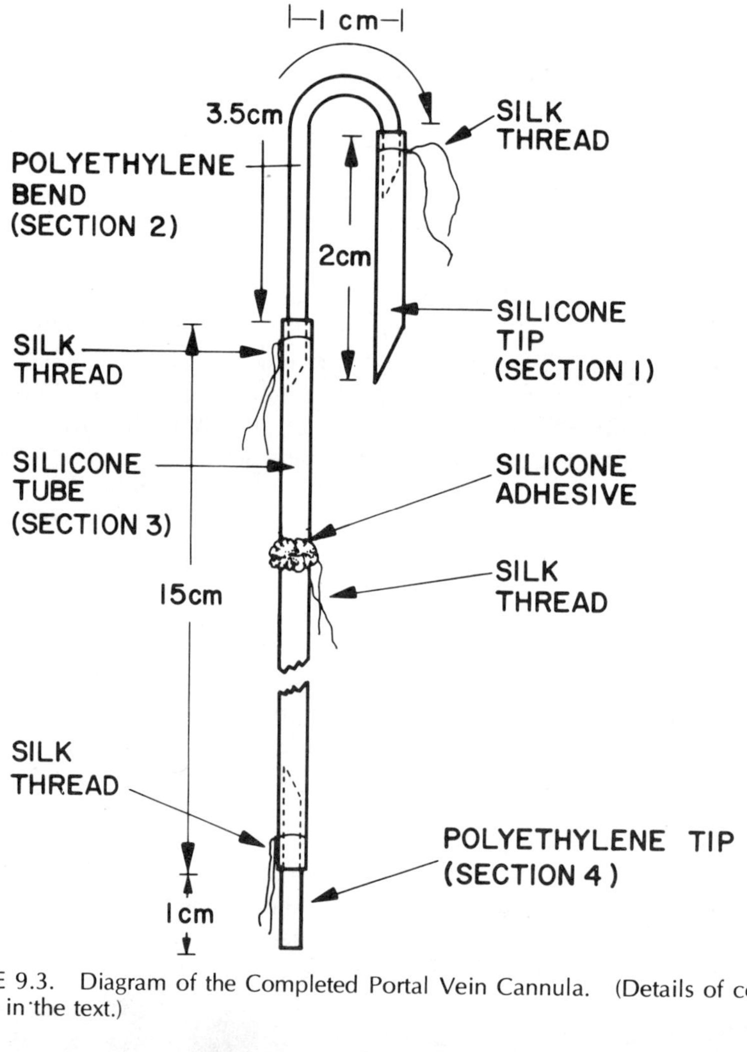

FIGURE 9.3. Diagram of the Completed Portal Vein Cannula. (Details of construction are described in the text.)

the silicone tubing about 2.5 cm from its junction with the "U"-shaped polyethylene tubing and anchored with silicone rubber adhesive. Finally, the silicone rubber intravascular tip is cut on a bevel to facilitate its insertion into the vein. The cannula should be washed in warm soapy water and throughly rinsed in distilled water. The cannula cannot be autoclaved, but it should be sterilized by soaking it in a Zepharin solution (1:1000) for at least 24 hours before use. Before implanting, it should be thoroughly rinsed in sterile normal saline to remove all traces of Zepharin.

Pedestal Construction

A pedestal design developed for several chronic cannulae is used in this preparation. This pedestal consists of an L-shaped piece of 26-gauge needle tubing, a sleeve of silicone tubing, and a 2 cm by 2 cm square of Fiberglas screen attached to the silicone-encased needle tubing with silicone adhesive. In addition, a piece of polyethylene tubing of the same size used for the cannula should be attached tightly to the needle tubing that protrudes from the animal's back. Since this tubing fits a 26-gauge needle so well, it greatly facilitates infusions.

Surgery

The animal is anesthetized, and a ventral incision is made across the midline, caudal to the ribs. To expose the portal vein, most of the small intestine is pulled carefully to the right out of the abdominal cavity. While it is out of the body, the viscera should be kept moist by covering it with gauze pads soaked in normal saline. The duodenum is then pulled to the right to expose its dorsal surface and the portal vein. The mesenteric vein of the portal system should then be clearly visible, from where it emerges posteriorly through pancreatic tissue near the duodenum to its termination at the liver.

The portal vein must at this time be isolated from its surrounding tissue at two locations. This must be done with extreme care because (1) the portal vein rests in pancreatic tissue that should not be damaged, (2) many easily damaged veins of varying sizes that are difficult to see join the portal in this area, and (3) the portal vein itself is fragile and easily punctured. All work in this area should accordingly be done by blunt dissection, avoiding the use of pointed instruments. Just anterior to where the superior mesenteric vein emerges from pancreatic tissue, it is joined by other tributaries and becomes the portal vein. There the vein should be separated from surrounding tissue, and the surface of the vein should be stripped of connective tissue. About 2 cm farther up the portal toward the liver, just anterior to the junction of the portal and the pyloric vein coming in from the animal's left, the vein should be separated from surrounding tissue but not stripped.

Next, a 2- to 3-mm stainless steel rod should be slipped under the vein where it first emerges from pancreatic tissue. By raising this rod, it can be used to stem blood flow in the portal temporarily if there is excessive bleeding from the hole into which the cannula is inserted. However, the blood flow must not be cut off for extended periods of time because this will cause the animal to go into shock and severely endanger its life. In addition, this can increase the chances of clotting in the vein around the cannula.

When the trocar is in place and the cannula is filled with normal saline, a tiny hole is made in the vein at the location of the trocar with a round intestinal needle. The cannula can then be slipped into the hole and inserted into the vein to the beginning of the polyethylene section of the cannula. The vein should be examined carefully to ensure that the cannula remains within the portal and does not branch off into one of its tributaries. If this occurs, the cannula should be pulled back slightly and reinserted along the correct vein. The presence of the cannula junction at the point of insertion should reduce bleeding. Loosely tying the sutures that are attached to this junction around the vein will secure its placement. The sutures must not constrict the vein to any extent.

The second set of sutures around the second junction should be tied loosely around the vein at the anterior location where it has been separated from its surrounding tissue. Throughout these procedures and until the operation is completed, the cannula should be flushed with physiological saline to prevent clotting at the tip. The third set of sutures, which are attached to the silicone section of the cannula, should be loosely tied to the underlying muscle of the rib cage around the midline. This should bring the cannula in a ventral, then posterior direction back to the abdominal incision and should anchor the cannula so that it is not pulled out by normal body movements. The incision can then be closed with the cannula emerging through it. The final position is illustrated in Figure 9.4.

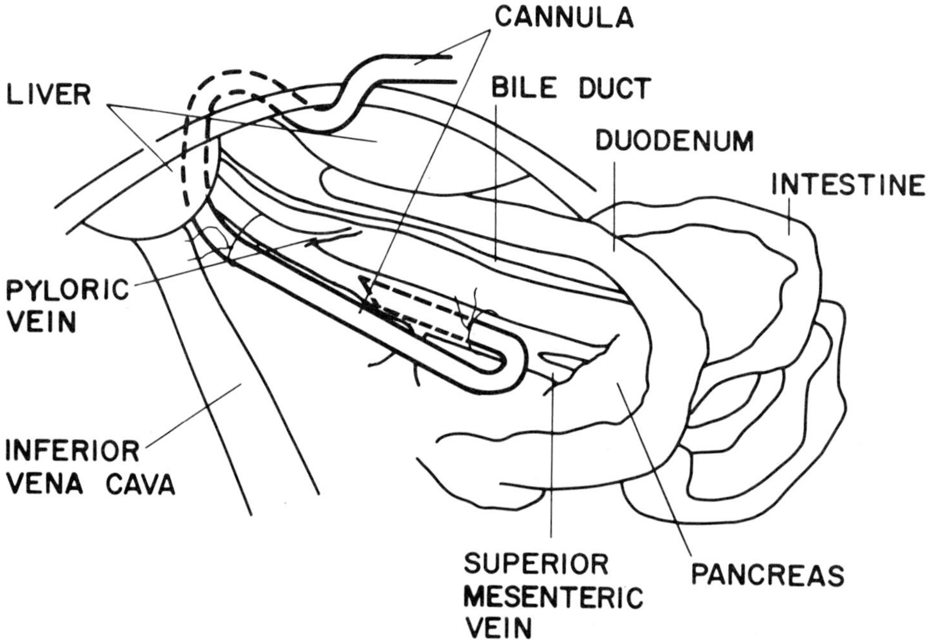

FIGURE 9.4. Schematic of the Position of the Portal Vein Cannula Immediately After Insertion and with the Duodenum and Small Intestine Deflected to Expose the Superior Mesenteric Vein.

The final step is to make an incision on the midline over the scapulae for the pedestal. An area surrounding the incision is blunt dissected, and hemostats are passed between the skin and muscle layers of the back of the midline and around the side to the abdominal incision. The cannula is grasped gently and pulled back under the skin to emerge through the dorsal incision. The polyethylene end is pushed onto the needle tubing of the pedestal and secured to it with sutures. It is imperative that this junction is tight and leakproof. The incisions are closed using conventional procedures.

Postoperative Care and Maintenance of the Cannula

The animals have usually recovered within 24 to 48 hours after surgery, unless a considerable amount of blood has been lost. There is no indication that the presence of the cannula impairs the animals' health, although infusions appear to cause changes in the respiratory rate.

To prevent clotting, the cannula should be filled with a mixture of PVP, saline, and Heparin (4 g PVP, 10 ml physiological saline, 1000 ml Heparin). This mixture is viscous enough to prevent blood from diffusing into the cannula but is too viscous to be pulled into the vein by heart action. However, it can be infused into the animal in small quantities without causing damage. During an infusion, the PVP mixture in the cannula is pushed into the vein with the injected solution, and the cannula is refilled with the PVP mixture to keep it patent. The cannula can be stoppered with a stainless steel plug if desired, but it is not always necessary.

If the cannula is to be used for withdrawal of blood from the vein, a larger diameter silicone (Silastic 602–151, .047-in. o.d., .025-in. i.d., Dow Corning) and polyethylene (Intramedic PE 60, .048-in. o.d., .030-in. i.d., Clay-Adams) tubing should be used, as well as a larger needle tubing in the pedestal (21 gauge). However, larger tubing has a greater tendency to cause clotting and stoppage of blood flow in the portal vein; thus, this cannula cannot be expected to remain patent as long as the smaller one.

As with all vascular cannulae, only sterile and preferably solutions passed through a Millipore filter should be infused. Care must be taken to prevent air from being injected along with the solution.

GASTRIC CANNULAE

A cannula implantation technique described by Epstein and Teitelbaum (1962) has been used extensively by a number of investigators to study the ability of the rat to regulate food intake in the absence of oropharyngeal stimulation (Epstein, 1967; Snowdon & Epstein, 1970). This cannula is relatively easy to implant surgically and has the particular advantage of avoiding surgical intervention of the stomach. Its major limitation is that small diameter tubing must be used to permit it to pass through the nasal cavity and esophagus without producing obstruction. This effectively prevents rapid injection of viscous solutions or sampling of all but the most dilute solutions in the stomach. The cannula described here was specifically designed to permit aspiration of the stomach of the rat without handling the animal or otherwise disturbing it (Davis & Campbell, 1973). It can be used also as an alternative to the Epstein technique when it is desirable to inject viscous solutions rapidly that would pass slowly or not at all through a small diameter tube.

Cannula Construction

For purposes of withdrawal, the cannula is constructed of flexible silicone rubber tubing (Meditube ST 212, Extracorporeal Medical Specialties, Inc.) with a relatively large diameter (0.048-in. i.d., 0.100-in. o.d.). The large size reduces the incidence of obstruction by food and hair, which occurs frequently with smaller diameter tubing. When the cannula is to be used only for infusion, a smaller size such as Silastic 0.025-in. i.d., 0.047-in. o.d. (Dow Corning) can be substituted. The outside circumference of the tip that lies within the stomach is coated with silicone adhesive (Silastic adhesive, Dow Corning) to round sharp edges that might damage the stomach lining, and two small holes are made in the sides of this tip to ease withdrawal and avoid obstruction. These holes must be placed near the tip since, if they lie near the inner stomach wall, there is a tendency for tissue to grow into them and seal off the cannulae. These holes can be made easily either with the point of a sharp-pointed scalpel blade or fine sharp-pointed iris scissors.

A circular piece of fiberglass screen (obtainable in most hardware stores) 1 cm in diameter is fixed to the cannula with silicone adhesive at a distance of 1 cm from the tip. This screen rests against the outside stomach wall and fixes the position of the cannula within the stomach permanently, preventing it from being pulled into the stomach by peristalsis or out of the stomach by the experimenter. From the stomach, the cannula extends 15 to 17 cm under the skin and is attached to a pedestal mounted on the back of the animal.

Pedestal Construction

A pedestal that provides a junction point between the cannula and the tube from the infusion device is placed under the skin just behind the neck of the animal on the back. The pedestal is constructed of 17-gauge, stainless steel needle tubing bent at a 90° angle (for the smaller, infusion-only cannula, 21-gauge needle tubing is used). One leg of this angled needle tubing lies under the skin and is attached to the cannula. The other leg protrudes from the skin, and a cap of silicone rubber tubing with a dab of silicone rubber adhesive on one end is slipped over it when the cannula is not in use. The bend in the needle tubing has a sleeve of silicone rubber tubing to which a piece of 2 cm by 2 cm square fiberglass screen is cemented with silicone rubber adhesive. This screen is placed under the skin and serves as an anchor (see Figure 9.5). During healing, scar tissue grows

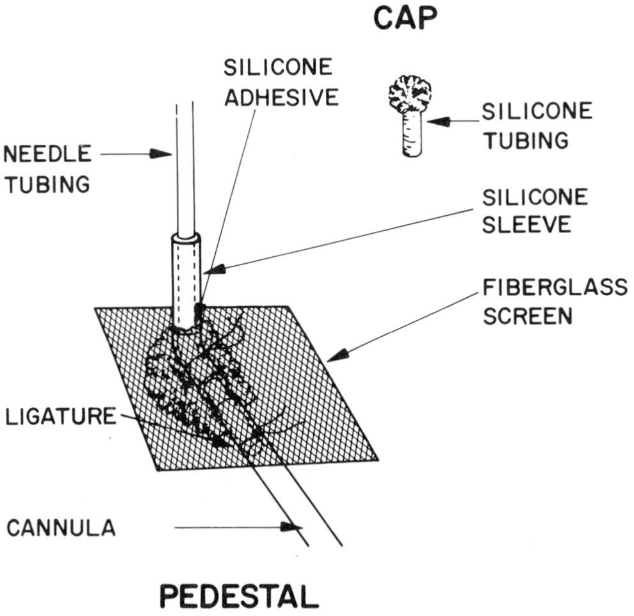

FIGURE 9.5. Construction of a Subdermal Pedestal for Use with Duodenal and Gastric Cannulae in Rats.

through the screen and holds the pedestal in place. After a month or two, the pedestal may sometimes grow out of the skin, but it is easily replaced.

Surgery

Before the operation, the animal should be deprived of food for 24 hours to be sure that the stomach is empty during surgery. An incision is made just below and parallel to the last rib running from the xyphoid process about 5 cm to the side. The intestines are gently moved aside, and the stomach is exposed, taking care not to damage pancreatic tissue lying close to the antrum. To maintain the stomach in a fixed exposed position, a 2- to 3-mm diameter stainless steel rod is placed beneath it. A circular set of purse-string sutures and a circular set of inverting sutures should be placed around an area about 6 mm in diameter and about 2 cm caudal to the junction of the esophagus and the stomach on the greater curvature of the fundus. These sutures ensure that the stomach muscle is inverted and held tightly around the cannula so that there is no leakage from the stomach. After the sutures are placed, a small incision is made in the stomach wall and in the underlying mucosa, and the cannula is inserted up to the screen, approximately 8 mm into the stomach. Care must be taken that the cannula extends through both muscle and mucosa, since the mucosa is not attached to the muscle at this location and the cannula can slip between these layers. If the cannula is correctly inserted, there will be an immediate and rapid flow of stomach contents into the cannula. After insertion, the surrounding sutures are tightened and tied so that no leakage occurs. Finally, omentum is brought from surrounding areas and placed between the screen and stomach wall, and the screen

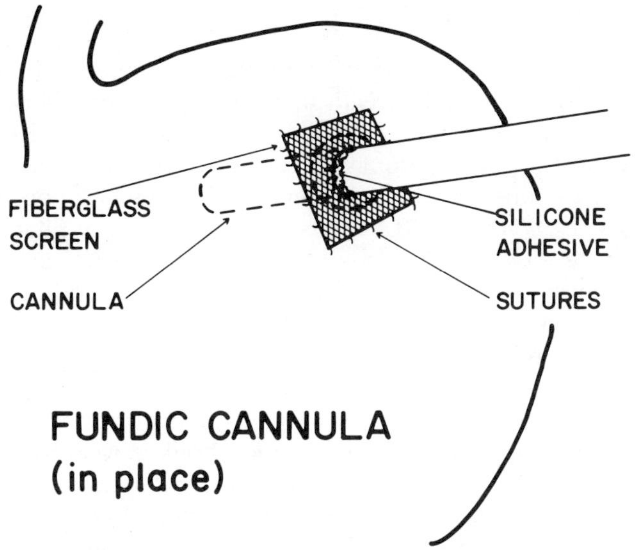

FIGURE 9.6. Placement of a Fundic Cannula in the Rat Stomach.

and omentum are loosely sutured to the stomach (see Figure 9.6). The omentum will also help prevent leakage by forming packing around the entrance of the cannula to the stomach. Throughout this procedure, it is important to prevent any flow of gastric contents into the abdominal cavity.

The cannula is then brought out through the abdominal incision and anchored firmly to the abdominal muscle with sutures. With the animal on its stomach, a small incision is made between the scapulae, and blunt scissors are used to separate the skin gently from underlying muscle layers. Hemostats are inserted between these layers and pushed gently until they emerge at the corner of the abdominal incision. The cannula is then gripped in the jaws of the hemostats and is pulled back under the skin to the dorsal incision. The cannula is then attached to the pedestal and secured there by wrapping a silk thread around the silicone rubber tube through the screen and tying it tightly.

Postoperative Care and Maintenance of the Cannula

Following the operation, the food intake of the animal may be diminished for as long as a week, but otherwise recovery is rapid and the animal soon appears normal. The plug on the external end of the pedestal is sometimes removed by the animals. If it is, it should be replaced as soon as possible, since the pressure of the stomach forces food and gastric juice out onto the animal's back where it irritates the skin. Occasionally, the cannula becomes clogged with hair or food, but it can easily be reamed out with a length of small diameter polyethylene tubing or flushed out with water. Infection may develop along the cannula under the skin and after a time will cause an eruption. Consequently, care should be taken to prevent infections and cure them quickly if they should occur. Barring accidents of this type, the cannula should remain patent indefinitely.

DUODENAL CANNULAE

The duodenal cannula was developed specifically to permit sampling of duodenal contents and to provide a route of injecting various chemicals directly into it without disturbing the animal. The only techniques previously known that allow sampling of the duodenum or direct injection into it require the use of a fistula and cannot easily be used for sampling or injection without disturbing the animal. The method described here also requires considerably less surgery and resulting trauma to the duodenum.

Cannula Construction

The cannula is designed so that it enters the gastrointestinal tract at the antrum of the stomach and extends through the pylorus, with its tip resting in the duodenum. This route is used because it is known that a tube passing through the pylorus into the duodenum does not change the normal gastric emptying time (Crider & Thomas, 1937). The length of the tip can be cut to end at any location in the 25-mm duodenum. The duodenal end of the cannula is constructed of silicone rubber tubing (Silastic, .025-in. i.d., .047-in. o.d., Dow Corning), which is pliable enough to rest in the lumen without abrading the mucosa. The length of this portion will vary depending on where the cannula enters the antrum and the desired location of the tip. This portion should be cut after inserting the cannula and observing where the tip rests. The second portion of the cannula, the S-curve, which is constructed of polyethylene tubing (Intramedic PE 60, .030-in. i.d., .048-in. o.d., Clay-Adams), is designed to lie flat against the outside of the antrum, bend inward through the incision, and bend again to pass through the pylorus and into the duodenum. The S-shaped bend is produced by holding the tubing in this shape with forceps in almost boiling water to soften the tubing and then in cold water to set the shape. Each of the ends of the polyethylene S-curve should be flaired slightly by holding the tip briefly near the heat of a flame. The silicone rubber duodenal portion should then be placed in trichloroethylene or chloroform for a few minutes to soften and expand it, after which it can be slipped over the flaired end of the polyethylene. The silicone will quickly shrink again and form a tight junction that can be reinforced with a piece of silk thread tied tightly above the flair. A similar junction should be made between the other end of the polyethylene S-curve and the 15- to 17-cm length of silicone tubing that leads to the pedestal. The curved portion and junctions can also be coated with Silastic adhesive (Dow Corning), but this is not essential (see Figure 9.7).

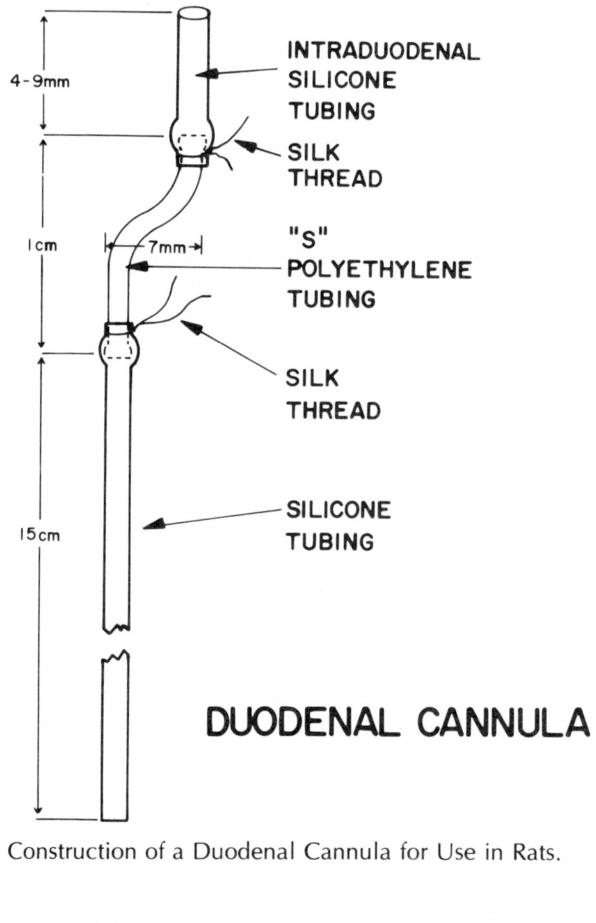

FIGURE 9.7. Construction of a Duodenal Cannula for Use in Rats.

For purposes of withdrawal, a larger size of tubing would be necessary (for example, Meditube ST 212) since food particles tend to block the smaller tubing. In addition, four to six small holes should be made in the duodenal portion of the cannula to facilitate fluid withdrawal in the event that the extreme tip becomes temporarily blocked.

Pedestal Construction

The same pedestal developed for use with the chronic gastric cannulae is used for the duodenal cannulae. It has 21-gauge needle tubing for the infusion cannula and 17-gauge needle tubing for the withdrawal cannula.

Surgery

Before surgery, the animal should be deprived of food for 24 hours so that the stomach will be completely empty during the operation. The animal is anesthetized, and an incision is made below and parallel to the last rib and rib cage. The intestines are gently moved aside to expose the stomach and duodenum. A 2- to 3-mm diam stainless steel rod placed beneath the stomach may help to hold it in a fixed, exposed position, although the rod should be placed with extreme care. On the exposed surface of the antrum, about 1 cm from the pylorus, one circular set of purse-string sutures and one circular set of inverting sutures are made (one on top of the other) with care being taken to avoid damaging the pancreas, which is attached to the antrum on its greater curvature. A small incision is then made within this double circle of sutures in the antral wall and in the underlying mucosa. The cannula is passed through the incision into the lumen of the antrum, through the pylorus, and into the duodenum (see Figure 9.8). It is important to ensure that the cannula passes into the

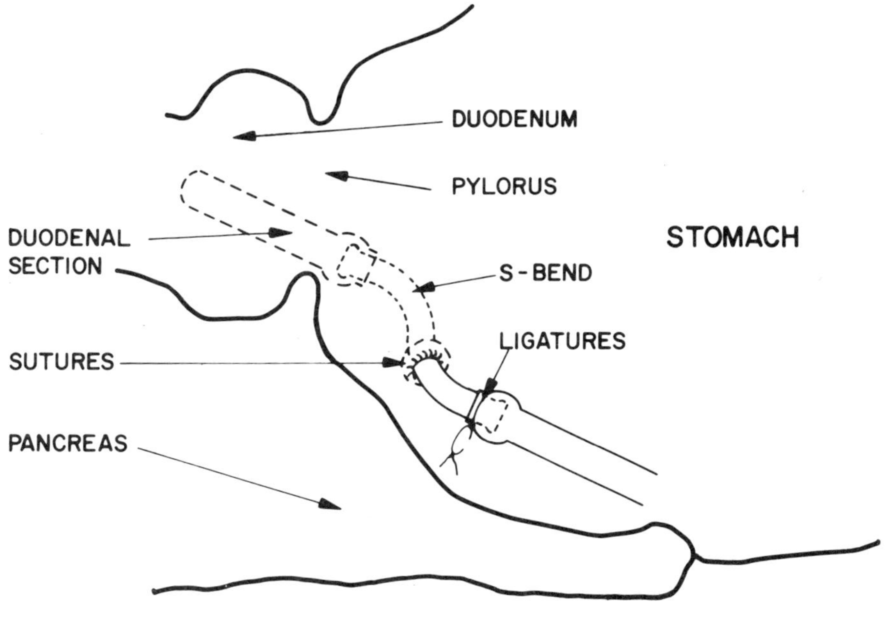

DUODENAL CANNULA

(IN PLACE)

FIGURE 9.8. Placement of a Duodenal Cannula in the Stomach and Duodenum of the Rat.

duodenum, since the mucosa is not attached to the outer muscle wall at this location, and the cannula can easily slip between the mucosa and the wall without ever entering the duodenum. The tip of the cannula is then removed, cut to the desired length, and reinserted. When it is again in place, the circular sutures are tightened so that the muscle wall inverts and fits tightly around the cannula. A ligature is tied to the cannula where it emerges from the incision and is sutured to the antral wall of the stomach for added reinforcement. The next step is to bring the cannula out through the abdominal incision and to anchor it to abdominal muscle with sutures. With the animal on its stomach, a small incision is made between the scapulae, and blunt scissors are used to separate the skin from the underlying muscle layers. Hemostats are inserted between these layers and gently pushed until they emerge at the corner of the abdominal incision. With the hemostats, the cannula is pulled back through the layers to the dorsal incision and slipped onto the pedestal. The cannula should be firmly secured to the pedestal with silk thread.

Postoperative Care and Maintenance of the Cannula

Feeding behavior becomes normal again after two to three days. The infusion cannula remains patent indefinitely, with blockage occurring very rarely. The withdrawal cannula occasionally becomes blocked with food, but it can usually be cleared by reaming it with polyethylene tubing or flushing it gently. Withdrawal through this cannula must be done slowly; the rate of gastric emptying and flow of digestive fluids determines the rate of withdrawal. Rapid withdrawal will collapse the duodenum. Although peristalsis tends to prevent flow up the cannula, the external end of the cannula should be covered with a stopper when the cannula is not in use to prevent air from entering the duodenum. Infusion rates can vary. The authors have infused at a rate of 0.2 ml per minute since this rate is tolerated well by the animal and is a reasonable approximation of the rate of flow of a milk meal into the duodenum (Campbell and Davis, 1974). Infusions of extremely hypertonic solutions (for example, 22 percent glucose) will cause distress to the animal and should be avoided.

REFERENCES

Adair, E. R., Miller, N. E., and Booth, D. A. Effects of continuous intravenous infusion of nutritive substances on consummatory behavior in rats. *Communication in Behavioral Biology,* 1968, **2,** 25–37.

Aziz, O., Haberich, F. J., and Nowacki, P. E. Technik der Daverkatheterisierung der Venaportae und Venacava caudalis an der Wachen Ratte. *Naturwissenschaffen,* 1964, **51,** 557.

Beattie, C. W., Campbell, C. S., Nequin, L. G., Soyka, L. F., and Schwartz, N. B. Barbiturate blockade of the tonic LH secretion in the male and female rat. *Endocrinology,* 1973, **92,** 1634–1638.

Bessman, S. P., Magnes, J., Schwerin, P., and Waelsch, H. Absorption of glutamic acid and glutamine. *Journal of Biological Chemistry,* 1948, **175,** 817–823.

Bradley, S. E. The hepatic circulation. In W. F. Hamilton (Ed.), *The handbook of physiology,* Sec. 2 Circulation, Vol. II. Washington, D.C.: American Physiological Society, 1963.

Campbell, C. S., and Davis, J. D. Licking rates of rats is reduced by intraduodenal and intraportal glucose infusions. *Physiology and Behavior,* 1974, **12,** 357–366.

Crider, J. O., and Thomas, J. E. A study of gastric emptying with the pylorus open. *American Journal of Digestive Diseases and Nutrition,* 1937, **4,** 295–300.

Davis, J. D., and Campbell, C. S. Peripheral control of meal size in the rat: Effect of sham feeding on meal size and drinking rate. *Journal of Comparative and Physiological Psychology,* 1973, **83,** 379–387.

Davis, J. D., Gallagher, R. J., Ladove, R. F., and Turavsky, A. J. Inhibition of food intake by a humoral factor. *Journal of Comparative and Physiological Psychology,* 1969, **67,** 407–414.

Davis, J. D., Lulenski, G. C., and Miller, N. E. Comparative studies of barbiturate self-administration. *International Journal of the Addictions,* 1968, **3,** 207–214.

Epstein, A. N. Feeding without oropharyngeal sensations. In M. R. Kare and O. Maller (Eds.), *The chemical senses and nutrition.* Baltimore: The Johns Hopkins University Press, 1967.

Epstein, A. N., and Teitelbaum, P. Regulation of food intake in the absence of taste, smell, and other oropharyngeal sensations. *Journal of Comparative and Physiological Psychology,* 1962, **55,** 753–759.

Jungblut, P. W., Lohmann, B., Schober, R., and Turba, F. Eine Methode zur for Haufenden Blutentnahme aus der Vena Portae von Hunden. *Experientia,* 1955, **11,** 241.

Smith, M. H., Jr. Effects of intravenous injections on eating. *Journal of Comparative and Physiological Psychology,* 1966, **61,** 11–14.

Snowdon, C. T., and Epstein, A. N. Oral and intragastric feeding in vagotomized rats. *Journal of Comparative and Physiological Psychology,* 1970, **71,** 59–67.

Steffans, A. B. Bloodglucose and FFA levels in relation to the meal pattern in the normal rat and the ventromedial hypothalamic lesioned rat. *Physiology and Behavior,* 1969, **4,** 215–225.

Terkel, J., and Rosenblatt, J. S. Humoral factors underlying maternal behavior at parturition. *Journal of Comparative and Physiological Psychology,* 1972, **80,** 365–371.

Weeks, J. R. Experimental morphine addiction: Method for automatic intravenous injections in unrestrained rats. *Science,* 1962, **138,** 143–144.

Appendix: Manufacturers and Suppliers

ANIMAL BREEDERS AND SUPPLIERS

Cats

California Caviary
10824 S. Prairie Ave.
Inglewood, California 90303

Morris Research Laboratories, Inc.
4000 Meridian Rd.
Topeka, Kansas 66617

Pratt Laboratories
1739 S. 54th St.
Philadelphia, Pennsylvania 19143

Monkeys

Amazon Animal Imports
919 N.W. 13th St.
Ft. Lauderdale, Florida 33311

Asiatic Animal Imports, Inc.
P.O. Box 8125
San Francisco International Airport
San Francisco, California 94128

Heath Research, Inc.
666 Elm St.
Buffalo, New York 14203

Rats

Charles River Breeding Laboratories, Inc.
251 Ballardvale St.
North Wilmington, Massachusetts 01067

Holtzman Co.
421 Holtzman Rd.
Madison, Wisconsin 53713

Simonsen Laboratories, Inc.
Rt. 1, Box 129
Gilroy, California 95020

Sprague-Dawley, Inc.
P.O. Box 4220
Seminole Highway, Rt. 2
Madison, Wisconsin 53711

ANIMAL CAGES AND ASSOCIATED EQUIPMENT

Acme Research Products
5500 Muddy Creek Rd.
Cincinnati, Ohio 45238

Amsco Industrial
2820 W. 23 St.
Erie, Pennsylvania 16506

Carworth
New City, New York 10956

Hoeltge
5242 Crookshank Rd.
Cincinnati, Ohio 45238

Wahmann Manufacturing
Box 6883
Baltimore, Maryland 21204

ANIMAL CARE AND FEED

Borden Co.
350 Madison Ave.
New York, New York 10017

General Biochemicals
Laboratory Park
Chagrin Falls, Ohio 44022

Hill Packing Co.
Topeka, Kansas 66601

ICN Nutritional Biochemicals
26201 Miles Rd.
Cleveland, Ohio 44128

Norden Laboratory
P.O. Box 80809
Lincoln, Nebraska 68501

Paxton Processing Co.
Paxton, Illinois 60957

Ralston Purina
Checkerboard Square
St. Louis, Missouri 63199

ANIMAL CARE AND FEED (CTD.)

Ross Laboratories
625 Cleveland Ave.
Columbus, Ohio 43216

Upjohn Co.
Kalamazoo, Michigan 49001

CANNULAE AND CANNULA COMPONENTS

Allied Electronics Corporation
Chicago, Illinois, and major cities throughout the United States

Bosco Fastening Service Co.
2570 31st St.
Denver, Colorado 80201

BRS/LVE
5301 Holland Drive
Beltsville, Maryland 20705

Flexi-Optics Laboratories
269 Mechanic St.
Marlboro, Massachusetts 01752

Harvard Apparatus
150 Dover Road
Millis, Massachusetts 02054

David Kopf
7324 Elmo St.
Tujunga, California 91042

Plastic Products, Inc.
P.O. Box 1204T
Roanoke, Virginia 24006

Travenol Laboratories
6301 Lincoln Ave.
Morton Grove, Illinois 60053

Tube Sales Inc.
1550 South Pearl
Denver, Colorado 80201

CONNECTORS

Allied Electronics Corporation
Chicago, Illinois, and major cities throughout the United States

Amphenol Connector Division
Amphenol-Borg Electronics
Chicago, Illinois

Winchester Electronics
19 Willard Rd.
Norwalk, Connecticut 06851

DRUGS AND PHARMACEUTICALS

Abbott Laboratories
14th St. and Sheridan Rd.
North Chicago, Illinois 60064

American Cyanamid
Pearl River, New York 10965

Dellens Laboratory
Omaha, Nebraska 68101

Diamond Laboratories
P.O. Box 863
Des Moines, Iowa 50304

Fort Dodge
P.O. Box 518
Fort Dodge, Iowa 50501

General Biochemicals
Laboratory Park
Chagrin Falls, Ohio 44022

Haver Lockhart
P.O. Box 390
Shawnee Mission, Kansas 66201

ICN Nutritional Biochemicals
26201 Miles Rd.
Cleveland, Ohio 44128

Jensen-Salsbery Laboratories
520 W. 21st St.
Kansas City, Missouri 64108

Johnson & Johnson
501 George St.
New Brunswick, New Jersey 08901

K and K
121 Express St.
Plainview, New York 11803

Knoll Pharmaceutical Co.
377 Crane St.
Orange, New Jersey 07050

Lederle Laboratories
Pearl River, New York 10965

Norden Laboratory
P.O. Box 80809
Lincoln, Nebraska 68501

Panray Division
Ormont Drug & Chemical Co., Inc.
223 S. Dean St.
Englewood, New Jersey 07631

Parke, Davis & Co.
P.O. Box 476 G.P.O.
Detroit, Michigan 48232

Pitman-Moore
P.O. Box 1656
Indianapolis, Indiana 46206

Sigma Chemical Co.
3500 DeKalb St.
St. Louis, Missouri 63118

DRUGS AND PHARMACEUTICALS (CTD.)

Upjohn Co.
Kalamazoo, Michigan 49001

Wyeth Laboratories
P.O. Box 8299
Philadelphia, Pennsylvania 19101

ELECTRODES AND ELECTRODE MATERIALS

Beckman Instruments
2500 Harbor Blvd.
Fullerton, California 92632

California Fine Wire Co.
Grover City, California 93433

Cleveland Tungsten Inc.
10200 Meech Ave.
Cleveland, Ohio 44105

Driver-Harris Co.
202 Middlesex St.
Harrison, New Jersey 07029

Epoxylite Corporation of New York
12 Breckenridge St.
Buffalo, New York 14213

Grass Instruments
101 Old Colony Ave.
Quincy, Massachusetts 02127

Harvard Apparatus
150 Dover Rd.
Millis, Massachusetts 02054

Insl-X Products Co.
115 Woodworth Ave.
Yonkers, New York 10701

Lafayette Instrument
Box 1279
Lafayette, Indiana 47902

Narco Bio-Systems
Box 12511
Houston, Texas 77017

FREEZING MICROTOMES

American Optical Co.
Sugar and Eggert Rds.
Buffalo, New York 14215

E. Leitz
Link Dr.
Rockleigh, New Jersey 07647

National Instrument
4119 Fordleigh Rd.
Baltimore, Maryland 21215

Optometric Instruments
111 N. La Cienega
Beverly Hills, California 90211

HISTOLOGICAL SUPPLIES

Clay-Adams
299 Webro Rd.
Parsippany, New Jersey 07054

W. J. Curtin & Co.
Major cities throughout the United States

LESION MAKERS

Burdick Corp.
Milton, Wisconsin 53563

Grass Instruments
101 Old Colony Ave.
Quincy, Massachusetts 02127

David Kopf
7324 Elmo St.
Tujunga, California 91042

Lehigh Valley Electronics, Inc.
Box 125
Fogelsville, Pennsylvania 18051

MICROINJECTION UNITS

Hamilton
Box 307
Whittier, California 90608

Stoelting Co.
1350 S. Kostner Ave.
Chicago, Illinois 60623

MICROSCOPES

American Optical Co.
Sugar and Eggert Rd.
Buffalo, New York 14215

Bausch and Lomb
77474 Bausch St.
Rochester, New York 14625

Circon
749 Ward Dr.
Santa Barbara, California 93111

International Micro Optics
5 Daniel Rd.
Fairfield, New Jersey 07006

E. Leitz
Link Dr.
Rockleigh, New Jersey 07647

Nikon
623 Stewart Ave.
Garden City, New York 11530

Scientific Products
1430 Waukegan Rd.
McGraw Park, Illinois 60085

Unitron
66 Needham St.
Newton Highlands, Massachusetts 02161

MISCELLANEOUS EQUIPMENT AND SUPPLIES

Armstrong Cork Co.
Industrial Adhesives Division
9600 Inland
Lancaster, Pennsylvania 19104

Dow Corning
Medical Products Division
Midland, Michigan 48640

Epoxylite Corporation of New York
12 Breckenridge St.
Buffalo, New York 14213

Extracorporeal Medical Specialists, Inc.
Church Rd.
Mt. Laurel Township, New Jersey 08057

Fischer Scientific Co.
711 Forbes Ave.
Pittsburgh, Pennsylvania 15219

Hamilton
Box 307
Whittier, California 90608

Microdot, Inc.
220 Pasadena Ave.
S. Pasadena, California 91030

Millipore Corp.
Ashby Rd.
Bedford, Massachusetts 01730

V. Mueller
6600 W. Touhy
Chicago, Illinois 60648

Sage Instruments
11 Blackstone St.
Cambridge, Massachusetts 02109

Service Supply Co.
1115 Seventh St.
Denver, Colorado 80204

Sigmamotor
14 Elizabeth St.
Middleport, New York 14105

Superior Tubing
P.O. Drawer 191
Norristown, Pennsylvania 16103

A.H. Thomas
Box 779
Philadelphia, Pennsylvania 19105

OPERANT PROGRAMMING EQUIPMENT

BRS/LVE
5301 Holland Dr.
Beltsville, Maryland 20705

Ralph Gerbrands
8 Peck Ave.
Arlington, Massachusetts 02174

Grason-Stadler Co., Inc.
West Concord, Massachusetts 01742

OSCILLOSCOPES

Analab Instrument Corp.
30 Canfield Rd.
Essex County
Cedar Grove, New Jersey 07009

Brush Instruments
3631 Perkins Ave.
Cleveland, Ohio 44114

Hewlett-Packard Co.
1501 Page Mill Rd.
Palo Alto, California 94304

Nuclear-Chicago Corp.
333 E. Howard Ave.
Des Plaines, Illinois 60018

Tektronix, Inc.
P.O. Box 500
Beaverton, Oregon 97005

RECORDING SYSTEMS

Beckman Instruments
3900 N. River Rd.
Schiller Park, Illinois 60176

Biological Electronics
10101 San Pablo Ave.
El Cerrito, California 94530

BRS/LVE
5301 Holland Dr.
Beltsville, Maryland 20705

Grass Instruments
101 Old Colony Ave.
Quincy, Massachusetts 02127

Harvard Apparatus
150 Dover Rd.
Millis, Massachusetts 02054

Hewlett-Packard
1501 Page Mill Rd.
Palo Alto, California 94304

Narco Bio-Systems
Box 12511
Houston, Texas 77017

Teledyne Geotech
Box 28277
Dallas, Texas 75228

STEREOTAXIC INSTRUMENTS

Baltimore Instruments
4610 Hartfort Rd.
Baltimore, Maryland 21201

BRS/LVE
5301 Holland Dr.
Beltsville, Maryland 20705

David Kopf
7324 Elmo St.
Tujunga, California 91042

STEREOTAXIC INSTRUMENTS (CTD.)

Scientific Prototype
615 W. 131 St.
New York, New York 10027

Stoelting Co.
1350 S. Kostner Ave.
Chicago, Illinois 60623

STIMULATORS

BRS/LVE
5301 Holland Dr.
Beltsville, Maryland 20705

Grass Instruments
101 Old Colony Ave.
Quincy, Massachusetts 02127

Harvard Apparatus
150 Dover Rd.
Millis, Massachusetts 02054

Narco Bio-Systems
Box 12511
Houston, Texas 77017

Stoelting Co.
1350 S. Kostner Ave.
Chicago, Illinois 60623

SURGICAL EQUIPMENT, INSTRUMENTS, AND SUPPLIES

Barnstead Co.
225 Rivermoor St.
Boston, Massachusetts 02132

L. D. Caulk Co.
Milford, Delaware 19963

Circon
749 Ward Dr.
Santa Barbara, California 93111

SURGICAL EQUIPMENT, INSTRUMENTS, AND SUPPLIES (CTD.)

Clay-Adams
299 Webro Rd.
Parsippany, New Jersey 07054

W. H. Curtin & Co.
Major cities throughout the United States

Dremel Co.
Dept. 350
Racine, Wisconsin 53406

H. D. Justi
32nd and Spring Garden
Philadelphia, Pennsylvania 19104

Labtron Scientific
341 Conklin St.
Farmingdale, New York 11735

Roboz Surgical Instruments
810 18th St. N. W.
Washington, D. C. 20006

Rodolfo P. Walther Co.
5321 Hollywood Blvd.
Los Angeles, California 90027

Sage Instruments
11 Blackstone St.
Cambridge, Massachusetts 02139

Sargent-Welch Scientific Co.
Major cities throughout the United States

Scientific Glass Apparatus Co., Inc.
735 Broad St.
Newark, New Jersey 07102

Scientific Products
1210 Leon Pl.
Evanston, Illinois 60201
and major cities throughout the United States

Indexes

AUTHOR INDEX

SUBJECT INDEX